COMPULSORY IRISH
Language and Education in Ireland
1870s–1970s

ADRIAN KELLY

IRISH ACADEMIC PRESS
DUBLIN • PORTLAND, OR

First published in 2002 by
IRISH ACADEMIC PRESS
44, Northumberland Road,
Dublin 4, Ireland

and in the United States of America by
IRISH ACADEMIC PRESS
c/o ISBS, 5824 NE Hassalo Street,
Portland, OR 97213-3644

Website: www.iap.ie

British Library Cataloguing in Publication Data

Kelly, Adrian
    Compulsory Irish : language and education in Ireland,
    1870s–1970s
    1. Language and education – Ireland 2. Irish language – Study
    and teaching – Ireland 3. Education, Bilingual – Ireland
    4. Language policy – Ireland
    I. Title
    491.6'2'071'0417

    ISBN 0-7165-2693-X (cloth)
    ISBN 0-7165-2747-2 (paper)

Library of Congress Cataloging-in-Publication Data

Kelly, Adrian, 1970–
    Compulsory Irish : language and education in Ireland, 1870s–1970s / Adrian Kelly.
        p. cm.
    Includes bibliographical references and index.
    ISBN 0-7165-2693-X (hb)
    1. Native language and education—Ireland. 2. Language and education—Ireland. 3. Irish
language—Study and teaching—Ireland. 4. Education, Bilingual—Ireland. 5. Language
policy—Ireland. I. Title.
LC201.7.I73 K45 2000
491.6'2071'0417—dc21

                                                                                00-059686

Typeset by Vitaset, Paddock Wood, Kent
Printed by
Creative Print and Design (Wales), Ebbw Vale

Contents

List of Tables

Foreword

THERE IS no doubt but that the publication of this book will bring the zealots out of the woodwork once again. The author had best invest in a suit of mail to prepare for the certain onslaught. We owe Adrian Kelly for this most comprehensive tour of policy over a period of a century, which presents damning evidence that the policy of compulsory Irish has been detrimental to the educational achievements of pupils. More worryingly, he shows that decision makers knew and discounted this fact as being an acceptable price to pay for the sake of aithbheochan na Gaeilge.

He clearly confirms that the policy on the revival was almost entirely school-based. He reinforces what primary teachers in particular have been saying for generations, that the current policy can never be successful and is unfair in the manner in which it places all responsibility on the teaching profession. Teachers have been the tools of social engineering in this matter. The school-based policy had no life outside the school as proven by the 1962 report which referred to 'the great intellectual and educational wastage when students who leave school with a good command of Irish lose that accomplishment through lack of opportunity for its use'. This book provides more and more evidence in support of this view from academics, Irish language writers and politicians. It is no surprise either to find time and again that people blamed for the lack of success in reviving the language are the teachers. In the 1960s more than half of my classmates were from the Gaeltacht and one of my abiding memories is being taught Latin through the medium of Gaeilge from an English language textbook. And nothing changes! In the year 2000 the Department of Education introduced a new Gaeilge curriculum in Gaeltacht primary schools and did this without there being even one new textbook printed, as Gaeilge, to support it.

Dr Kelly is also to be congratulated on being, as far as I know, the first academic to show conclusively that Gaeltacht areas were given no special treatment in the revival policy. His statistics, which show that 50 per cent of Gaeltacht children were being taught through English in the 1930s, are damning indeed. They prove that over the decades successive Governments have been more interested in getting a few extra people in the Galltacht speaking Gaeilge than in supporting and developing the inhabitants of the Gaeltachts which are in essence foinse na Gaeilge. Gaeltacht people have in my view been the continuing victims of government policy, they have never been recognised as central to any prospect of a revival and have never received the resources or been given the opportunity to exercise their human and civil rights tré Gaeilge.

Those of us who love both the language and the Gaeltacht people who breathe life in it will always be angry at the fact that they have never received appropriate consideration in any official policy document on Gaeilge.

This work also captures the inflexibility and intolerance of those who condemn anyone who questions policy or regulation on compulsory Irish. This is nowhere clearer than in the report on the Language Freedom Movement's Mansion House meeting in 1965. Arising from that meeting the writer John B. Keane was demonised as anti-Irish and West Brit to boot. Anyone privileged to know John B. will also know of his great love for and fluency in Gaeilge as well as his support for the Gaeltachtaí. The fact that he could be presented as the enemy of the Irish language is proof enough of the bankrupt thinking of his mindless critics.

The book is a good reminder of the difficulties in influencing Irish language policy. It would appear that successive governments are not prepared to take on the well-organised fundamentalists who present themselves as the protectors of all things Irish. It is a pity that some Government would not ignore them and listen to and take advice from Muintir na Gaeltachta as to the support required by them. We would be far more successful if we concentrated resources on the Gaeltachts than on the Galltachts.

Those of us who have over the years questioned the compulsion aspect of Gaeilge in Education have been seen as pariahs. But strangely enough the attacks always come from outside the Gaeltachts. Every Gaeltacht friend of mine hates to see Gaeilge being used as a political weapon and is always uncomfortable with seeing Gaeilge, the language they love, 'á bhrú siar scórnaigh ár dhaoine'. So much so that when two Gaeltacht people are joined by a non-Irish speaker they will invariably and out of courtesy change to English, because they would never see their language as being exclusive or unwelcoming of people though they would most willingly help any person trying to improve his or her Gaeilge.

It is a pity that this dignified and openly positive attitude of Gaeltacht people has never been allowed to inform and mould the State's policies towards the Irish language.

SENATOR JOE O'TOOLE
General Secretary, Irish National Teachers' Organisation
President, Irish Congress of Trade Unions
October 2001

Acknowledgements

ONE IS afforded few opportunities to acknowledge publicly debts of gratitude accumulated during the course of one's academic development and one's life. It is therefore with enthusiasm that I record here my sincerest thanks to those who have contributed so much of their experience, time and knowledge over the past number of years while I worked upon this volume, initially as a Master of Arts degree in the History Department at the National University of Ireland, Maynooth.

My warmest thanks to Professor R.V. Comerford who supervised the original thesis for his generosity and support in so many ways. My thanks also to the other members of the History Department for their support over a number of years, and to the other members of the teaching staff in NUI Maynooth, particularly in Roinn na Nua-Ghaeilge.

I am indebted to the staff of several institutions where I carried out research, including the staff of the John Paul II Library, Maynooth, the National Archives, the Irish National Teachers Association and the National Library. The enduring patience and politeness of the staff in these institutions made researching a pleasure, and I am in their debt.

During the course of researching and writing a number of individuals offered practical support and critical comment, and I wish in particular to acknowledge the assistance of Paula Coonerty, Dr Enda Delaney and Bill Tinley. The task would have proved much more difficult were it not for the ground-breaking work of those who have already published histories and critical analyses of the education system in Ireland, and I owe my thanks to them. I am also grateful to the staff of Irish Academic Press, particularly Linda Longmore for her much valued guidance, and to the staff in the Houses of the Oireachtas and my colleagues in the Official Reporting Section.

I am conscious that it is easy for historians to be critical in hindsight of policies and policy makers. I hope I have used with fairness throughout the work the benefit of hindsight and the privilege of critical comment while not having to act.

Finally, I acknowledge the enthusiasm and support of my parents over the years as I wrote this work. Their gentle encouragement has made this, and so much more besides, possible. Glad of the opportunity, I dedicate this work with respect and thanks to them, and to Cóilín, Hilary and Enda.

INTRODUCTION

Language and Education,
1870s–1920s

WITH THE establishment of the Irish Free State, the revival of the Irish language was taken from the sole care of cultural pressure groups and placed firmly on the agenda of an independent Irish government. For the first time the native language had a native government behind it, a government united in its determination to revive Irish and undeterred by the economic, social and cultural realities of early twentieth-century Ireland. The approach of the government to the language revival was two pronged: the preservation and expansion of the Gaeltachtaí—Irish speaking, mainly scattered, rural and comparatively poor communities on the western and southern seaboard—and the use of the education system, particularly the primary schools, as the chief means of reviving the language in the Galltacht (the English speaking area which comprised most of the Free State). While policies directed towards the Gaeltacht have received much attention and were a central part of the revival effort, the attempt to revive the Irish language through the education system has received scant analysis, despite being the single most important policy in shaping the education system of independent Ireland. The huge qualitative and quantitative differences between the two elements of the revival policy should also be noted. While inhabitants of Gaeltacht areas were often to the forefront in demanding State intervention to preserve the economic, social and linguistic fabric of their communities, the revival policies based on the education system were often imposed through compulsion on pupils, teachers and parents who were not prepared for nor necessarily accepting of the extent to which the schools were being Gaelicised. It was also overwhelmingly monolingual English speakers who saw the post 1922 education system beginning to revolve around the attempts to make them fluent in Irish.

While the desire and determination to revive the Irish language in the Galltacht was both clear and logical, a number of other issues were less so.

In particular, why were the schools chosen as the chief instrument which could best effect a revival? Why was it thought both necessary and acceptable to trade educational achievement for linguistic ability? Why was the policy such a failure in terms of what it set out to achieve? What were the long-term costs of the strategy, culturally and educationally? While these questions are central to the ensuing analysis, the way in which the schools became the central focus of the language revival is outlined below.

The ideology connecting the schools with language had its origin in pre-Independence Ireland. In the same way that the 1960s was a period of unprecedented metamorphosis in approaches to education generally, so too was the period before the founding of the Free State. The nineteenth century had seen the pattern of education in Ireland change with the extension of schooling on a more popular basis. This followed the trend of the rest of Europe where the State was becoming involved in the provision of education on a broad basis. Ireland experienced this trend from the 1830s with the new national school system being established in 1831 under the auspices of Lord Stanley, the Chief Secretary of Ireland. Later the new system would be described in the *Saorstát Éireann Official Handbook* of 1932 as 'opposed to anything savouring of Irish sentiment'.[1] The board of commissioners of the national system, under the Duke of Leinster, consisted of three representatives from the Established Church, two from the Catholic Church and two representatives from the Presbyterians. Despite such initial representation, by 1839 the Established Church had set up its own school system in opposition to the national system while three years before this, in 1836, the Christian Brothers, who had initially put a few schools under the system, had withdrawn from it. By 1849, the year in which Paul Cullen became Archbishop of Armagh, the Catholic Church had begun a concerted opposition to the national school system on the grounds of disagreeing with mixed education, banning Catholics from attending the model schools and the central training college of the State system. From the 1850s, a more confident and aggressive Catholic Church began to demand a denominational, State supported national school system for Catholics. By the mid 1860s the Catholic hierarchy had won many concessions which resulted in the establishment of a royal commission to investigate the national education system and to make recommendations on reform. The ideal of non-denominational education, aspired to by the founders of the system, was abandoned in the face of opposition from the Catholic Church while Catholic clergy came to control individual schools at local level resulting in the national system 'ostensibly [being] under the control of the commissioners of national education, but actually [being] dominated by the proclamations of the Roman Catholic hierarchy'[2] by the end of the nineteenth century.

The main curriculum changes in the system as introduced occurred in 1872 when the payment by results system was established, presumably in response to the Powis Commission of inquiry into primary education established in 1868 which was critical of the progress being made by children; and in the 1900s with the introduction of a child centred educational programme.

As the nineteenth century drew to a close, dissatisfaction on various grounds was being expressed with the national schools. The Recess Committee's report of 1896 had urged reform. As a result of the Commission on Practical and Manual Instruction, established in 1897 and commonly referred to as the Belmore Commission, a revised programme for national schools was implemented in September 1900. In 1918 two further committees were set up to examine both national and intermediate education— the Killanin Committee and the Molony Committee. The MacPherson Education Bill of 1919, which never became law, contained many reforms proposed by these committees.

Meanwhile the intermediate school system had been established in 1878 with the passing of the Intermediate Education (Ireland) Bill of that year. After this development some national schools called 'secondary tops' offered the secondary school programme.

The nineteenth century also brought dramatic changes to university education in Ireland, which was associated with the élite and the upper class in society. Prior to the nineteenth century the only colleges in existence in Ireland were the Protestant dominated Trinity College, Dublin, founded in 1591, and a few Catholic foundations of which St Patrick's College, Maynooth, founded in 1795, was the largest. However, this position changed in the first half of the nineteenth century. A Select Committee on Foundation Schools and Education in Ireland, established in 1835, recommended in its report of 1838 that four provincial colleges should be established to provide higher education for the middle classes in Ireland. The recommendation was followed by the Queen's Colleges Bill of 1845 which established colleges at Cork, Galway and Belfast. Denounced by Daniel O'Connell's Repeal Association as 'godless colleges' they were opposed by the Catholic hierarchy. In 1854 a Catholic university was formally established while in 1879 the Royal University of Ireland, an examining body, was established. The next development came in 1908 with the passing of the Irish Universities Act which established the National University of Ireland (NUI). Now the Queen's Colleges of Cork and Galway—renamed University College,

Cork and University College, Galway—joined with University College, Dublin in a new federal structure, with Maynooth College affiliating two years later.

Paralleling these significant changes in educational structures in nineteenth-century Ireland was the dramatic linguistic change in the same period, the Irish language declining as rapidly as the use of English was increasing. What is of central importance is the extent to which the changes in education and linguistic patterns were linked: did the educational structures precipitate or contribute to the nineteenth century witnessing the greatest linguistic shift ever recorded in Ireland? The perception in independent Ireland was that the education system did indeed cause the demise of Irish as a spoken language. The governing body of the national school system was said to have 'crushed the Irish language',[3] while evidence gathered by the Folklore Commission in 1954 suggested that it was 'school that finished Irish … Those who didn't go to school kept their Irish.'[4] This perception sprung partly from the use of the 'bata scóir' or tally stick, by parents and teachers as a method of ensuring that children did not speak Irish during school hours. Being a punishment system for the speaking of Irish, it helped discredit the language among the younger generation. Equally, growing school attendance resulted in greater levels of literacy and the bias towards English in the schools meant that literacy became equated with knowledge of English. Much of what appeared on the school curriculum was culturally anachronistic in the Irish context. While the main aim of the schools was to provide a grounding in literacy and numeracy, the whole system had a British cultural emphasis. Padraic Pearse in the *Murder Machine* described the system as 'grotesque and horrible' aimed at the 'debasement of Ireland'.[5]

Much of this correlation between the developing education system and the declining status of Irish was justified. In particular, it is difficult to agree with the idea that the national school commissioners were simply unaware of the Irish language.[6] However, it seems equally spurious to suggest that English was 'imposed' on the majority of the population.[7] Rather, the British policy of cultural assimilation was strengthened by the desire of Irish people, springing to a large extent from economic necessity, to learn English. To this extent only can the schools be seen as participating in the linguistic shift of the nineteenth century. Of greater importance was the fact that the Irish people were surrounded by a world whose business was carried on through the medium of English, a world which was seen as economically more prosperous than Gaelic-speaking Ireland, Irish often being associated with poverty.[8] In the words of the poet Michael

Hartnett, English became 'a necessary sin/the perfect language to sell pigs in'.[9]

However, economics was not recognised as an agent of linguistic change by the Free State government, and the idea that the schools alone had brought about the use of English as a vernacular was the central premise on which the whole revival effort of the independent Irish government was based. The philosophy of the revival movement was founded on the incorrect assumption that if English had replaced Irish as the language of the country primarily because of an anglicised education system, then the reverse could be brought about by a native government.

This perception was fostered by the Gaelic League (Conradh na Gaeilge), an association fired by a philosophy based on cultural nationalism and all its ramifications. Mirroring developments in Europe in the nineteenth century, where a sense of nationality and the concomitant traits of nationality became eminent, the League had its origins in 1879 when some members of the Society for the Preservation of the Irish language founded Aondacht na Gaedhilge, the Gaelic Union, heralding Ireland's emergence from 'lár geimhridh na Gaedhilge'.[10] According to *An Claidheamh Solais*, the official newspaper of the Gaelic League first published in March 1899, the object of the League was to make Ireland a bilingual country by restoring the language and cultivating a modern Irish literature.[11] In 1912 Padraic Pearse, in answer to the question: 'Cad is cuspóir do Chonnradh na Gaedhilge?' replied: 'Gaedhil do chur ag labhairt Gaedhilge'.[12]

The League's emphasis on education and the education system as the most powerful, practical means of reviving the language was evident from the beginning. It provided its own opportunities for learning the language through the work of the Coiste Oideachais set up in June 1902, through Irish lessons in the columns of *An Claidheamh Solais*, and through 'rapid sale'[13] publications such as *Simple Lessons in Irish*, written by Eugene O'Growney, a founder member of the Gaelic League and Professor of Celtic Literature and Language in Maynooth from 1891–94. However, the League quickly turned its attention to the State education structures as conduits for the language revival. Resolutions, such as the one below, were passed by various branches of the League, underlining the importance it attached to the schools in reviving Irish:

We call upon the Commissioners of National Education to (1) introduce into all schools under their control in predominantly Irish-speaking districts a frankly and unreservedly bilingual system of education; (2) we regard their doing so as a simple act of

> justice to the children of those schools, and as the removal of an intolerable educational wrong; and (3) we ask them to grant the fullest facilities for the teaching of Irish in all their schools, to suitably remunerate its teaching in all classes and to abolish the present vexatious regulations regarding it.[14]

One of the first public controversies entered into by the League was with the Intermediate Education Commissioners over the lack of prominence given to the Irish language in the secondary schools. To the forefront in this controversy was Douglas Hyde, a co-founder of the Gaelic League and its president until 1915.

The first indication of how vehemently the League was attached to the idea of the schools being central to the revival, and the extent to which it was prepared to see educational achievement sacrificed for the sake of the language, may be seen in the works of another prominent member of the League, Fr. M.P. O'Hickey. In 1899 he wrote:

> Even though half the subjects in the programme should have to be sacrificed, the language of the country should be taught in all the schools of Ireland. On this question we can have no parley; we can entertain no compromise.[15]

O'Hickey succeeded O'Growney as Professor of Celtic Literature and Language at Maynooth in 1896. Nevertheless, the Maynooth trustees forced his resignation from the Gaelic League in 1903 as a result of his pamphleteering in support of Irish in the curricula of the schools. In 1909, following a campaign to have Irish made compulsory for matriculation in the newly established National University of Ireland, he was dismissed from his professorship. Having unsuccessfully appealed his dismissal to the Holy See, he retired to his brother's home in Carrick-on-Suir.[16]

The efforts of the Gaelic League and its predecessor language groups were successful even before the establishment of the Free State. In 1879 the teaching of Irish outside ordinary school hours was permitted in national schools, fees being payable for such instruction. By 1895, out of 8,557 schools, sixty-three schools were presented for examination in Irish, 737 of the 1,176 pupils, achieving a pass standard.[17] In 1900, with the introduction of a new school programme, managers and teachers could, within certain constraints, arrange their programmes to suit the needs of the localities in which the schools were situated. Irish could now be taught as an optional subject during ordinary school hours or as an extra subject for fees outside ordinary school hours. These regulations depended on the inspectors who had to be happy that the standard obtained in the other school subjects was satisfactory. The problem was that a large number of schools were not reported as satisfactory. In 1902, for example, only half of the schools were reported as attaining an adequate standard in other subjects.[18]

In April 1904 the Commissioners of National Education announced their approval of a bilingual programme for use during ordinary school hours in Irish-speaking districts. The programme was to start in the school year 1906–7 with thirty-six bilingual schools. By 1921–22 there were 239 such schools operating.[19]

The demand that 'the secondary schools must become the servants of the Irish nation'[20] was satiated more rapidly than was the case with the national schools, the Irish language securing a footing in the intermediate system from its inauguration in 1878. However, in that year less than 10 per cent of pupils presented it for examination. Following the representations made by Douglas Hyde on behalf of the Gaelic League to the Royal Commission of 1899, the status of Irish was enhanced with 20–30 per cent of students taking it within a few years.[21] However, it was only with the introduction of compulsory Irish for matriculation within the NUI in 1913 that the number of second level students taking Irish increased substantially. By this time Sinn Féin was strongly reinforcing the work of the Gaelic League in ensuring that the schools became the servants of the language revival. Its party constitution, adopted at its Ard Fheis in October 1917, committed Sinn Féin to 'the reform of education, to render its basis national and industrial by the compulsory teaching of the Irish language'.[22]

With the coming of Independence, the last obstacles to implementing an official schools-based revival were removed. Based on the unquestioned nationalist assumption that the education system of the nineteenth century had caused the spread of English and was the major factor in the decline of the Irish language, Dáil Éireann committed itself not just to a language revival programme but to a language revival programme based on the preservation and extension of the Gaeltachts and, in English-speaking areas—comprising the greater demographic and geographic portion of the Free State—based predominantly on the education system. The possibility of complacency once a native government had committed itself at policy level to the language revival, or the fact that the national symbolic defiance associated with the language was no longer a spur, were not aired. It was simply presumed that the language, long 'neglected and despised',[23] would again occupy a pre-eminent position in Irish society. The words of the Young Irelander, Thomas Davis—'A people without a language of its own is only half a nation' and 'To have lost entirely the national language is death, the fetter had worn through'—were never more loudly or more often echoed.

The job of overhauling the intermediate and national education systems, part of the *damnosa hereditas*[24] left by the English administration, was given to John J. O'Kelly ('Sceilg') who was appointed Minister for Irish in November 1919 in the first Dáil and later Minister for Education in August 1921. A noted republican and author of many Irish books, he was president of the Gaelic League.

Following the formation of the first Dáil in 1919, the Irish National Teachers Organisation (INTO) passed a resolution at its annual congress of Easter 1920 directing its central executive committee to convene a representative group in order to frame a programme for the national schools in accordance with Irish ideals and conditions. Part of the urgency in introducing a new curriculum stemmed from reports that Sinn Féin cumainn throughout the country were visiting schools in order to ensure teachers were using Irish. The resulting National Programme Conference, which met for the first time in January 1921, was composed of representatives from the Department of Education, the General Council of County Councils, the National Labour Executive, the Gaelic League, the INTO and the Association of Secondary Teachers. Máire Ní Chinnéide, one of the two Gaelic League representatives, was elected chairperson and T.J. O'Connell, secretary of the INTO from 1916–48 and leader of the Labour Party from 1927–32, was elected secretary. It is interesting to note the organisations which declined an invitation to attend: the Professors of Education, the Catholic Headmasters' Association, the Catholic Clerical Managers, the Christian Brothers and the Schoolmasters' Association.[25]

It was decided from the outset that where the majority of parents objected to having either Irish or English taught as an obligatory subject, their wishes would be complied with.[26] However, this proviso was seemingly ignored in the final recommendations (see below). No consideration was taken of the teachers who had to teach the programme, many of whom had no Irish themselves. This is especially surprising in light of the fact that the INTO had five representatives at the conference. Even before the final report was signed Michael Hayes, the Minister for Education in the second Dáil from January to September 1922, (and subsequently a lecturer in Modern Irish at University College, Dublin) in a letter dated 6 January 1922 stated that every manager and teacher was at liberty to put the programme into operation immediately.[27] The following February the Provisional Government issued 'Public Notice Number 4' concerning the teaching of

Irish in all national schools. Its recommendations were to come into effect from St Patrick's Day 1922. The four central regulations were that:

(1) The Irish language was to be taught, or used as a medium of instruction for not less than one full hour each day in all national schools where there were teachers competent to teach it.

(2) The hour was to be divided (a) a half hour not earlier than 10.00 a.m. and (b) a half hour not later than 2.30 p.m.

(3) If there was but one or two competent teachers in the school, special arrangements were to be made to facilitate their teaching of the language.

(4) In cases where there were any difficulties in carrying out the regulations statements were to be submitted as a matter of urgency to the Inspector of Irish Instruction, National Education Office.[28]

In April 1922 the National Programme officially came into operation after being submitted to and approved by the provisional government. The new programme was welcomed by a broad spectrum of people (at least initially) as going some way towards redressing the cultural balance in the national schools. More and more it was becoming the norm to associate the revival of Irish almost exclusively and certainly primarily with the schools. As William Cole, T.D., pointed out in December 1922:

Many of the ills from which we suffer today and perhaps most can be traced to the fact that the education of the children for generations past has never been on the right lines, nationally speaking. We want to make the Irish population in the future an Irish speaking nation.[29]

There was little room afforded to honest scepticism. One of the few doubting voices raised was that of Cathal O'Shannon, TD, in 1923, a former leader of the Socialist Party of Ireland and a member of the I.R.B. and Gaelic League, when he expressed the fear that his faith had been shaken 'in the likelihood of Irish becoming a dominating language in Ireland within my time'.[30] The prevailing sentiment was captured more accurately by another Dáil Deputy, Seoirse Ghabhan Uí Dubhthaigh, in his appeal: '*Ná tréigimis an chúis*'.[31]

In September 1921, a few months after the establishment of the First National Programme Conference, the Department of Education convened a conference on secondary education. Like its national school counterpart, it recommended a greater alignment between the curriculum of the secondary school and the culture of Ireland, especially in relation to the Irish language.[32] As a result of a preliminary meeting in August 1921 in the Mansion House (the location of the Department of Education) a thirty strong commission was established in September of the same year 'to draft a programme which would meet the national requirements, while allotting its due place to the Irish language'. Chaired by Michael Hayes, the commission consisted of representatives from the INTO, the AST(I), the Incorporated Society of Assistant Masters, the Catholic Headmasters' Association, the Christian Brothers and the Irish Schoolmasters' Association. Also on the commission was Timothy J. Corcoran, the single most important individual impetus behind the Gaelicising of the schools. In 1925 Corcoran published a seminal article in *Studies* outlining the importance he attached to the schools in reviving the language. Described by a contemporary as having 'a passionate conviction of the continuity of the Ireland of today with the old Gaelic Ireland [and] an intense desire to make this manifest in the curricula and methods of our schools',[33] Corcoran was the first Professor of Education in University College, Dublin, having spent a number of years teaching at second level. In the *Studies* article he persuasively argued that 'the Irish language will have to be acquired, and thoroughly acquired, as a vernacular within the school and within the school-hours. This is a plain fact as regards all areas not effectively Irishspeaking: and effectively means devotedly.'[34]

Corcoran suggested that there was 'an abundance of historical evidence' to suggest that Irish could be restored through the schools as a 'real vernacular'. The fact that such evidence did not exist was a point lost in the midst of Corcoran's powerful, nationalist rhetoric which greatly appealed to the revivalists. Once again, the great inadequacy and simplicity of the argument that if English displaced Irish then a linguistic and cultural reversion could equally be precipitated, was overlooked. Not only did Corcoran see the schools as the mainstay of this reversion, but he contributed to the decrease in importance attached to the promotion of Irish outside the schools: 'the popular schools ... can restore our native language. They can do it even without positive aid from the home'.[35]

The fact that Corcoran had no Irish himself was not seen as an issue, a stark contrast to the verbal lambasting which those who questioned the policy received for similar linguistic ignorance. The centrality of Corcoran's thesis, an affirmation of pre-Independence nationalist thought, but now with the weight of a professional and widely respected educationalist, was an enduring one: as late as 1963, the final report of Comisiún um Athbheochan na Gaeilge said of the nineteenth century that:

> The extension of popular education, especially through the setting up of national schools, provided the means whereby the diffusion of English could be effected in every corner of the land.[36]

The report of the commission on secondary education, completed in December 1921 and circulated to teachers and headmasters, recommended the establishment of a junior and senior Leaving Certificate examination. The subjects for the former were to be compulsory Irish or English, a second language, mathematics, science, history and geography, with Irish, history and geography constituting the Gaelic core of the curriculum. Following the receipt of criticisms and suggestions from teachers, the recommendations were adopted through the Secondary School Programme of 1924 which emphasised the Gaelic element of the curriculum.[37] With the establishment of the Intermediate and Leaving Certificate examinations in 1924 either Irish or English had to be passed before the certificate could be awarded.

Owing to certain problems in the national schools regarding the First National Programme, especially the failure of the government to introduce compulsory school attendance (which did not come about until 1926) the central executive committee of the INTO decided in March 1924 that a second conference on primary education was necessary. However, Eoin MacNeill, the Minister for Education, refused to take part until a meeting was convened in November 1924 between representatives of the INTO and the Department of Education at which the INTO delegation asked the minister to convene the conference and agreed that MacNeill would choose the delegates. The second conference, finally convened in June 1925 by MacNeill, was far more representative than the first conference of 1921 and included a large proportion of clerical school managers.

The second conference made numerous recommendations regarding the teaching of Irish in the national schools. One of the leading characteristics of its deliberations was the insistence on the principle of teaching the infant classes through Irish:

> The work in the infants' classes between 10.30 a.m–2.00 p.m. is to be entirely through Irish where the teachers are sufficiently qualified. Teachers able to teach Irish, but not through Irish, are to teach Irish as a subject for one hour per day at least and to use Irish as much as possible as the school language.[38]

Every aspect of class work was to go into 'training the children to understand Irish and to speak it distinctly and correctly as their natural language'.[39] While it was anticipated that many schools would not be in a position to carry out the recommendations of the second programme, it was expected that all schools would work towards a situation where the higher course in Irish would be taken in both junior and senior infants:

> Where the attainment of both teacher and pupils justify the use of Irish as the school language, the higher course is to be taken in Irish together with the lower course in English; otherwise, the higher course in English and the lower course in Irish. Those who take the lower course in Irish will be expected to advance gradually towards the higher course in Irish, less English in proportion being taken.[40]

The weaknesses in instruction which necessitated the convening of the second conference were blamed on the teachers: 'we received evidence that—as often happened—teachers were insufficiently prepared, the effort to teach history, geography, or mathematics through Irish resulted in an indifferent teaching of these subjects and consequently in giving colour to some adverse criticism of the general teaching standard of our schools'.[41]

The last meeting of the conference was held in March 1926 and two days later the report was signed. In May the new Minister for Education, John O'Sullivan, stated that he was prepared to accept the Second National Programme as the official programme for use in the national schools. The central position of the Irish language in the education system had now been secured.

The huge impact that this emphasis on Irish had on the schools, both as a subject and as a medium of instruction, is the central focus of the following chapters. There is little doubt that the implications of the language revival effort from 1922 for the Irish education system were enormous and enduring. An attempt is made to analyse the gulf between nationalist ideals and pragmatic realities, and the extent to which the education revival policies remained largely untainted by practical considerations. This was seen most clearly in the failure to deal with such issues as the adequate provision of Irish language text books, the absence of a standardised spelling or grammar, the almost non-existent structures to train the many monolingual English-speaking teachers already in the service and the near absence of any drive to Gaelicise the wider society in the face of public apathy.

The policy was also the most significant one in shaping popular perceptions of the language and its status within society. The work examines the 'gombeenism' which came to surround the language, evident in the increasingly complex system of grants and increments available to those who used the language and the strong defence of their necessity, and the increasing association between—and resentment towards—the necessity of passing Irish examinations both in and out of school in order to succeed in education or employment.

Another area explored is the extent to which the nationalist rhetoric from the early twentieth century never translated into popular, practical support for the language. Yet, despite this, criticism of the language movement could still evoke the strongest of nationalist feelings up to the 1960s and beyond, among a population which often chose ignorance of its national language over knowledge of it. Perhaps this national cultural irony best underpins the complexity of identity in relation to language in Ireland. What is attempted here is to trace the single most important element in that complexity, the attempts to revive the Irish language through the education system.

CHAPTER ONE

Compulsory Irish, 1922–1973

THE HOPE of successive governments and Ministers for Education was that if teachers and pupils realised the importance and significance of the Irish language, they would bring an enthusiasm to its learning. With the introduction of compulsion at curriculum and examination level the potential for achievements through enthusiasm was copperfastened by enforcement; enthusiastic or not, the teachers had to teach Irish as a compulsory subject. Compulsion was the most consistent trait of the language revival policy both inside and outside the education system. Irish was being imposed as an obligatory requirement for many civil and public service posts. It was also obligatory in entrance examinations for NUI and teacher training colleges. These latter issues are debated in subsequent chapters in the context of Irish in the broader society and teacher training. Here the focus is on Irish as a compulsory subject on the school curriculum and in certificate examinations, issues of great argument and debate, almost to the point of divisiveness.

Like so many other aspects of the revival policy, the teaching of Irish as a compulsory subject was fraught with inherent contradictions, with a huge disparity between theoretical aspiration and practical application. This becomes evident when examining teaching methods and the competency gained by students: while it might be expected that the emphasis of the Irish class would be on oral exercises, the Irish course was to develop in other directions. Of course, there were schemes to encourage the spoken language, the establishment of Irish summer colleges for pupils, the first of which pre-dated Independence, being one example. The chapter revolves around these issues—the ideology behind compulsion and its introduction; the methodology of teaching and its level of success; the balance of oral as against written work in the schools; the founding of summer colleges and the eventual curbing of compulsion in the early 1970s.

Contemporary arguments for compulsory Irish

To justify making Irish a compulsory school subject it was first necessary to demonstrate that the language had an inherent value and significance, and many arguments were put forward in this context. The three most widely used arguments were based on the historical significance of Irish and the idea that extinction would constitute a betrayal of previous generations of Irish people and history; its significance as a cultural badge marking the Irish out from all other cultures, particularly the Anglo-Saxon; and the practical, namely that the Irish nation would not survive or prosper without its own language. Other reasons were also put forward: the 'high spirituality' of the Gaelic language and outlook was put before teachers by the Department of Education as one of the reasons why they should fully commit themselves to the language revival.[1] However, it was the emphasis on the historical significance of the language which was most often stressed and which summed up the inherent flaw in the language revival campaign: it was backward looking. Its philosophy was based on an unsound interpretation of history. It was part of an attempt to revive not just a language but an imaginary early Irish Utopia:

> Ná bíodh sé le rá go ndéanfaimis faillí anois i dteanga Phádraig,
> Bhríd is Cholmcille, Bhrian Boirmhe is Eoghan Ruaidh, Eoghan
> Ó Gramhnaigh is Pádraig Mac Piarais ...[2]

Allied to this historical argument was the one based on nationhood, namely, that Irish served as an expression of a separate nationality, as a tangible difference between the Irish nation and the British Crown. Harkening back to the rhetoric of Thomas Davis, revivalists were constantly making this connection between the language and nationality:

> A people without a language is not worthy to be called a nation.[3]

> Ní hé amháin gur mian linn an Ghaeilge a shábháil toisc gurb
> í ár dteanga féin í ach ní féidir an náisiún a shábháil má cailltear
> an Ghaeilge.[4]

While this latter reason could be loosely interpreted as practical—the revival of the language to ensure the survival of the nation—it was practical only in the most nebulous and abstract sense. No reasons were put forward based on economic or social development, the areas of life of most immediate concern to the people. And considering that Irish culture was finding very full and adequate expression through English at this time, the abstract arguments based on cultural significance were less than convincing when left unqualified.

Yet, it was these reasons which were put before teachers in an effort to galvanise them into activity. Department of Education circulars and rule books particularly hyped the significance of the language in ensuring the survival of the nation:

> That Gaelic attitude … gives us our individuality as a nation, without it we become an amorphous or a hybrid people.[5]

Neither was there any doubt but that, based on the arguments outlined in the Introduction of this book, 'the effort to revive Irish as a spoken language undoubtedly rests very largely with our schools' to quote Tomás Ó Deirg, the Minister for Education for all but nine months between 1932–1948.[6] This would result, it was hoped, in making natural and fluent Irish speakers of all pupils within the retrospectively ambitious timescale of twenty to forty years.[7] The Department of Education's *Notes for Teachers: Irish* (1933), made this expectation clear to teachers, saying that students from the Galltacht on leaving the primary school should, by the age of fourteen, be able to converse freely in Irish.[8] All the teacher's efforts were expected to go into the achievement of this aim. The efforts of some city schools in this regard were cited as an example of how this might be achieved: some schools had set up special playgrounds, called 'Gaeltachts', for pupils willing to speak Irish voluntarily during break time.[9]

Teachers were encouraged to cultivate a love for the language among their pupils. It was thought that the best means of doing this was to explain the ideals and reasons behind the revival campaign. As John Goulding, a Fianna Fáil TD from Waterford and a prominent worker in the Irish-Ireland movement, which developed in the 1890s promoting a type of cultural nationalism, pointed out: 'unless there is an effort made to teach the children what they are being taught Irish for it will be a failure'.[10] By doing this a 'Gaelic outlook' could be fostered in the schools and in the minds of the pupils.[11]

To help inculcate the ideals of the language revival, it was suggested at an early stage that school text books should reflect the national spirit 'agus ní amháin sin, ach gur fíor-Éireannaigh na daoine a sgríobhas iad'.[12] It was thought that not just books written in the Irish language should serve this purpose, but that books written in English should also reflect 'obair na tíre'.[13] This was seen as particularly important in the teaching of history: Irish history should be taught in the context of the Irish language revival.[14] There seemed an open acceptance that the history taught should be geared specifically to the backing of the revival campaign and the search for a separate national identity. According to one observer, the Irish Christian Brothers, founded by Edmund Rice in 1802 with the aim of teaching those who could not otherwise afford an education, were already doing this by teaching 'the Irish language and Irish history ... with a bias matching the bias displayed by the British in their renditions of history'.[15] As late as 1965 the history of 'the national aim' to be taught in the schools was defined as 'the forces which caused its [the Irish language's] decline, the purpose behind its revival, its imprint on placenames, on personal names, on the English that is spoken in Ireland ...'.[16]

The success in fostering this Gaelic mentality in the schools, so important to revival efforts, was limited. As early as July 1924 the Minister of Education, Eoin MacNeill, a founder member of the Gaelic League, was being warned that proceeding too far in haste was dangerous. One of the consequences of the initial and enthusiastic effort in reviving the language was that nobody quite knew what was expected from them—neither teacher, nor pupil, nor parent. Enthusiasm seemed to be outrunning practical consideration.[17]

By 1930 the Department of Education was complaining that pupils were not being encouraged to learn Irish as a 'national duty',[18] a fact attributed in part to teachers not understanding the importance of the language in national affairs.[19] It appears little progress was made in this direction over the next thirty years. By 1960 the Department of Education still saw a greater role for schools in encouraging pupils, especially in the primary school, to carry out this 'national duty' to a greater degree:

> Meastar ... nach mór iarracht níos fearr a dhéanamh chun a chur in iúl do na daltaí an fáth a mba chóir dóibh meas a bheith acu ar an Ghaeilge, gurb í a dteanga féin agus teanga an Náisiún Gaelaigh í agus gurab í an teanga náisiúnta an comhartha Náisiúntachta is bunúsaí dá bhfuil ag aon tír.[20]

These sentiments were echoed two years later in the *Report of the Council of Education: Curriculum of Secondary Schools* (1962), which observed that it was only when pupils were aware of the reasons for learning Irish that they would bring an enthusiasm to the task, making the learning of the language a pleasure rather than a burden.[21]

The introduction of compulsory Irish

The obvious lack of enthusiasm for the language which reports and commissions from the 1920s to the 1960s implied can be taken as an early indication of how successful the schools-based revival policy was in achieving its aim. However, enthusiasm or not, with the introduction of compulsion Irish became a very definite part of school life. Not relying on arguments based on nationality and history, compulsion ensured that the schools carried out the wishes of the legislature. Enthusiastic or otherwise, teachers were compelled to teach Irish and pupils were compelled to learn it and what parents thought did not matter. The compulsory policy was tripartite—Irish was made a compulsory subject for the curriculum, a compulsory examination subject and a necessary subject to pass in certificate examinations in order to pass the examinations overall. In time, the presentation and carrying out of this policy was to prove one of the major *faux-pas* of the language revival effort. The reversion of a native government to a policy popularly associated with British rule alienated people from the revival policy. There was a feeling that English had been rammed down the throats of the Irish people and that now a native government was attempting the same with Irish.[22] The reason for compulsion rather than a voluntary effort was that the legislators and the revival pressure groups which exerted considerable influence over them were afraid that if schools were left to teaching the subject on a voluntary basis, many would not bother teaching it at all.[23] Indeed, the view was that it would be extraordinary if Irish was not an obligatory subject for children attending school and taking examinations.[24]

As a subject Irish had been compulsory for matriculation in the National University of Ireland since 1913. From St Patrick's Day 1922, Irish was made compulsory in all standards in the national schools. From then at least one hour per day had to be spent teaching Irish. From the school year 1927–28 Irish became a necessary subject for the award of the Intermediate Certificate[25] in accordance with the 'requirements and suggestions of the programme of the first Dáil'[26] while Irish also became a necessary subject on the curriculum, replacing the previous regulation which required the teaching of Irish or English.[27] From 1934 Irish became a necessary subject for the award of the Leaving Certificate examination.[28] Beginning in the school year 1934–35 schools were expected to examine entrants in Irish by means of a written examination which was combined with an oral examination from the school year 1937–38.

It was decided at the National Programme Conference in 1922 that if the majority of parents objected to their children being taught Irish (or English) as an obligatory subject then their wishes would be respected.[29] However, as we shall see, this never became government policy in practice. The evidence of Father Quinlan of Belvedere College is illuminating in this regard. It was reported in the INTO publication *Irish Schools Weekly* in December 1924 that amidst the differing views and interpretations of government policy 'he was glad to see that in their school the standard of proficiency in the language today was very high and the boys were bound to learn it whether their parents liked it or not'.[30] Tomás Ó Deirg was to echo this sentiment as Minister for Education when parents expressed dissatisfaction with compulsion: 'I cannot see that parents, as a body, can decide this matter'.[31]

The move towards compulsory Irish was greeted as a positive development by many. The only complaint of revivalists was that the policy of compulsion could not be implemented at an even more rapid pace.[32] It was seen as a *sine qua non* if Irish was to be revived: 'it is clear that once the principle of reviving Irish is accepted, compulsion must in some degree be employed'.[33]

It was not long, however, before two divergent views emerged on the issue. In 1924 Professor William Thrift, an Independent Dáil Deputy for Dublin University and a member of the Commission on National Education, entered a 'mild protest'[34] against compulsory Irish in response to which Eoin MacNeill said that if Irish was put outside the list of compulsory school subjects, 'you will also put it outside the schools'.[35] Within a decade of its introduction, James Dillon, then a member of the National Centre Party, was calling on the minister to 'get it into his head that [if he thinks] he can dragoon this country into the learning of the Irish language before public opinion is ready for it, he will kill the Irish language absolutely, finally and irrevocably'.[36] Dillon went on to warn of the growing public opinion against compulsory Irish outside the Gaeltachts. He found many adherents among the politicians and academics of Free State Ireland for his views. Right across the political divide, Deputies were advising that the compulsory approach to Irish was causing a general resentment among the people.

Irish Schools Weekly highlighted some of the problems of compulsion from the teachers' point of view, the most important being that 'the teacher was frequently penalised by the inspector for his inability to rise to the high standard set on examination day, a proceeding which tended to damage, and had damaged, the enthusiasm of many efficient teachers for the language'.[37] Other groups stressed other problems. The Irish Association of Accountants at its inaugural dinner in 1927 called for an end to compulsion on the grounds that it was hindering trade and commerce, and suggested a redirection of energy and finances away from compulsory Irish and towards some more fruitful policy.[38]

By the late 1930s the arguments against compulsion were becoming more numerous as their proponents were becoming more vocal. It was developing into a divisive element in the revival campaign. Part of the division on the issue was political, the policy of compulsion being associated more and more with Fianna Fáil, a fact underlined by James Dillon in 1936:

> The truth is that the great majority of deputies in Fianna Fáil would not dare to speak the truth because they have a kind of pious hope that the Gaelic League has in it a good many extremists, and that if they upset the Gaelic League some of the boys would give them a stab in their respective constituencies ... The more precarious their seats become in this house, the more daring they are on the subject of compulsory Irish because they are afraid of the extremists' views and it is always safe when dealing with the left wing supporters of the Fianna Fáil Party to hold out as an irreconcilable Gael. Of course the Gaels are very valuable persons to keep with them. Not knowing 'B' from a bull's foot about the education problem themselves, so long as they remain in the Fianna Fáil Party they will take good care to be on the right side.[39]

Dillon remained vociferous in his condemnation of the compulsory Irish policy, calling for an end to compulsory Irish for State examinations in 1945.[40] He found many supporters. In 1951 an article in *The Bell* called for an end to 'all compulsion or any process remotely related to it'.[41] In an article in the *Sunday Independent*, Myles Dillon, then Professor of Celtic Studies at the Dublin Institute of Advanced Studies and a brother of James, asked: 'What then should we do to save the language?' to which he answered: 'I should like to remove all compulsion in the schools.'[42] Not only was compulsion not assisting in the revival of the language, but it was being argued that it was disadvantageous to the revival effort.

The question of compulsion went further than the teaching of Irish as a school subject. There were calls for an end to compulsory qualifying examinations in Irish for entry to the Civil Service, an issue which will be raised in a later chapter. Suffice to say at this point that the general perception was abroad that Irish was being used as a stumbling block in appointments to the Civil Service. Even if Irish was no longer compulsory in the schools, it would still be necessary to learn it to enter the Civil Service. No matter how highly qualified an individual was, insufficient Irish to pass the Civil Service or local authority appointment exams[43] meant failure. By 1960 James Dillon was talking about the 'awful resentment' this created among students and parents. One group, the Cahirciveen Farmers' Association, requested that alongside the referendum on PR of 1958, a referendum should be held on the question of compulsory Irish, partly in the context of 60,000 people having to emigrate annually to English speaking countries in order to make a livelihood.[44] Dillon concluded that: 'the extent to which Irish is becoming the instrument of inefficiency is a public scandal'.[45]

The kernel of the argument against compulsion was perhaps best summed up in an article by 'Captain Mac' (the pseudonym used by William Carr, an ex-clerical student from Maynooth College) in the *Irish Press* in September 1957 under the headline 'Do you like school?' Of catechism and Irish he said:

> These are the two subjects that should, above all, be not connected with slaps in the child's mind. It would be better if a child was to learn less and love more in any subject ... Those that are against Irish are, I'm afraid, as often as not people who got too many slaps at school themselves.[46]

The teaching of Irish and its level of success

Implicit in the criticism of compulsion was a questioning of the success of the teaching of Irish. It was obvious that the schools were falling spectacularly short of the goal with which they were burdened: had they been more successful there would undoubtedly have been less criticism. However, responsibility for the lack of success lay not with the teachers but with the government—while urging the schools to do everything possible to restore the language, the Department of Education refused to implement or even assess any of the practical suggestions which could have ensured greater success.

The methods to be used in teaching Irish in the primary school were set out in *Notes for Teachers: Irish*. In it teachers were advised that 'the only way to teach Irish is through the "direct method"',[47] where new expressions in Irish would be used in such close connection with the experience that the relationship between them could be in no doubt and easily recalled when necessary. Other suggested methods were the phrase method for the junior classes, the series method and the triangular conversation method. The idea of the latter was to split the class into three groups—a group of actors and two groups of onlookers. Presumably this method would be used in the teaching of oral Irish. Its application, however, was deemed limited while the method of dramatisation 'transcends all of these devices in interest and utility'.[48] The *Notes* stressed the necessity of conversation in the Irish class. Above all it asked teachers to ensure that Irish did not become 'merely a school subject'.[49] The importance of using Irish in teaching games was stressed in this regard.

Armed with these suggestions, the teachers implemented the policy of compulsory Irish. Nevertheless, it became apparent that teachers were relying too heavily on the 'ceist agus freagra' method of teaching.[50] Worse still, according to the Department of Education, 'bídhtear sásta le h-aon fhreagra a bhíonn ceart gan bacaint le cruinneas nó líomhthacht'.[51]

Yet, the Department paid no practical attention to what is possibly the most important consideration when teaching a language, namely, the balance struck between oral and written exercises. The lack of such a balance in the teaching of Irish is one reason for the limited success of the language revival. Since the idea of teaching Irish was to make it a vibrant and living language, it might have been expected that the emphasis would be on spoken Irish; that, as *Notes for Teachers: Irish* pointed out, 'continuous speech must be practised'.[52] The stated aim of reviving the language through the schools was to make Irish the normal language of conversation outside the schools. It might also have been expected that examinations in proficiency would have meant oral examinations to a very large extent. However, despite the repeatedly stated aim of reviving the language as a spoken tongue or a second vernacular, the emphasis in the schools, the primary instrument of the revival campaign, was on the written word. It was one of the many paradoxes underlying the revival policy and con-tributed greatly to the failure of the revival effort.[53] The gap between the stated aim and what was actually being done in the schools in this respect is indeed surprising.

Eoin MacNeill in his preface to Eoghan O' Growney's *Simple Lessons in Irish: Part IV*, which had gone through its tenth edition by 1918, wrote that 'to teach the student to speak should be the main object' of the Irish class.[54] The *First National Programme of Primary Instruction*, issued by the National Programme Conference in 1922, made little mention of oral Irish however. In naming Irish as one of the obligatory subjects in the primary school curriculum, it divided the subject into its teaching components: reading and spelling, writing, composition and grammar. The only mention of an oral content was in the explanation of what was meant by 'composition'. For third standard it meant teaching pupils how to 'form short consecutive statements orally about familiar subjects, or to describe a series of actions'.[55]

In a circular to managers, teachers and inspectors from the Department of Education on the subject of teaching through the medium of Irish, dated July 1931, the Department stated the intention of the programme was that schools 'do their part in reviving the language as a spoken tongue by giving the pupils such a mastery of Irish as will go a long way towards ensuring that revival'.[56] The programme in question here is presumably the Second National Programme of 1926 which differed little from the Programme of 1922. Again, the written word took precedence over the spoken word. At the same time, most academics were in agreement that the only way to promote a living language was to teach the spoken word first and then the written word. Shán Ó Cuív, a journalist and educationalist from Cork and first director of the Government Information Bureau, at a lecture in Harcourt Terrace in December 1936 entitled 'Múine beo-theangthacha' quoted Harold Palmer in this regard. Palmer, author of *The Scientific Study and Teaching of Languages* (1917), explained the four steps necessary in the learning of a new language. Ó Cuív emphasised these steps as:

1. An teanga nua do thuisgint agus í á labhairt fé mar a labharfadh cainteoirí dúchais í.

2. An teanga nua do thuisgint agus í sgríte fé mar a sgríbhfadh cainteoirí dúchais í.

3. An teanga nua do labhairt fé mar a labhrann cainteoirí dúchais í.

4. An teanga nua do sgrí fé mar a sgríonn cainteoirí dúchais í.[57]

In the same year that Ó Cuív gave this lecture, the Department of Education again circularised inspectors and school managers, reminding them that 'the main purpose of the teaching [of Irish], particularly in the lower standards, is to secure that pupils *speak* the language freely and fluently'.[58] This re-enforced the revised Programme of 1934 which emphasised the use of 'dialogues and of conversational lessons bearing directly on the occupations of the people'.[59] Despite such guidelines, however, little practical attention was paid to the teaching of 'labhairt na Gaeilge' with the result that the objective of making Irish the 'gnáth theangan teinteáin agus sráide' was not being achieved.[60] It was a complaint that appeared from time to time in Department of Education reports. (Indeed one is inclined to wonder what exactly was being taught in the Irish class in the early years of the Free State, as the teaching of written Irish had limited success according to the Department report of 1927–28: 'I mórán sgoileanna, go mór mór ins na sgoileanna lae, ní déintear maoirseacht cheart ar na cleachtaithe sgríobhtha.'[61]) The reason given in the report for the school year 1929–30 for the lack of progress in making Irish speakers of the pupils was that: 'Níl ár ndóthan múinteoirí cliste againn agus níl na córacha acu'.[62] Yet, the teachers were only following departmental guidelines and the practical necessities of departmental regulations. There were adequate numbers of 'múinteoirí cliste'; the lacking was elsewhere.

Despite the apparently negative evidence there were those who were praising the positive developments in the teaching of 'labhairt na Gaeilge'.[63] In 1941 Tomás Ó Deirg, the Minister for Education, noted that 'i labhairt na Gaedhilge tá tugtha faoi ndeara ag na roinn chigirí go bhfuil dul chun cinn éigin déanta'.[64] The report of the Department of Education for that year expressed satisfaction that the teaching of 'labhairt na Gaeilge' was developing satisfactorily in the higher classes of the national schools.[65] Four years later, however, the Department report had mixed feelings about progress: while satisfied on the one hand that primary school pupils were able (despite a limited vocabulary) to speak Irish easily, it was concluded that teachers were not putting enough effort into the teaching of spoken Irish. The thrust of the Department's argument now was that while Irish was being used in the school as the language of conversation, little effort was being made to make it the common language outside the school.[66]

The report of the Council of Education acknowledged that the progress made up to 1950 in making the Irish language a living language through the medium of the schools was not satisfactory.[67] To remedy this the report recommended that oral expression should take precedence over other elements of the Irish programme:

> The first and paramount case of the primary school in relation
> to Irish should be to ensure that the child can speak it.[68]

It described reading merely to acquire the technique of reading as a waste of time and recommended that, in order to devote more time to oral Irish work, less time should be spent on written exercises.[69] Tomás Ó Deirg, reading a prepared statement to the Fianna Fáil Ard Fheis in 1952 on behalf of Eamon de Valera, stressed the sentiments expressed in the Council of Education report. The tenor of the statement was that if the 'national objective' was to be attained, then it was crucial that the Irish language class involved the pupils in 'everyday conversations': 'Purely written tests in examinations give a completely wrong bias to the teaching.'[70]

However, the teachers felt as helpless in the 1950s as they had done in the 1920s with regards to oral Irish, some writing directly to the government complaining of the lack of oral Irish in the classroom of the primary school.[71] Meanwhile the Department of Education began praising the increased emphasis on oral Irish in the classroom. Obviously someone was becoming increasingly 'cliste'! The report of the Department for the year 1955–56 said that in standards one and two of the primary school, it was usual to spend a half an hour a day on written work and 'a dhá oiread' on oral work. While somewhat more time was spent on written work in standards three and four, the proportion of time spent on oral work was also greater. In standards five and six two hours per week were spent on written exercises in the Irish class, while twice that amount of time was spent on oral work.[72]

The ideal ethos of the language class was elucidated in the Dáil by Dr Noel Browne (who could not speak Irish himself) in 1957. A founder of Clann na Poblachta, Browne by this time was an Independent Deputy, having failed in his attempt to join the Labour Party and having been expelled from Fianna Fáil. Widely known for the controversy his 'Mother and Child' scheme aroused when he was Minister for Health in the first Inter Party administration, Browne said that the ideal attitude of the Irish class should be that 'we will relax now and we will talk the language' rather than 'we will get down and flog this into them and they will learn the genders and the past participles'. It was Browne's opinion that there should only be a simple oral test in Irish and that there should be no written examination in the language.[73]

In 1960 the newly appointed Minister for Education, Patrick Hillery, praised the efforts of everyone involved in the teaching of the language. He said it was a great pleasure for him to announce that the emphasis in the teaching of the language was now on the oral side.[74] In January of that year Dr Hillery issued a circular to all teachers saying that future assessment of their work would depend largely on their own efforts in the teaching of oral Irish:

> In this connection the minister wishes to stress his desire that the teachers should make every effort to advance as far as possible and as quickly as possible the speaking of Irish amongst their pupils.[75]

However, in 1965 it was still necessary for the INTO at their annual congress to ask, as Noel Browne had in 1957, that written Irish be no longer expected from primary school pupils.[76] The following year Fine Gael in its *Policy for a Just Society* also asked for an increased emphasis on oral as against written Irish in the primary school, pledging itself to what it termed a 'liberal Irish language policy'.[77]

What called into question official departmental complaints about the lack of oral Irish in the primary schools and the suggestions by Tomás Ó Deirg, Eamon de Valera and Patrick Hillery about infusing a greater oral element into the teaching of Irish in the primary school, was the Primary Certificate examination. Introduced in 1929 on a voluntary basis, the examination was made compulsory for pupils in sixth standard in 1943. It was purely a written test thus necessitating an emphasis on written exercises in the teaching of Irish which the legislators, among others, complained so vigorously about. It meant that while oral Irish may have been the ideal, concentration on written Irish was a necessity. Despite many requests made to various Ministers of Education, the Primary Certificate examination remained unreformed until its abolition in 1967. The result, according to Micheál Ó Síoradáin, who became an inspector with the Department of Education, was that, harkening back to his own experience:

> Bhíos ábalta aistí a scríobh agus bhí an ghramadach agam go seoigh; ní raibh labhairt na teanga ag mo mhúinteoir ná agam féin ámh.[78]

Calls for the introduction of an oral examination into the Primary Certificate were ignored by those who were calling for a greater emphasis on oral Irish in the primary school. For example, de Valera did nothing to change the format of the examination while at the same time stating in February 1949 while in Opposition that:

> precedence must be given at all times to the spoken tongue, particularly in the schools. The reading of the language and the writing of it will follow in due course.[79]

Not surprisingly the anomalous situation led many people to question the seriousness of the whole revival campaign. While in 1950 Tomás Ó Deirg said from the Opposition benches that the 'bun-chuspóir' of the revival campaign should be 'labhairt na Gaeilge d'fheabhsú',[80] the Department of Education, where Ó Deirg had served as Minister for all but nine months from March 1932 to February 1948, had stacked the odds against it.

From 1952 the INTO annual congresses discussed motions and passed resolutions calling for the abolition of the Primary Certificate 'on the grounds that it is educationally unsound and detrimental to the teaching of oral Irish'.[81] Its 1963 Congress authorised the central executive committee of the INTO to enter negotiations with the Department of Education and school managers with a view to changing the format of the Primary Certificate, rather than abolishing it. The new format, it was proposed, would attach greater importance to the teaching of oral Irish.[82]

Comisiún um Athbheochan na Gaeilge (1963) advised that at least 50 per cent of the marks for the Primary Certificate should be reserved for an oral Irish examination.[83] Nevertheless, it was another four years, in 1967, before the Primary Certificate examination was finally removed by the Fianna Fáil government at the same time that free primary and secondary education was introduced under the new and dynamic Minister for Education, Donough O'Malley. However, it was perhaps reform rather than removal that was called for. The abandonment of the Primary Certificate did not ensure that oral Irish would in future be emphasised in the primary schools. Had the examination been restructured to include an oral assessment, the results may have been more positive.

The teaching of oral and written Irish in the secondary and vocational schools became as much a point of debate as it did in the primary school. In September 1921 Dáil Éireann established a commission on secondary education 'to draft a programme which would meet the national requirements, while allotting its due place to the Irish language'.[84] Its recommendation that the Irish course should contain an oral examination was ignored in the *Rules and Regulations* for 1924–25, however, which obliged schools to teach either Irish or English together with a second language. Outlining the content of the Irish course, the guidelines stressed the importance of the spoken language:

> I bhfíorthosach na h-oibre dob' fhearr gan leabhar ar bith do chur i láimhaibh na sgoláirí agus gan iad do dhíriú ar léightheóireacht nó go mbeidís ábalta ar roinnt mhaith Gaedhilge do labhairt.[85]

Meanwhile an oral examination was introduced for the position of junior clerkship in the Civil Service in 1928. There seemed to have been the hope abroad that the introduction of oral tests into Civil Service examinations would encourage the teaching of oral Irish in the classroom, but official recognition in the form of an oral exam was very far off for the secondary schools.

In 1935 the Minister of Education, Tomás Ó Deirg, expressed satisfaction with the position of oral Irish in the secondary schools in Connaught. However, he instructed the inspectors to carefully examine the position of oral Irish in all secondary schools.[86] Many people shared Ó Deirg's general satisfaction. While speaking on the motion 'That in the opinion of the Dáil, the methods of the Government for preserving the Irish language need to be reconsidered and rationalised', Frank MacDermott, a Fine Gael Deputy for Roscommon, expressed the opinion that all the talk about oral Irish was 'part of … the vicious plan of putting the talking of some kind of Irish before everything else'.[87] It was feared that the continuing development of 'Dublin Irish' as distinct from what was perceived as proper 'Gaeltacht Irish' would go on interminably. Nevertheless, as there was no oral exam in Irish in the secondary schools, 'a grave injustice to the Irish language',[88] MacDermott's anxiety was unfounded.

In 1949 Richard Mulcahy, the Minister for Education in the first Inter Party Government, praised the secondary schools for their success in teaching oral Irish. While he was of the opinion that the secondary school 'must by its very nature emphasise the literary side', he believed that 'secondary schools in general have made considerable progress in the cultivation of oral Irish during the last twenty-five years'.[89] Yet, the truth was that Ireland was as far away as ever from becoming an Irish-speaking nation. To further promote the language, Mulcahy developed a scheme based on an existing scheme established under the Fianna Fáil government in 1945–46 whereby special grants were given to schools judged to be doing the most to make Irish not just the language of the classroom but the common language outside the classroom. Such stop gap measures, however, were a poor substitute for an oral examination, the introduction of which would have ensured that the energies of the Irish class would be spent on speaking and conversing in the language. The pressure for such a test was mounting by the mid 1950s. In March 1953 the *Irish Times* pointed to the importance of incorporating an oral element into Irish examinations.[90] The previous October, in a letter to the Department of the Taoiseach, the Department of Education spelled out the reasons for not introducing such a test in secondary schools, concluding: 'nach mbeadh a leithéid de scrúdú ion-oibrithe agus nárbh é leas, ach aimhleas na Gaeilge iarraidh a thabhairt ar a leithéid a chur i bhfeidhm'.[91] At this time the Department was providing £4,600 in grants to secondary schools which most encouraged the speaking of Irish. The request by Comhdháil Náisiúnta na Gaeilge at a meeting with the Taoiseach, Eamon de Valera, in August 1952 that a compulsory oral Irish examination be introduced into all secondary schools, was turned down.[92]

In 1953 the Department of Education circulated a very detailed document outlining its negative response to the calls for an oral examination.[93] It ruled out the introduction of an oral examination in either the Intermediate Certificate or the Leaving Certificate examinations on the basis of practicality and desirability. Its first argument was based on numbers. In 1952 over 6,000 pupils sat the Leaving Certificate while 11,000 sat the Intermediate Certificate, the pupils coming from 450 secondary schools. Such numbers, the Department argued, eliminated the possibility of a fair and common assessment of marks. This ruled out the possibility of awarding any marks for any future oral examination. The oral exam would, instead, have to be a qualifying exam. Even with that the Department foresaw many problems.

The second argument, perhaps surprisingly, concerned sectarianism. The Department of Education claimed that in Protestant secondary schools the standard of spoken Irish was very poor. This was due to many factors, not least of which was the difficulty encountered by Protestant schools in finding teachers suitably qualified in Irish. Unionist in outlook, the constant association of the Irish language with a certain type of cultural nationalism could only have diluted any existing enthusiasm among Protestants for the revival of the language, especially among those believers in the two nations theory.

From the introduction of compulsory Irish, the Protestant community had made no secret of their opposition to it. Even before Independence, it was clear that they found it difficult to adapt to the narrow concept of nationalism cultivated around the language and which presented Irish as an exclusively Catholic-nationalist appendage. Among those who objected to the policy of the Free State were Revd. A.A. Luce of Trinity College Dublin who claimed that compulsory Irish 'tends to drive a wedge between them [the Protestant parents] and their children. Compulsory Irish … is a wrong to the religion of Protestants.'[94] Bishop Orr, the Anglican Bishop of Tuam, expressed similar sentiments. *The Catholic Bulletin*, reinforcing the Catholic/Gaelic brand of nationalism, accused him and the 'New Ascendancy' of wanting to see Irish become a dead language, 'for philological dissection'.[95] The comments of M.E. Knight, who presided over the presentation of prizes at the Clones High School in 1926 did nothing to allay nationalists' fears. Knight warned that half a million 'of the States most loyal subjects' were in 'revolt against the government scheme of compulsory Irish … because the scheme is ruining Protestant schools'.[96]

To an extent Protestants were unable to understand the nationalist psyche which demanded that the Irish language at the very least deserved an honorary status in Irish life. The Protestant inability to comprehend this is possibly best illustrated by the remarks of J.E. Floyd, headmaster of the

Bishop Foy Grammar School, the total sum of whose contribution to the revival debate was that the Aborigines of Australia had their own language, but were still reported as being in the Stone Age.[97]

In the light of these circumstances and attitudes the introduction of an oral test would, according to the Department of Education, 'create an educational cleavage between Protestants and the rest of the community'.[98] It was foreseen that such a situation could in the future be used as an argument against the whole idea of restoring the language.

Religious considerations were also important in the context of élite Catholic schools. It was claimed that the pupils in these schools 'are not very much more proficient in oral Irish than Protestant pupils'.[99] To offend the wealthy patrons of such schools was not considered wise. An oral examination would mean that the government:

> would have to either stand firm in the face of 99 per cent of Protestant parents, of, say 20 per cent of Catholic parents, and these from the most influential and vocal section of society, and possibly of the ecclesiastical authorities—or else withdraw in confusion.[100]

The Department mentioned some other minor difficulties which would arise in the event of an oral test being introduced in post-primary schools. These included the case of the very good student who became tongue-tied; the problem with differing dialects; the problem of earnest pupils from the 'Six Counties' who had no chance of becoming proficient in spoken Irish; the problem of external candidates who were not attending the school and the problem of accommodation for the holding of the tests. There was also an opinion within the Department that an oral Irish examination would 'make no great difference to the pupils' command of Irish' and would instead 'upset, irritate and confuse the schools'.[101]

The report suggested that an oral Irish test would only become viable when Irish finally became the vernacular or second vernacular of the majority of the people. (Following the logic of this argument, it would appear unusual that there was no oral examination in English!) Rather than instituting an oral examination in Irish the Department suggested that the grant of £4,600 should be trebled and that the number of inspectors of Irish should be doubled to six. Short of these measures the Department took solace from the fact that 80 per cent of secondary schools were already spending much time on oral Irish. However, this statistic seems highly questionable, especially given that students were leaving the secondary school without ever having had an oral Irish examination. The claim was contradicted by, among others, Dr Noel Browne in 1957. It was Browne's opinion that there was little or no emphasis on spoken Irish. Certainly his assertion that in the Intermediate or Leaving Certificate 'a person could get high honours in Irish and not speak a work of the language'[102] is credible. It is a point backed up by the report of the Council of Education.[103]

Proving Adam Smith's dictum that there is a deal of anomaly in a nation, Jack Lynch, five years after the circulation of the Department of Education document explaining why an oral examination was not feasible, announced his intention as Minister for Education to introduce a 'béaltriail Gaeilge' in the Leaving Certificate from 1960.[104] The Department of Education claimed that teachers were satisfied with the introduction of the test.[105] It was a significant advance, facilitating not an entire change in emphasis but at least a significant degree of balance between the oral and written content of the Irish class.

The *Report of the Council of Education: Curriculum of the Secondary School* (1962) was satisfied that the new revised syllabus in Irish introduced in 1959–60, together with the oral examination, would prove beneficial in encouraging spoken Irish.[106] The Council of Education had begun its investigation of the secondary school curriculum in 1954. It recommended in the preface to the syllabus that the importance of oral Irish should be stressed as follows:

> The restoration of Irish as a living language in general use among our people is an integral part of national policy. The language, therefore, should have exceptional status in the achievement of the national objective (a) by creating in the school an atmosphere favourable towards the use of the language and (b) by providing such instruction as will enable our youth to extend and perfect the knowledge of the oral and written media already acquired by them.[107]

In 1963 the Irish Labour Party, in its document, *Challenge and Change in Education*, called for the introduction of an oral exam in the Intermediate Certificate.[108] In the same year, the English summary of the final report of Comisiún um Athbheochan na Gaeilge called for an oral examination in the Intermediate Certificate to help shift the emphasis further towards spoken Irish.[109] It also suggested that students should spend one month in the Gaeltacht to improve their command of spoken Irish.[110] The Commission, far from agreeing with Richard Mulcahy's assertion that teaching in the secondary school was by its very nature literary, stressed the necessity of tilting the balance in favour of oral Irish, a recommendation accepted by the government.[111]

The *Páipéar Bán um Athbheochan na Gaeilge*, [White Paper on the Revival of Irish], laid before both houses of the Oireachtas in December 1966, confirmed that the new syllabus for the Intermediate Certificate examination, applicable from September 1966, would include an oral Irish examination for which one-third of the overall marks would be allotted. The new syllabus became fully operational in 1969 when an oral test finally became part of the Intermediate Certificate examination.

These developments were partly a symptom and partly a result of the first attempts to approach the revival and teaching of the language from a scientific perspective. In December 1962 Dr Colmán Ó Huallacháin, OFM, was appointed adviser on linguistics to the Minister for Education. A graduate of Louvain and Georgetown universities, Ó Huallacháin had spent a number of years lecturing in University College, Galway, and St Patrick's College, Maynooth.

Comisiún um Athbheochan na Gaeilge urged the government to gear its policy over the following decade towards improving teaching methods.[112] By this time the amount of time being spent teaching the vernacular languages in the primary school was ten hours per week, the division between Irish and English being roughly 2:1. This compared with five hours spent teaching mathematics and five hours spent teaching the other subjects on the curriculum.[113] It recommended that this be done by fostering research into the nature and teaching of the language. The Irish Labour Party's pamphlet, *Challenge and Change in Education*, recommended that more time be spent teaching children to speak Irish rather than turning Irish class into a form of 'grammatical drudgery'.[114] Fine Gael's *Just Society*, outlining a more progressive social and economic policy for the party, called for more attention to be paid to such educational research, committing the party to encouraging and supporting such research when in government:

> There are few kinds of expenditure which could yield such a high return in human terms. We shall not allow any vested interest, or any fear that the results of such research would reflect on past policies or achievements of this or any other political party, to stand in the way of psychological, educational, sociological or economic studies which would help to improve our education system.[115]

While promising great things for the future this statement amounted to a recognition that past policies as regards the Irish language were detrimental to the educational development of the child.

An Páipéar Bán Um Athbheochan na Gaeilge, drawn up following the report of the commission of inquiry into the revival of Irish, saw great promise in the scientific approach to language learning,[116] Comhlacht Comhairleach na Gaeilge being established in March 1965 with the aim of pursuing this. Consisting of twenty-three members appointed for a period of three years its role was as a consultative council to advise on future policy regarding the language.

In June 1966 *Buntús Gaeilge* was issued by the Government Publications Office, the result of Colmán Ó Huallacháin's research and on which the multi-volume *Buntús Cainte*, published in 1967, was based. *Buntús Cainte* was the first multi-media, graded course in Irish for beginners based on books, audio tapes and radio and television series. Together with the setting up of Institiúd Teangeolaíochta na hÉireann in 1967, of which Ó Huallacháin was appointed director, it was considered a major contribution to linguistic research. In 1967 the first audiovisual Irish language courses became available to primary and secondary schools. All this evidence suggests that by the late 1960s there was an effort being made to develop scientific language teaching methods. However, the changes of the 1960s far from justified the previous forty year period when successive governments refused to submit their teaching policies to scientific scrutiny, despite calls on them to do so. And the days were not yet gone when 'creid nó ná creid is trí bhéarla a mhúineas an Ghaeilge', as one inspector reflected as he looked back on his own years as a pupil, teacher and inspector.[117]

Summer colleges

To improve their command of oral Irish pupils were encouraged to spend time in the Gaeltacht. The first official scheme, Sgéim na Roinne, established in 1932 under the direction of the Department of Agriculture and Fisheries, provided an opportunity for children between the ages of eight and twelve who could speak Irish fairly well and who had the capacity to gain fluency in the language, to spend a period of time in the fíor-Ghaeltacht. Students attended school in the Gaeltacht if it was open during the time of their stay, an examination deciding qualification for scholarships.[118]

In 1934 the first organised voluntary effort to send children to the Gaeltacht was set up in the form of Coiste na bPáistí. Established in Dublin in 1934, its official notepaper showed the influence of Thomas Davis on its work, quoting his dictum that 'a people without a language of its own is only half a nation'. Its aim was to bring English-speaking pupils between the ages of eleven and fourteen years whose parents had insufficient means, to the Gaeltacht for a period of at least four weeks during the summer. In the first year eighty children were sent to the Gaeltacht. This increased to 216 the following year. This number had more than doubled by 1936 and in 1937, 644 children were sent to the Gaeltacht.[119] By this time there were branches of Coiste na bPáistí in Dún Laoghaire, Navan, Tipperary, Limerick and Dundalk.[120]

The organisation received funding from the Department of Education in recognition of the fact that there was not 'éinnidh is mó a rachaid chun tairbhe d'aithbheochaint na Gaedhilge sa tír seo ná caoi a bheith ar fáil do pháistí na Galltachta chun seal a chaitheamh ins na ceanntair 'na mbíonn labhairt mar ghnáth theanga na ndaoine'.[121] Although the Department at first suggested a grant of £3 per student (half the entire cost), because of conditions outlined by the Department of Finance, it was finally agreed that for every pound collected by Coiste na bPáistí the Department would contribute £1 up to a limit of £1,000 per year—a sum which the Department of Education still felt was too small in the context of the 'obair náisiúnta' of the coistí.[122]

The other important group which brought children to the Gaeltacht was Clann na h-Éireann which started by bringing a group of pupils to Na Forbacha, County Galway, in 1935. The scheme was formed by a group of Dublin parents anxious that their children should be given every opportunity to learn Irish. By 1939 the parents, with the help of a government loan, had built 'Brú na Midhe' at Gibstown, County Meath, which was officially opened by Eamon de Valera. The Brú was geared towards the ten to sixteen age group and had accommodation for 100 children. Those attending the Brú had to possess a fair grasp of Irish in order that the 'inviolable rule' of Irish only be kept. Each course at the Brú lasted two weeks, attendance at which during school term was considered by the Department of Education as school attendance. Demand for places in the Brú became intense. In 1952, by which time the Department of Education was subsidising each child between ten and fourteen years of age by £3 or half the cost of the visit to the Gaeltacht,[123] all the places were filled within a fortnight of being offered, the Brú embarking upon an expansion programme in 1953.

The *Láimh-Leabhar* of Clann na hÉireann, under the motto 'Do chum Glóire Dé agus Onóra na hÉireann' listed the promises of the Clann:

1. Geallaim a bheith dílis do Dhia ár n-Athar agus do Chríost ár mBráhair.

2. Geallaim a bheith dílis do'n Ghaedhilg agus do'n náisiún Gaedhealach.

3. Geallaim a bheith dílis do Chlann na hÉireann agus d'á chuspóir.

In 1954 the Department of Education accepted the recommendation of Oifig na Gaeltachta agus na gCeanntar gCúng that the State should provide 1,000 scholarships to the value of £15 each for children under fourteen years to attend an Irish college. It was hoped that the scheme would show children that Irish was a living language. To avoid the possibilities of the children spreading English in the Gaeltacht (according to an *Irish Press* report in March 1952 'several complaints have been made in recent years that the girls and boys, while in the Gaeltacht, persist in speaking English'[124]) the Department of Education made it a condition of receiving the scholarship that a certain proficiency in Irish be attained beforehand.

In 1959, 1,129 students attended a Gaeltacht course, a number of whom were attending by virtue of scholarships offered by all sorts of organisations and clubs throughout the country. In 1955, for example, the Fianna Fáil Comhairle Cheantar Dhún Laoghaire began offering scholarships, sending five students to Cnoc na nAille and eight to Brú na Midhe in 1960. The Garda Síochána and army authorities also provided scholarships for children of Gardaí and army personal while commercial companies like New Ireland Assurance, Fry-Cadbury and National City Bank subscribed to the funds of Coiste na bPáistí.

By 1965 the government was providing grants of up to 80 per cent for the erection, extension and improvement of Irish colleges in the Gaeltacht and was paying £5 per pupil for each twenty-four to twenty-eight day course and approximately half the cost of enabling children attend primary school in the Gaeltacht for terms of three months.[125]

While the Irish colleges were both successful and valuable in terms of the Irish revival, it is difficult to judge to what extent they were so. Coiste na bPáistí was certainly overstating the fact when it spoke about students putting 'the capstone on their learning of Irish, so well begun in the schools, and return[ing] home ... with a fluent conversational command of Irish'.[126] In 1951 Domhnall Ó hUallacháin, an inspector with the Department of Education, visited Knock, County Galway, where a group of Dublin students were learning Irish. He returned disappointed with the progress being made:

Ní mór dom a rá go raibh díomá orm ... Shíl mé go raibh cuid mhaith idir a haon déag agus a ceathair déag lag go leor agus nár bhain siad aon ró-thairbhe ó thaobh Gaeilge dhe as an

> tréimhse a chaith siad san Ghaeltacht ... bhí na fuaimeanna go
> bacach agus bhí an stórfhocal an-chúng.[127]

Ó hUal"lacháin was of the opinion that the summer colleges should be more
structured with an increased emphasis on formal classes. Two years later
another inspector visited the Knock Gaeltacht where 201 students were
staying under the care of Coiste na bPáistí and returned equally dissatisfied.
He mentioned three factors that were particularly disappointing, namely,
that some children admitted to speaking English among themselves; that
no formal classes in Irish were organised and that very few children could
understand the native speakers. In the light of this it would appear that
Breandán Ó hEithir's comments about the Irish colleges were in some
respects justified. Writing in the *Irish Times* in April 1977 he concluded that:

> They are now Big Business and to criticise them is to be classed
> as a poitín informer. Most of the large ones have departed so far
> from the original excellent idea as to be worse than caricatures
> of the originals.[128]

However, the Gaeltachtaí did provide an opportunity for students to
speak and hear the language. Although not an opportunity that was always
taken advantage of, it was important for students to see that Irish was
more than an academic subject. Also, Ó hEithir's comments failed to take
account of the genuine and voluntary enthusiasm of non-State run Irish
summer colleges, an enthusiasm which may be taken as a measure of the
tangible commitment to the language in some quarters at least, albeit one
spurred on by State grants. Similarly, attendance at courses in the Gaeltacht
underpinned the extent to which children and their parents were prepared
to voluntarily invest in the language. This encouragement of voluntary
scholastic effort in the learning of Irish was to become increasingly
important in the 1960s when a non-compulsory approach was being urged
by many people.

Conclusion: Towards the curbing of compulsion

In the mid 1960s the white paper on the revival of Irish stated that:

> The parent or other person who conditions the mind of a child
> by constantly associating the adjective 'compulsory' with Irish
> is doing a disservice not only to that individual child but to other
> children and the nation in general ... The inclusion of Irish in

school curricula as an essential subject doesn't merit denigration
as a form of compulsion any more than the inclusion of English
or mathematics.[129]

It was not the first time that a call was made to abandon the term 'compulsory Irish'. Neither was it the first time that such an argument, based on the compulsion to study other subjects, was proffered: Seán Lemass had used it at a Fianna Fáil meeting in November 1961.[130] However, the equating of the position of English and mathematics with the position of Irish in the curriculum was not altogether justified. English and mathematics formed part of the essential, practical led curriculum; Irish was part of the culture led curriculum. Equally questionable was the implication by those opposed to compulsion that students were failing the Intermediate and Leaving Certificate examinations because of Irish. Of the 8,000 pupils who sat the Leaving Certificate examination in 1961, only seventy-eight failed by reason of Irish while 163 failed because of English.[131] Neither did those who objected to the policy take into consideration the fact that at least some students did become bilingual as a result of the compulsory Irish language policy,[132] while many students gained a reasonable reading and writing command of Irish. Nollaig Ó Gadhra claims that

> I got the opportunity to learn Irish in primary school. In my
> parish [Feenagh, Co. Limerick] there were no native Irish
> speakers by the time I was born in the 1940s. But because of the
> efforts that were made by the Irish State, and because of the
> policy of compulsory Irish, most of us at the age of twelve or
> thirteen left primary school in those years, bilingual.[133]

In an effort to give weight to its support for Irish as an 'essential subject' on the curriculum, the Commission used the example of Northern Ireland as showing what the alternative to a compulsory policy in Irish would mean. It claimed that only 7.7 per cent of pupils in primary schools in Northern Ireland were taught Irish in 1960–61:

> We have not the slightest hesitation, therefore, in recommending
> that the present universal teaching of Irish to all Irish children
> be maintained.[134]

Nevertheless, the relevance of the Northern Ireland situation is arguable and no direct comparison can feasibly be made.

Partly in response to this recommendation and partly as a reflection of the growing concern over compulsory Irish, the Language Freedom Movement (LFM) was founded in Autumn 1965 two years after publication of the UNESCO Report on Foreign Language in Primary Education, which envisaged only fifteen to thirty minutes per day being spent on learning a second language. The aim of the LFM was to have compulsory Irish abolished in the schools as it constituted an educational policy which was, in its view, 'objectionable'. It was obvious at this stage that compulsion as an element of the revival campaign was having very limited success.

During the General Election of 1961 Fine Gael, under its new leader James Dillon, made it clear that on entering government it would abolish compulsory Irish in the schools. The perception, as enunciated by some of the provincial newspapers, was that this stance would gain Fine Gael electoral support. It is particularly interesting that this was the opinion of the *Galway Observer*, a newspaper which served one of the largest Gaeltacht areas. Despite increasing its share of the vote by over 5 per cent to 32 per cent (forty-seven seats), Fine Gael again occupied the Opposition benches, Fianna Fáil forming a minority government with the aid of a few independents. However, Fine Gael's commitment to abolishing compulsory Irish remained. In June 1966 the party issued a policy statement on Irish calling for an end to the mandatory pass in Irish necessary to qualify for the award of the Intermediate and Leaving Certificate examinations. It also requested an end to the mandatory tests in Irish for appointment to the Civil Service and local authorities.

It was Liam Cosgrave's government that acted on these issues. In 1973 when Richard Burke, a former secondary school teacher, was Minister for Education the necessity to pass Irish in order to pass the Leaving, Intermediate and Group Certificate examinations was dropped. While Irish was still one of the necessary curriculum and examination subjects of the secondary schools, the previous rule regarding the Intermediate Certificate that candidates 'who obtain Grade D or a higher grade in at least five subjects ... the five subjects to include Irish'[135] was changed to candidates 'who obtain Grade D or a higher grade in at least five subjects from the approved list of subjects'.[136] The rule regarding the award of the Leaving Certificate was changed from 'candidates who obtain Grade D or a higher grade in at least five subjects ... to include Irish',[137] to 'candidates who obtain Grade D or a higher grade in at least five subjects or in four subjects including Irish'.[138] Now only the National University of Ireland required a pass in Irish for matriculation. The change concluded a decade of substantial rethinking of the Irish language revival policy, a decade preceded by an eventful and often divisive forty years of compulsory Irish. The decision to make the passing of Irish a qualifying requisite for the passing of certificate examinations which were the keys to future education, career and life-style, a signal of language revivalists' triumphalism, was perhaps the most repugnant element of the revival campaign and the most damaging to the perception and status of Irish.

CHAPTER TWO

'Education in the Proper Sense':
Irish as a Medium of Instruction

T HE PROMOTION of Irish as a medium of instruction in primary and
secondary schools was based on the premise that teaching Irish as a
subject was not in itself sufficient to ensure its revival. As Tomás Ó Deirg
explained when Minister for Education:

> Muna bhfuil d'aidhm againn ach díreach an Ghaeilge do
> choimead beo, ina dara theangain ornáidigh gur cheart í do
> bheith ar eolus, a bheag nó a mhór, ag gach Éireannach, amhail
> agus a bhíodh eolas ar Laidin agus ar Fhrainncis ag daoine
> léigheanta san naoú aois déag—féadfaimid an aidhm sin do
> shroicint ach an Ghaedhilg do mhúineadh ar feadh aon uair an
> chluig amháin sa ló i ngach scoil—agus an chuid eile den obair,
> nó a furmhór, do dhéanamh trí Bhéarla ... Níl mise sásta
> glacadh leis agus ní dóigh liom go bhfuil an Rialtas ach oiread.[1]

The policy was aimed at not only increasing students' oral grasp of the
language, but at inculcating the idea that Irish was more than an academic
subject, that it was a 'living speech fully capable of adjusting itself to the
needs of modern life'.[2] It was for this reason that the use of Irish as a
medium of instruction became a cornerstone of the revival policy.

The first indepth discussion of using Irish as a medium of instruction
was contained in Padraig Pearse's *Murder machine*. Pearse argued that Irish
should be the medium of instruction in both the Gaeltacht and Galltacht
if the revival campaign was to be successful.[3] There was no perception of
practical considerations limiting the possibility of this. As Shán Ó Cuív
claimed: 'Irish can't be taught through the medium of algebra, but algebra
can certainly be taught through the medium of Irish.'[4] Despite complaints
that the use of Irish as a medium of instruction interfered with the
educational progress of pupils, the policy found many adherents whose

arguments were summed up by the Department of Education as revolving around the fact that the depletion in educational achievement, if such was a result of the policy, was a reasonable price to pay for the revival of the language; that instruction through Irish was more beneficial than instruction through English when English was the vernacular and that the results of teaching through Irish or English were commensurate.[5] Far from agreeing with accusations that the policy was resulting in people being illiterate in two languages, there were claims that not only could pupils taught through the medium of Irish develop impressive written communication skills, but that their communication skills in English were better than those who received instruction solely through English.[6] This was an idea cultivated by the Gaelic League which claimed that Irish, in particular when studied or used as a medium of instruction, provided a unique intellectual training which went far beyond the possibilities of modern languages.[7] Not surprisingly, the Department of Education supported the idea.[8]

The idea that studying through Irish was conducive to training the mind was widespread. Seán T. Ó Ceallaigh, actively involved at various levels in the Gaelic League and President of Ireland from 1949 to 1959, cited the better examination results obtained by those pupils who received their education through the medium of Irish,[9] while Shán Ó Cuív claimed that where issues of comprehension did not arise, Irish as a medium 'tends to clarify the meaning and give the children a better grasp of the subject'.[10] Of course, there were critics and of course, following the pattern established in relation to compulsion, they were ignored if not derided. However, the speed with which the supporters of Irish as a medium of instruction in the schools felt it necessary to become entirely defensive is telling. Fianna Fáil and the *Irish Press* were to the fore in this defensiveness, de Valera saying that:

> I do not believe our people, intellectually, culturally or otherwise will suffer. I believe that through the Irish language, education in the proper sense can be given to our people as effectively as in any other way.[11]

The *Irish Press* claimed that criticism came mostly from 'people who, for one reason or another, have no language but English',[12] while the Department of Education, acknowledging the criticisms, claimed that most critics failed to understand what they were talking about and were unfamiliar with the work of the schools.[13]

The lack of scientific investigation and the non-circulation of analyses commissioned by the Department which questioned the policy, facilitated the arguments in support of instruction through Irish, a language largely unfamiliar to students.[14] When scientific evidence did become available it was ignored or presumed inaccurate and part of a plot to subvert the language revival. The arguments that instruction through Irish caused mental, emotional, physical and psychological distress and educational disadvantage were countered with the argument that 'if children are dull in other subjects, they will naturally be dull in Irish too'.[15]

Right through the period there was a strong official adherence to emphasising the benefits of both the teaching of Irish and its use as a medium of instruction. The *Report of the Council of Education: Curriculum of the Secondary School* (1962) argued that any student leaving the secondary school without a 'suitable knowledge of Irish' could not claim to be properly educated,[16] while *An Páipéar Bán um Athbheochan na Gaeilge* (1966) expressed the government's view that no Irish child could be regarded as fully educated unless they had a knowledge of the national language.[17] The 'sound policy' described by Ó Cuív in 1936 was set for a long history.[18]

Irish as a medium of instruction in primary schools

On Wednesday, 1 February 1922, as Ireland stood on the brink of civil war, the government issued Public Notice Number 4 which announced that from 17 March of that year the Irish language was to be taught or used as a medium of instruction for not less than one full hour per day in every primary school in which the staff were competent to give such instruction. The following month the First National Programme Conference was introduced as the official government programme for the primary schools, copperfastening the government's commitment to the revival of Irish. Despite criticism from as early as 1923 that a reversion to the 'error' of Whately's National Board (of giving instruction to children in a language they did not know) was wrong,[19] and the labelling of the policy by one Dáil Deputy as a 'method of the Stone Age',[20] the position of the language in the education system was further copperfastened under W.T. Cosgrave's second administration (September 1923–June 1927). Eoin MacNeill, a founder member of the Gaelic League and first Professor of Early and Medieval Irish History at University College, Dublin, was appointed Minister for Education, a position he resigned from in November 1925 on the request of Cosgrave following the political storm which erupted over his signing of the Boundary Commission Report. John O'Sullivan, Professor of Modern History in University College, Dublin, took over from

MacNeill and it was under him that the Second National Programme Conference of May 1926 was adopted with the recommendation that all instruction in the first two years of primary school should be through Irish. Indeed the great emphasis was on 'gaelicising' in every way possible the infant classes and then the remaining standards, as it was thought that the earlier Irish was introduced as a medium of instruction, the better. The reasoning on which this was based was often questionable however. One supportive Dáil Deputy claimed:

> Tá fhios againn go léir nach mbíonn eolas ag páist, nuair a théas sé ar scoil ar a ceathair nó a cuig bliana d'aois, ar theanga ar bith. Is cuma leis an bpáiste cén theanga in a múintear é.[21]

Described as a maximum minimum[22] the Second National Programme Conference of 1926 set out in detail what teaching through the medium of Irish in the primary schools involved. The work of the infant classes between 10.30 a.m. and 2.00 p.m. was to be entirely through Irish, 'where the teachers are sufficiently qualified'. Those not sufficiently qualified were to teach Irish as a subject for one hour per day and to use it as much as possible during school hours. In junior infants, every aspect of learning— conversation, object and picture lessons, storytelling and recitation—was to be used for the purpose of training children to understand Irish 'and to speak it distinctly and correctly as their natural language'. The work of senior infant classes was to be of a similar nature with a similar end result. When teacher and pupil alike were sufficiently qualified, the higher courses of the primary school together with the lower courses were to be taken in Irish. Where neither pupil nor teacher was sufficiently qualified, the higher course was to be taught through English and the lower course through Irish, with the gradual phasing out of English in the higher course in favour of Irish.[23]

In a clear statement of the importance and primacy it attached to Irish, the National Programme Conference advised the elimination of drawing, elementary science, hygiene, nature study and needlework as obligatory subjects on the primary school curriculum in order to facilitate concentration on the language. Increasingly, primary education was being defined in terms of the Irish language.

Initially there was little objection to the changes. The dropping of other subjects to facilitate Irish was seen by many as part of the price to be paid for restoring the language and being patriotic.[24] More difficult to assess was the effect the promotion of Irish would have on the subjects remaining on the curriculum. The Irish National Teachers Organisation, to the forefront in calling for the conference, expressed its fears in a submission to the conference that the new regulations would mean that the teaching of history, geography or mathematics would be second in importance to the teaching of Irish if Irish was used as a medium of instruction.[25] However, in 1928 the leader of the Labour Party, Thomas O'Connell, a member of the National Programme Conference and general secretary of the INTO, claimed that the standard of subjects remaining on the curriculum had not been adversely affected by the status afforded to Irish.[26]

A major point of concern in the new programme was that a working definition of a suitably qualified teacher and a suitably knowledgeable pupil—the prerequisites necessary for the use of Irish as a medium of instruction—was never explained or clarified. The rule stood in its original form that only when teachers knew the language sufficiently well enough to use it and children knew it sufficiently well enough to understand it could Irish be used as a medium of instruction.[27] The INTO pointed out on numerous occasions that this instruction 'means nothing at all. It is simply a window phrase.'[28] Indeed, even if the pupil was able to understand Irish and the teacher was 'sufficiently' qualified to give instruction through Irish, the INTO believed that this still did not mean Irish was a suitable medium of instruction.[29] The fact that these comments were coming from an organisation deeply committed to the language revival and a core participant in the National Programme Conference is highly significant, although the government paid no attention to them.

By 1928, 1,240 primary schools were giving instruction entirely through the medium of Irish at infant standard, while in a further 3,570 schools, instruction in infant classes was bilingual. Only 373 primary schools were using English as the sole medium of instruction for infant classes.[30]

Promoting enthusiasm among teachers for the use of Irish as a medium of instruction, the Department of Education under O'Sullivan issued a circular in June 1931 equating the level of Irish used with the rating of teachers as 'efficient' or 'highly efficient'. This was followed in July of the same year by circular 11/31 which clarified the guidelines of the Second National Programme Conference of 1926, stating that the aim of the programme was to secure the full use of Irish as a teaching medium in all subjects in as short a time span as possible. The teaching of Irish was confirmed as compulsory when 'the teacher is competent to give instruction and the pupils are able to assimilate the instruction so given'. It was expected that schools falling short of these conditions would take active transitional measures to ensure that at a future date Irish became the chief language of instruction.[31] The INTO had suggested three transitional phases in its submission to the First National Programme Conference, namely, the use of both languages in teaching certain subjects; the gradual extension through the standards, beginning at the lowest, of instruction through Irish and the gradual extension through the subjects of the use of Irish as a medium of instruction.[32] Elaborating on these transitional stages, circular 11/31 suggested that all disciplinary arrangements of the school should be in Irish and that drawing, nature study, cookery, singing, cartography lessons in geography and mathematical revision should be carried out through Irish.

Continuance of the policy was guaranteed with the change of government following the General Election of March 1932 when Fianna Fáil began what became a sixteen-year period in office. One of the first actions of the new government was to circulate *Rules and Regulations for National Schools* (August 1932) which stressed the importance of extending the use of Irish, especially in infant classes.[33] The rules went as far as allowing for the provision of a separate school where instruction would be through Irish for pupils who had a good grasp of Irish but where the local school was not using it as a medium of instruction.[34] These rules combined with circular 11/31 heralded a greater drive towards extending the use of Irish at primary level. The Taoiseach, Eamon de Valera, an avid supporter of the language movement, took the opportunity of a radio broadcast on St Patrick's Day 1932 to speak of his interest in progressively increasing the use of Irish in the schools.[35] He appointed Tomás Ó Deirg as Minister for Education, a position Ó Deirg held for all but nine months from 1932 to 1948. Born in Westport, Ó Deirg was first elected to the Dáil in 1921 for West Mayo. Having been educated by the Christian Brothers, he qualified with a B. Comm. and Higher Diploma in Education at University College, Galway and University College, Dublin respectively and subsequently taught at Ballina technical school from 1918 to 1925.

Despite the increased activity in promoting Irish as a medium of instruction Ó Deirg expressed disappointment in 1934 at the level of achievement under Cumann na nGaedheal,[36] an early indication of how the language policy was to become a party political issue. In the same year the INTO met with officials of the Department of Education to express its concern that both pupil and teacher were suffering adversely because of the use of Irish as a medium of instruction. As early as 1930 the INTO had passed a resolution at its annual congress saying that:

> The time is now ripe for an educational assessment of the use
> of Irish as a teaching medium in schools in English-speaking
> districts.[37]

The response of the Department of Education following the conference in 1934 between its officials and the INTO, was not to review the Irish policy but rather to again lighten the curriculum.[38] A circular issued by the Department in February 1934 assured teachers that if they failed to cover the entire syllabus in history and geography due to their efforts in Irish, their marks in efficiency would not be affected. Already implicit in earlier regulations, this explicit statement justified the concerns expressed by the INTO in 1926 that the teaching of history, geography and mathematics would come second in importance to the teaching of Irish. It was followed by the publication in September 1934 of a *Revised Programme of Primary Instruction* which considerably lightened the curriculum with the explicit aim of promoting Irish. Rural science was omitted as a compulsory subject. In mathematics, algebra and geometry were made optional in one and two teacher schools, three teacher mixed schools and 'in all classes taught by women', a provision it was not thought necessary to explain.[39] Algebra and geometry were now only taught in 'large boys' schools'.[40] Perhaps more alarmingly, English became compulsory no longer for first standard while it was 'permitted' in infant classes for half an hour each day. Throughout the standards, the new programme in English was described as 'less ambitious in scope than that hitherto in operation'.[41] In effect this 'simplification' meant a lowering of standards so that those books previously used in fourth class would now be used in sixth class: 'an t-am a sábháilfi mar sin bheadh ar na hoidí é a thabhairt do mhúineadh na Gaedhilge'.[42] It was expected that the revised programme, which remained largely unchanged until 1971,[43] would 'make for more rapid progress and more effective work in the teaching of Irish and in the development of teaching through Irish'.[44] There could be no question but that the standard of education was being sacrificed to the goal of revival. The nonsensical situation, described two years earlier in the Dáil by a Fine Gael Deputy, Eamon O'Neill, a prominent member of the Gaelic League in the early days, now seemed complete:

> Is éagcóir ar na leanbhaí sa Ghalltacht gan aon Bhéarla do
> labhairt leo i scoileanna na naoidheanán, ná aon Bhéarla do
> mhúineadh dhóibh agus gan aca féin ach Béarla, agus gan ach
> Béarla á labhairt agus á chlos aca lasmuigh de'n scoil. An fhaid
> atá an sgéal mar sin sa Ghalltacht, tá na múinteoirí sa

Ghaeltacht ag briseadh a gcríodhe ad' iarraidh Béarla do mhúineadh do leanbhaí na Gaeltachta![45]

Those supporters of the policy who recognised the deleterious effect it was having on the education system simply explained it in terms of a necessary sacrifice.[46]

The report of the Department of Education for the school year 1934–35 expressed satisfaction that the new *Revised Programme of Primary Instruction* was a 'céim maith chun tosaigh'.[47] However, inspectors were still unhappy with the teaching of Irish in infant classes. The problem was that use of Irish was almost entirely restricted to the formal class atmosphere while children once outside the classroom invariably reverted to English.[48]

Two years after the changes Tomás Ó Deirg expressed satisfaction that in places where English and Irish were heard previously Irish was now the common tongue, while in areas where Irish was seldom heard except among the older people, 'anois tá an Ghaedhilg á h-úsáid go coitchiannta mar ghnáth-úrlabhra 'na lán tighthe'.[49] Yet, the price of achieving this, if we accept the accuracy of Ó Deirg's statement, was seen as unnecessarily and unacceptably high by, among others, the former Minister for Education, John O'Sullivan.[50]

Success, criticism and investigation

By the 1930s there was an increasingly widespread opinion that not only was the policy of instruction in a non-vernacular in the primary sector unsound from an educational point of view, but that it was killing Irish.[51] James Dillon, Vice-President of the new Fine Gael Party formed in 1933 from the merging of the National Centre Party and Cumann na nGaedheal, argued that no matter how successful the policy of using Irish as a medium of instruction was, it still would not preserve Irish as a living language outside the schools.[52] He used terms like 'crime', and 'victimised' to describe the pupil and teacher who were coerced into receiving or giving instruction through Irish:

> You must make it possible to teach Irish and provide education at the same time. It is an intolerable proposition that this whole generation of our people should be denied education in order that they should be used for the purpose of handing on Irish to the generation to come. The thing is grotesque.[53]

Dillon found many supporters of his views among colleagues in his own party,[54] who argued that the policy being sustained by the Department of Education under Fianna Fáil was resulting in people being illiterate in two languages.[55]

The INTO became increasingly opposed to the use of Irish as a medium of instruction. As early as 1923 its magazine, *Irish Schools Weekly*, commented on an article in the *British Journal of Psychology* which examined the question of bilingualism and which concluded that monoglot children between the ages of eight and eleven years made better progress than bilingual children in their power of expression, choice of vocabulary and accuracy of thought. An unacceptable conclusion in the Irish context, *Irish Schools Weekly*, while prefacing its remarks by commenting on the lack of such research in Ireland, called into question the value of the survey:

> educational experiments of this kind may easily be made to yield any results that the experimenters desire them to yield. As far at all as events in Ireland are concerned, we have now irrevocably adopted the bilingual system, and hope confidently for the best results from it.[56]

However, in 1930 *Irish Schools Weekly* returned to the issue of disadvantage in relation to the use of Irish as a medium of instruction in schools in English-speaking districts. Mentioning the fact that 'some people hold that there is a retardation of progress' it said that it was inevitable that pupils' educational achievement was being considerably hampered.[57] Some years earlier John O'Sullivan as minister acknowledged that damage could be done to both the education of the child and to the language revival movement if Irish was used as a medium of instruction where 'conditions were not present that could ensure success'. He referred in particular to the use of Irish as a medium of instruction in standards higher than infants. In the infant classes themselves he was satisfied that the instructions of the National Programme Conference ensured educational achievement would not be damaged.[58] Such an acknowledgement stopped well short of dealing with the issues subsequently raised in *Irish Schools Weekly*.

In 1936 Shán Ó Cuív, commenting on the attitudes of teachers where knowledge of Irish among pupils was insufficient, spoke about the 'repressive' atmosphere of the Irish-medium class leading to a slowing of the mental development of pupils and an impaired power to express themselves or to learn.[59] In particular, there was growing concern over evidence suggesting that pupils' grasp of numeracy was being adversely affected.

Thomas O'Connell, although expressing satisfaction in general with the National Programme Conference, warned as early as 1924 of the dangers to children who had a poor grasp of Irish being taught arithmetic through the medium of Irish.[60] There was also the problem of the teacher who had excellent Irish but a poor grasp of maths, teaching children who had a poor grasp of Irish, resulting in them knowing neither Irish, English nor mathematics.[61] A further problem was that often the child started learning how to add in Irish in the junior standards of the national school but in the senior standards was expected to do addition through English, a process unfamiliar to them. If the child then proceeded to secondary education the possibility was that skills in numeracy would be taught and learned again through Irish. It hardly seems unreasonable that Charles Fagan, a Fine Gael Deputy for Longford-Westmeath, saw this as resulting in quite an amount of confusion.[62]

Perhaps as a reaction to this growing questioning of the policy, the Department of Education issued a circular in March 1936 to inspectors and managers referring them to circular 11/31 and 'the warning it contains against using Irish as a teaching medium in schools or classes where the conditions set out in the circular as necessary for the success of such teaching are not present'.[63] However, calls for an investigation into the effects the policy was having on the accomplishment of children, the quality of education being received and attained, and the position and status of the language remained unanswered.

It was in this context and after having calls for investigations ignored, that the INTO carried out its own investigation, initiated in 1936 and published in 1942 as the *Report of the Committee of Inquiry into the Use of Irish as a Teaching Medium to Children whose Home Language is English*. It was the first attempt to examine the consequences of the language revival for the quality of education, the standard of education achieved by pupils and the status of the language. Based largely on a questionnaire circulated among national school teachers rather than a scientific investigation,[64] the survey findings were to prove a damning indictment of government policy. Based on 'firsthand evidence' the Committee of Inquiry was established in May 1936, two months after the Department of Education's inadequate response to growing fears about the policy and following a resolution at the INTO Congress of that year:

> That as it seems a widely accepted opinion that the use as a teaching medium of a language other than the home language of a child in the primary schools of Saorstát Éireann is

educationally unsound, we instruct the CEC to select a committee of teachers representative of different types of schools in each electoral area to make a full examination of the whole question and to issue a detailed report of the results of their deliberation.

Questionnaires were distributed to teachers in September 1936. Unsurprisingly, those who returned questionnaires were generally of the opinion that pupils in infant classes would derive more benefit if English was used as a medium of instruction in Galltacht areas. In response to what subjects could, with advantage, be taught through Irish, 288 of the 483 teachers who replied said none.[65]

The report of the Commission of Inquiry was particularly strong in its condemnation of the use of Irish as a medium of instruction in the teaching of mathematics which, according to the Department of Education, 'should be the first subject taught through Irish'.[66] It pointed out that the child's attention was divided between the mathematical problem and their understanding of the language with the danger of a lessening in the process of thinking consecutively, clearly and logically. Having already gained some grasp of maths at home in their vernacular, pupils could easily become confused if they were compelled to do their conceptualising through Irish. Sixty-eight per cent of teachers who participated in the inquiry were of the impression that mathematical tables, while reproduced readily when taught through either language, were not produced as accurately or as quickly when learned in a language other than the vernacular,[67] while 73 per cent of those who replied said that pupils' grasp of numerical processes when Irish was the medium of instruction was not at all equal to, or as thorough, as if the home language was used. The report concluded that the value of mathematical training in Irish to English-speaking pupils was largely lost while the increased grasp of fluency in oral Irish was not commensurate with that loss.[68]

Apart from the teaching of mathematics, it was clear from the replies that the majority of infant teachers opposed the use of Irish as a medium of instruction and believed that the majority of pupils did not benefit to the same extent when instruction was not in the home language. The problem lay in the fact that pupils had to divide their attention between understanding the language and the subject in hand, something which led to the pupil's life being one of 'repression, confusion and unhappiness'.[69] The use of Irish as a medium of instruction in the teaching of history had the effect of turning 'what may be a very interesting study into a difficult grind', while instruction in geography amounted to 'memorisation of a mass of names, which is so wholeheartedly condemned in the Department's *Notes*'.[70] It was explicitly stated that these comments concerned all standards in primary schools.

Regarding the effectiveness of the policy in reviving the language the report suggested that the use of Irish as a medium of instruction was having the opposite effect to that which was desired:

> Living as he does during the school day in an atmosphere of repression, there is the further danger of his associating the language with what is unpleasant and distasteful. In this way a positive dislike for the language may easily be developed.[71]

The majority of teachers were of the opinion that it was possible to revive the language while ending its use as a medium of instruction.[72]

In addition to assessing the prevailing situation, the report made a number of recommendations. It suggested a greater emphasis on conversation in the Irish class itself thus increasing pupils' oral command of the language. In the teaching of other subjects it suggested a bilingual approach: a half hour of instruction in Irish followed by half an hour through English. It further suggested that the school leaving age be increased from fourteen to fifteen years to facilitate the revival of Irish. Lest there be any doubt, the report concluded by stressing that teachers were wholeheartedly committed to the revival effort.[73]

Official responses to the report were scathing. Conradh na Gaeilge dismissed it as worthless and took solace from the belief that the majority of teachers did not support either its recommendations or its findings.[74] The Department of Education's response was equally dismissive, pointing out the importance of the fact that no female teacher and 'no teacher with any worthwhile experience' of infant teaching was on the committee of inquiry. The importance the Department attached to the views of female teachers on this occasion was highly questionable in light of the government's decision in 1932 to ban from the profession females recruited after 1 October 1934 who married on the basis that there was a high rate of absenteeism among married women, that married women must either neglect their families or their work and that the employment of married women led to job shortages for other qualified teachers.[75]

The Department's Chief Inspector highlighted many other criticisms of the report: of 9,000 questionnaires distributed only 1,347 had been returned representing 10 per cent of primary teachers; no mention was made of many infant school activities including singing, drill, games and hand work, 'as if the whole day were devoted to cramming the children with Irish and maths'; the position of mathematics in senior classes was greatly over stressed and no school was visited before recommendations were made.[76] Turning to the finding that use of Irish as a medium of instruction dulled the natural receptivity of the child's mind, leading to unnatural physical demands on the child and signs of uneasiness and listlessness,[77] the departmental inspectors questioned teachers' competence to assess physical strain or to trace its origin:

> Underlying the teachers' statement is a sort of suggestion to the outside reader that, if English alone were to be made the medium of instruction in infant classes, a complete transformation would be effected, the health of the children would improve—no more defective teeth, and no more malnutrition; the furniture and equipment would at once be adequate; and the atmosphere of every infant school would immediately become bright, cheerful and home like.[78]

The Department concluded that the report represented the views of the writers and was not based on the material supplied in response to the questionnaire:

> there was even a suggestion that they had made up their minds at an early stage … From our discussion with the framers of the report we gathered that they themselves found teaching through Irish a strain—largely due, it appeared, to their own lack of proper command over the medium and lack of energy or time to make the necessary previous preparation. It appears to represent the voice of the middle-aged, somewhat tired, and not too well linguistically equipped teachers.[79]

The report was further invalidated by the Department of Education on the grounds that between 1936 when the questionnaire was issued, and 1941 when the results were compiled, 1,270 more teachers had bilingual or higher qualifications.

Undoubtedly, there were weaknesses in the report. The number of questionnaires completed represented the views of only 10 per cent of teachers. A more important question concerns why the majority of teachers did not return the questionnaire: were they complacent or largely satisfied with the status quo pertaining in the schools? Whatever the implications of these issues, the importance of the report cannot be diminished and the Department's personal attack on the compilers of the report, coupled with a lack of willingness to comment on the effects that the teaching of arithmetic through Irish had on pupils, betrayed among other things the emptiness of the trenchant crusade against the report. One gets the strong feeling that what the inspectors objected most strongly to was the calling into question of the orthodoxy of departmental policy. Also, the fact that the report was published against a background of increased tension between teachers and the Department of Education over the issue of salaries can only have detracted from its potential impact on policy.[80]

However, the government did ask Dr Johanna Pollak, a Czechoslovakian educationalist, to investigate the effect of the schools-based revival policy on the education system. Czechoslovakia was an example of a country where previously 'language and tradition had fallen into decay' but which—unlike Ireland—developed a successful language movement.[81] In her unpublished report of May 1943 Dr Pollak concluded that 'strange as it sounds Irish is a foreign language for the Irish'; that 'to the childish mind its use seems to be restricted to the school and its knowledge only necessary for an examination when applying for a job in the Civil Service'; and that

> the children get an overdose of it at school when they are still too young to benefit by it ... Children are too young to benefit by the intense work that is done in Irish in the national schools.[82]

Such a hard-hitting report from an external expert, which largely agreed with the INTO analysis published the previous year, was not what the government wanted to hear and was, therefore, never published or referred to publicly by the government or the Department of Education. Tomás Ó Deirg continued to express satisfaction with the process of 'gaelicisation' that was taking place in all classes in the primary school up to standard three and urged teachers to increase their efforts in the higher standards, despite the fact that the INTO report was particularly critical of this.[83] Despite Pollak's view that children in infant classes 'are still too young to benefit' either educationally or linguistically from instruction through Irish, Ó Deirg continued to claim that the use of Irish in teaching infant classes was 'based on the sound maxim that, if young people are to acquire the language, the sooner they begin, the better'.[84]

In February 1948 Ó Deirg's long tenure as Minister for Education came to an end with Fianna Fáil's failure in the General Election. John A. Costello became Taoiseach of the first Inter Party government comprising Fine Gael, Labour, National Labour, Clann na Poblachta, Clann na Talmhan and a number of independents, with Richard Mulcahy, the leader of Fine Gael, being appointed Minister for Education. An active member of the Gaelic League, Mulcahy had worked closely with Michael Collins as Deputy Chief-of-Staff of the Irish Volunteers. A supporter of the Treaty, he was a founder member of Fine Gael. Unacceptable as Taoiseach, he served instead as Minister for Education in the first (Feb. 1948–June 1951) and second (June 1954–Feb. 1957) Inter Party governments. One of his first actions in this capacity was to assess the position of the Irish language in the schools. In order to ensure that the Department of Education could not be accused of formulating and implementing policies without visiting the schools to see their effects—an accusation levelled at the INTO report— Mulcahy, former chairperson of Comisiún na Gaeltachta (1926), set about examining the use of Irish as a medium of instruction in national schools. Four inspectors visited twenty-nine schools in fourteen counties in the Spring of 1948. The mission was explorative in nature, it was to ascertain how the rules concerning the position of the language in the schools were being adhered to. The inspectors found that few schools actually observed the rules. This was a problem which had existed for some time but which received little indepth or sustained attention, almost as though there was a tacit acceptance that the rules and regulations concerning Irish were not being implemented in all schools. In 1928 Tomás Ó Deirg expressed concern that teachers in some schools receiving grants for teaching Irish were paying little or no attention to the language,[85] while Shán Ó Cuív found that:

> English has … been used in secular instruction when the eye of the inspector was not on the teacher. This surreptitious use of English was a lesson in deceit in so far as it was done in defiance of the regulations and of the inspectors.[86]

Now inspectors were of the opinion that the rules should be simplified. As a result the regulation that, 'Is i nGaedhilge a déanfar an obair go léir i mbuidheanta na Naoínán má's leor chuige cáilíocht na múinteoirí' was replaced by a new phraseology:

> I ngach scoil ina bhfuil dóthain cáilíocht chuige acu sé an aidhm is ceart a bheith ag na múinteoirí an pointe a shroicint, chomh luath agus is féidir é, ina bhféadaí an Ghaeilge amháin a úsáid san naí-scoil mar theangain chaidrimh agus theagaisg.[87]

While the former implied the compulsory use of Irish as a medium of instruction, the changed phraseology of the latter implied delayed though inevitable compulsion. The perceived and satisfactory result was that now the practice and theory were more aligned, while English could in future be taught for half an hour a day in the infant classes if the principal so desired. However, the revised programme for infants issued in July 1948 and resulting from the observations of inspectors, still used the undefined term 'sufficiently qualified' when referring to teachers expected to use Irish as the sole language of instruction in the infant school.

Apart from these largely semantic changes, it was not until the 1950s that any concrete scientific investigation into the entire policy became available, an indictment of governments up to then which were quite prepared to implement a policy that was, according to some significant sources, dangerous to the mental health and educational development of the school-going population and which, furthermore, was falling remarkably short of its aim. The 1950s began with the publication of the report of the Council of Education, a conservative, unremarkable document which reinforced the status quo in the absence of coming up with anything better. Its analysis and recommendations were confused: while arguing that the introduction of a second language as a medium of instruction did cause educational disadvantage, it stated that Irish could not be regarded as a second language 'in the ordinary meaning of the term'. In the light of this and 'common experience' it supported the use of Irish as a medium of instruction from the infant class. Despite a few dissenting voices who held that 'a child is not ordinarily capable of benefiting fully from instruction through the medium of the acquired language',[88] the majority of Council members were happy to recommend 'that the teaching of Irish be introduced at the beginning of the primary school'.[89] Such a recommendation demanded reassurances that it resulted in no educational or psychological problems and the Council of Education quoted the conclusions from a number of research experiments carried out by the Welsh Central Advisory Council of Education in this respect:

> It appears wisest at the present juncture to accept that body of opinion that maintains that bilingualism in itself is neither an advantage nor a disadvantage to the mental development of the child.[90]

What was not mentioned was that in Wales the call for bilingualism was based on the needs of the child rather than any cultural imperative.[91]

Part of the Council's argument in favour of Irish as a medium of instruction was similar to that used in 1926 by the National Programme Conference, namely, that Irish when used as a medium of instruction helped pupils see the language as something more than a school subject. Nevertheless, in the period that had elapsed since the conference, Irish had become progressively associated with school and education, a fact alluded to by Dr Pollak, and this stance by the Council of Education flew in the face of reality. Emphasising its conservativeness, the report, like the Second National Programme of 1926, circular 11/31, the rules of 1932 and the various amendments to the rules, stressed the necessary condition which had to apply before Irish could be used as a medium of instruction, i.e. that:

> The teacher must always have such proficiency in Irish as will enable him to use it with effect at the level of the child's knowledge of both the subject being taught and of Irish. Equally the child must possess competence in the language fully to understand what is being said and to express his thoughts in Irish.[92]

While the latter condition is expressed with greater clarity than before, the conditions pertaining to teachers are expressed in even more nebulous terms than formerly. In conclusion, the Council called for 'flexibility in the use of Irish' as a medium of instruction while recommending its extension in the teaching of other subjects 'from standard to standard'.[93]

Many people felt thoroughly dissatisfied with the report of the Council of Education. Described by the *Irish Times* as 'a very confused and confusing document',[94] its most strenuous critic was the INTO, a motion before the union's annual congress in April 1955 castigating the report for 'its failure to face pertinent issues' and 'deprecating' its recommendation that the existing methods of teaching Irish be continued.[95] Its failure to address the central issues surrounding Irish in the curriculum resulted in more vehement calls for serious examination and change. The General Synod of the Church of Ireland called the Department of Education's policy a 'psychological outrage; it is a violation of all recognised educational principle',[96] and asked for religious instruction to be given through English,[97] something that was, significantly, already happening in most schools.[98] By the time of the Council's report, Irish was being used as a medium of instruction in all fíor-Ghaeltacht schools while less than 5 per cent of schools in the Galltacht were using Irish as the sole medium of instruction. In the official breac-Ghaeltacht the figure was 16 per cent. At the same time only twenty-five schools out of a total of 4,876 used English as the sole medium of instruction.[99]

With the return of Fianna Fáil to government after the collapse of the second Inter Party administration in March 1957, Jack Lynch was first appointed Minister for the Gaeltacht and subsequently in June became Minister for Education. When it was put to him that there was evidence that the policy pursued in the schools was injurious to the psychological and emotional life of pupils, he referred to the divergence of views on the subject, saying that any such pronouncements should only come after 'a great deal more research'.[100] However, like previous ministers, he was adamant that the Department of Education was not going to carry out the necessary research. What the *Irish Times* described as the 'suicidal policy'[101] was to continue without investigation into its success in reviving Irish, its effect on the standard of education, or its effect on the educational development of pupils.

It was not until the late 1950s that the 'easpa eolais agus taithighe ar oideachas dá theangthach',[102] as described in *Irish Schools Weekly*, was rectified. In March 1958, following publication of his book *Reform in Education* the previous year,[103] Dr John O'Meara, Professor of Latin at University College, Dublin, delivered a lecture entitled 'reform in education' under the auspices of the Research and Information Centre of Fine Gael in which he attacked the teaching of Irish, especially in the primary schools. However, it was Professor E.F. O'Doherty's address in September 1957 to the British Association for the Advancement of Science on 'the educational, psychological and administrative problems of bilingualism'[104] and published the following year, that garnered most attention. Arguing that bilingualism was 'one of the most difficult psychological and educational problems to discuss dispassionately',[105] O'Doherty, Professor of Logic and Psychology in University College, Dublin, concluded that, 'our present pseudo-bilingual policy is based on emotional, political and historical factors, to the neglect of pedagogical, psychological and social consideration'.[106] This was the kernel of the problem. His investigation showed that the achievement of monoglots exceeded that of bilingual or pseudo-bilingual children and he recommended that the *langue maternalle* should be the *langue vehiculaire* in the school.

At the same conference J.R. Morrison, a lecturer in education at University College, Aberystwyth, delivered a paper on 'Bilingualism: Some Psychological Aspects', published with O'Doherty's paper in *Advancement of Science*.[107] Like O'Doherty's paper, Morrison's findings deeply challenged the assumptions on which the schools-based revival was founded. For one thing, he found that bilingualism was of no educational advantage and that bilingual children 'tend to score less than monoglots of the same age in existing intelligence tests'.[108]

Like the INTO report of 1942, O'Doherty's paper in particular drew the wrath of the revival lobby. Speaking at the Children's Day of Oireachtas na Gaeilge, organised by Conradh na Gaeilge, a month after O'Doherty's address, Jack Lynch said he found it difficult to understand how anyone interested in the country's welfare could take such hostile attitudes.[109] It was a reversion to the tactic of *argumentum ad hominem.* However, Lynch felt it necessary to respond with more than rhetoric to O'Doherty's claims and in February 1958 the government announced its intention to establish Comisiún um Athbheochan na Gaeilge to inquire into the position of Irish in the schools. In May the terms of reference of the inquiry were widened to include the status of the Irish language in general. While at least one contemporary civil servant saw the inquiry as having the aim of shielding the minister from accusations of inactivity, it had major potential once not squandered in the way the Council of Education had done with the opportunity afforded it.[110]

The first breach in the use of Irish as a medium of instruction in national schools came in November 1959 when the new Minister for Education, Patrick Hillery, in reply to a Dáil question expressed the view that more success could be achieved by concentrating on teaching Irish well rather than teaching through the medium of Irish.[111] The previous June the new Taoiseach, Seán Lemass, had moved Jack Lynch from Education to Industry and Commerce, appointing Hillery to Education. First elected to the Dáil in 1951, it was Hillery's first ministerial post.

In January 1960 the Department issued a circular which ended the use of Irish as a medium of instruction in all but a minority of national schools.[112] In October 1962 Hillery appointed a survey team to examine, among other things, the use of Irish as a medium of instruction. Consisting largely of people involved in economic development and carried out in co-operation with the OECD, its report, *Investment in Education,* showed that out of 4,550 Galltacht schools, only 135 used Irish as a sole medium of instruction while in a further 404 schools two or more consecutive standards other than infants were taught through Irish.[113]

In 1966 Dr John MacNamara, a lecturer in St Patrick's teacher training college, Drumcondra, published the results of an investigation he carried out into the language policy during research for his Ph.D. at the University of Edinburgh.[114] He set out to discover the effect on children's mathematical attainment when taught through Irish where Irish was a non-vernacular and the effect of the revival policy in primary schools on the level of English attainment. Commenting on the INTO report, MacNamara said:

> It seems but common sense … English-speaking children cannot be given a vernacular-like command of Irish in one or two years in infant classes, even though all the school time is devoted to Irish.[115]

On the question of problem mathematics as distinct from mechanical mathematics, MacNamara concluded that poor standards were obtained in a bilingual situation:

> The retardation in problem arithmetic is estimated at about eleven months of arithmetic age. While teaching arithmetic in Irish appeared at first sight to have a beneficial effect on attainment in Irish, closer study of the data revealed that such was not the case.[116]

This was in stark contrast to the Department of Education's recommendation in 1933 that 'maths should be the first subject taught through Irish'.[117] His findings in the second area of research pertaining to attainment in English were equally discouraging and a poor reflection on the language policy. Possibly his most alarming finding, however, was in relation to children from the Gaeltacht whose attainment in English and arithmetic was 'the poorest of all'. MacNamara saw this as particularly worrying as for most of these children, 'the adult world, in Ireland and England, will be an English-speaking one—and they appear to be ill-equipped for life in it'.[118] Overall, the findings proved what the INTO had been saying since the 1930s, that the emphasis on Irish as a medium of instruction had the effect of reducing the standard of education while doing nothing to increase the status or level of use of Irish. As late as 1965, the year before MacNamara published his work, the INTO at its annual congress adopted a resolution calling on the Department of Education to institute a 'new realistic programme in Irish' as the one in operation was seen as detrimental to all other subjects.[119]

The influence of the abundance of fresh evidence combined with a heightened public interest in and awareness of educational issues, and 'wider social and attitudinal change' in Irish society, marked the period from 1960 as a 'transitional epoch'.[120] The influence of these factors on policy could be first seen in Fine Gael's *Just Society* policy committing the party to a more progressive social policy and marking the growing rift within the party between the dominant conservative wing and the younger group led by Declan Costello and Garret FitzGerald. Following the 1966 General Election the policy was broadened to include an extensive review of education. The review concluded that too much time was being devoted to the use of Irish in the schools to the detriment of other subjects, the proof being that British students were higher achievers than their Irish counterparts.[121] This emanated from the pursuance of an 'educationally unsound' policy by the Department of Education.[122] Yet, it was 1973 before Fine Gael came to power and had a chance to introduce change, although change was then geared primarily towards Irish in the secondary schools.

Irish as a medium of instruction in post-primary schools

The importance of Irish as a medium of instruction in secondary schools must be seen in terms of the secondary school population which was far smaller than that of the primary school sector. In the school year 1929–30, for example, there were 504,427 pupils in 5,401 primary schools but only 26,792 pupils in 290 secondary schools.[123] It was only in the 1960s with the advent of free education in 1967, that this ratio changed in any substantial way. However, while the emphasis on Irish in the secondary schools was less and the arguments not as intense, the use of Irish as a medium of instruction was seen as a 'logical postulate of the movement to restore the language as a vernacular'.[124]

There was also a number of practical issues favouring the use of Irish in secondary schools even before the Free State policy of compulsory Gaelicisation was embarked on, with over 80 per cent of all secondary school students studying Irish as a subject for the Intermediate Examination by 1922.[125] The reason for such a high figure was twofold. First of all Irish was necessary for matriculation in the National University of Ireland from 1913. More importantly, one teacher qualified in Irish was sufficient per school to teach Irish to all classes, unlike the situation which prevailed in primary schools where competency was required by each teacher.

Nevertheless, despite this existing support, the government predictably moved to consolidate the position of Irish in the secondary school and its use as a medium of instruction, chiefly through the provision of financial inducements to both schools and teachers. From 1 August 1924 when the recommendations of the Commission on Secondary Education established in 1921 came into effect, the first tranche of such inducements were provided. The Department of Education provided additional grants equalling one-quarter of the capitation grants to schools using Irish as a sole medium of instruction, while those using Irish as a medium of instruction in at least half of all subjects qualified for a 10 per cent increase in capitation. In the school year 1925–26, two schools received the 25 per cent bonus while nineteen received the 10 per cent bonus.[126] Although compulsion could never be used in the secondary schools in the same way as in the primary sector due to their independent nature, the encouragement provided through additional grants by the Department was strong and successful. The number of students taking Irish in examinations increased by 15 per cent to 95 per cent within the first ten years of Independence.[127] The Intermediate Education (Amendment) Act, 1924, which introduced the Intermediate and Leaving Certificate examinations, required pupils to pass either Irish or English in order to be awarded the certificate. These figures were also buoyed by the decision from 1927 to deny schools capitation where a 'reasonable proportion of pupils' were not taking Irish as a subject on the curriculum.[128] By the school year 1941–42, 102 out of 362 recognised secondary schools taught all subjects through Irish while a further 113 used Irish as the medium of instruction in some subjects.[129]

The system of grant payments, established in 1924, was based on the division of secondary schools into three categories, namely, Class A, Class B (B1 and B2) and Class C, each category designating the level of Irish used. Class A schools were those 'in which all teaching is done through the medium of Irish and in which Irish is the ordinary language used by pupils and teachers'.[130] The experience of one pupil who was later to become a departmental inspector underpinned what this could mean in practice:

> Ní hamháin gur múineadh na gnáth-ábhair trí Ghaeilge ach múineadh an Béarla féin tríd an mheán sin. Bhí drámaí de chuid Shakespeare ar an gcúrsa 'When shall we three meet again! In thunder, lightning, or in rain, or on the heath there to meet with … Mac a' Bheatha'. I kid you not. Léití an dráma i mBéarla, ach bhí an tráchtaireacht agus an míniúchán—an 'explication' ar fad trí Ghaeilge. Ní hionadh go ndeireadh De Valera 'its a great little country'.[131]

Class B were bilingual schools in which Irish was taught as a subject to everyone while certain subjects or certain classes were also taught through Irish while Class C schools were those in which Irish was taught only as a subject.[132] By 1931 there were thirty-four A schools with sixty more applying for A status by 1934. By the same year, 1934, there were 113 B schools,[133] Tomás Ó Deirg informing the Dáil that 19 per cent of the 314 secondary schools were using Irish as a sole medium of instruction while 55 per cent were offering bilingual instruction.[134]

Richard Mulcahy, however, questioned the success of A schools, suggesting that English was the language of the playground:

> There are 'A' schools in the city of Dublin which, while they profess to teach and do teach their subjects through the medium of Irish, do not comply with what, I think, is the regulation and what certainly ought to be the regulation—that Irish should be the language of the recreation hours of the children as well as of the school hours.[135]

Yet, if statistics prove anything, the grants system based on the three-way classification of schools according to the levels of Irish used was successful in promoting the increased use of the language to the maximum practical level, at least for official purposes. In 1928 the Department of Education heralded the 'méadú is leathnú' in the use of Irish,[136] the number of schools using Irish as a medium of instruction and the number of students attending such schools continuing to increase through the 1930s and 1940s. As late as 1946 Tomás Ó Deirg was claiming 'go bhfuil borradh ag teacht go seasamhach faoin teagasc tríd an nGaeilge',[137] though he was of the opinion that there was much room for improvement in making better Irish speakers of the students. To this end, his Department announced an additional grant system for schools in which pupils were able to speak Irish well. This came into operation from the school year 1946–47.[138] By 1949 more than 25 per cent of the total number of schools were in the 'A' category.[139]

However, as in the primary schools where, for example, changes in the language of instruction from Irish to English and back again caused problems, practical difficulties were experienced and by 1962, the year that the *Report of the Council of Education: Curriculum of Secondary Schools* was published, the number of A schools was in decline. This was attributed to the lack of facilities to continue education through Irish in the universities and to the shortage of suitable text books. Both issues had been raised from the early 1920s but remained largely unaddressed. In 1928 the Department of Education described the lack of text books as one of the 'constaicí is mó' facing the policy,[140] while as early as 1923 Thomas Johnson, for example, was questioning the wisdom of having one level of education with Irish as a medium of instruction, while subsequent levels did not offer education through the same medium.[141] These two issues are examined in more detail in later chapters.

The Council of Education also noted that 'English is almost the sole language of business and commerce in this country'—hardly a startling insight—having a negative influence on the promotion of Irish as a medium of instruction.[142]

Clearly what was sustaining the use of Irish as a medium of instruction in the secondary schools—and elsewhere—were the financial inducements which the government offered to those willing to use Irish to the greatest extent possible within the schools. 'Use' became the key word, because the majority of grants were based on quantity of time spent rather than quality of instruction given or standard attained in the language. The fact that constant use did not always result in fluency is clear from Ó Deirg's observation in 1946, cited above, that while the use of Irish as a medium of instruction was increasing, there was much room for improving the oral Irish skills of students. Financial inducements were the sweetener in a progressively souring policy; they maintained the 'interest' in the Irish language.

The reaction to the government's proposal to reduce the grants available to Class A schools from 1941 is enlightening. The Chairperson of the Coiste Oideachais of Conradh na Gaeilge said:

> Gur ab iongadh linn go mór go bhfuil sé i gceist mar réidhteach tioghbhásach ag an Rialtas na deontais do na meádhon-sgoileanna i Roinn A a laghdú. Badh mhaith linn a rádh nach bhfuil an teanga bunuighthe chomh láidir sin fós 'nár sgoileanna go mbadh cheart aon chuid de'n chongnamh airgeadais a tugagh do lucht stiúrtha na meádhon-sgoileanna seo le na neartú a tharraing siar agus iarraimid ar an Rialtas ath-smaoineadh a dhéanamh ar a mbreitheamhas faoi'n gceist seo mar gheall ar an gcuspóir atá rompas, mar atá, an Ghaeilge a ath-bhunadh mar ghnáth-theanga labhartha an Náisiún.[143]

Obviously, the deep commitment of some schools to the language was tempered by the availability of grants, and while it is reasonable to assume that any increase in capitation was a welcome relief to school managers, the manner in which Irish became the means of gaining extra capitation was far from ideal. Despite protests the decrease in capitation went ahead along the lines of the following table.

Table 2.1

PERCENTAGE INCREASES ON ORDINARY CAPITATION[144]

	Prior to Emergency	After 1941
A schools	25%	15%
B^1 schools	10%–16.66%	10%*
B^2 schools	2.5% –10%*	2%–6%*

*These percentage increases reflect the extent of the instruction given in Irish.

Apart from the schools, teachers and pupils also received incentives to teach and use the language. Primary school teachers in Gaeltacht schools competent to give instruction through Irish, following calls as early as 1927,[145] qualified for a special grant of up to 10 per cent of the net scale salary, subject to a maximum of £25 per annum.[146] Similarly, additional increments were provided for secondary school teachers in Class A and B schools amounting to between £15 and £30 per year depending on the level of instruction given through Irish.[147] In the case of students, those from the fíor-Ghaeltacht were eligible to apply for one of the eighteen secondary school scholarships and subsequently for university scholarships while all pupils were encouraged to answer State examinations through Irish by the awarding of 10 per cent in bonus marks for all subjects answered through Irish except mathematics which was given a 5 per cent bonus.[148]

However, what government policy failed to achieve by other methods, it was not going to achieve by providing extra remuneration or examination marks for teachers and pupils willing to use Irish. Whatever amount of Irish was being used in the schools one thing is clear—the means employed were not producing the ends desired. In addition there was growing evidence throughout the period, eventually recognised in part during the 1960s although not addressed until later, that in the primary schools the use of Irish as a medium of instruction was detrimental to the standard of education and to the achievement of students.

CHAPTER THREE

Teacher Training: Irish in the Preparatory Colleges, Training Colleges and Universities

THE GOVERNMENT faced a number of huge practical difficulties in 1922 which needed urgent attention if the Irish language was to gain a foothold in the schools. Perhaps the most significant of these problems concerned the lack of qualifications in Irish among teachers, the majority of whom had little knowledge of the language. However, with idealism outrunning practical considerations, there could be no postponing the introduction of compulsory Irish or the promotion of Irish as a medium of instruction, and teachers with 'only a half-knowledge of Irish … and possibly only able to read it', were expected to teach it and use it as a medium of instruction, with pupils 'possibly, not understanding a quarter of what he (sic) [was] saying'.[1] Rectifying this situation would be crucial for the morale of teachers and concomitantly their enthusiasm for the language, for the attitude of pupils to the language, and for the standard of Irish being taught and learned. The government set about addressing the problem at two levels. First of all, it ensured that newly qualifying teachers were competent in Irish, a move which over time would provide an adequate supply (at least in theory) of competent teachers and secondly, it facilitated additional language training, mostly through the provision of Irish summer colleges, for teachers already in the service who had little or no knowledge of Irish.[2] The summer colleges, together with the teacher training colleges, preparatory colleges and to a lesser extent the universities became the institutions around which the teaching force in Ireland would become competent to implement the new emphasis on Gaelicisation in the education system.

Irish summer colleges for teachers

In the context of Irish becoming an optional extra subject on the national school curriculum and with the teacher training colleges offering Irish only as an optional subject, the benefit of providing Irish language courses for teachers during school holidays was appreciated before the founding of the Free State by both promoters of the language in the schools such as the Gaelic League and, subsequently, by the Commissioners of National Education which from 1907 provided grants of £5 in respect of each teacher who received a certificate in Irish and who was capable of teaching Irish satisfactorily.[3]

Coláiste na Mumhan, opened in Ballingeary in 1904, was among the first of the organised summer colleges and was followed shortly afterwards by colleges in all the main Gaeltacht areas, the first courses being subsidised by the London branch of the Gaelic League.[4] For many teachers these summer colleges were their only means of improving their Irish language skills, ensuring that by 1922 at least some teachers were in a position to cope with the new emphasis of the post-Independence curriculum. The Free State government's decision to further develop the summer college idea for teachers was, therefore, a natural progression, and in 1922 longer school summer holidays were introduced to facilitate teachers' attendance at such courses in the Gaeltacht, a move seen in some quarters as 'drastic'.[5] Student teachers in teacher training colleges were also expected to spend four weeks in the Gaeltacht when the colleges closed at the end of May.[6]

The emphasis on summer colleges would be significant for practical purposes only until such time as teachers qualified in Irish emerged from the training colleges, which would be in a matter of a few years. During the first few years attendance was subsidised by the Department of Education[7] and oscillated between being voluntary and compulsory. In 1922, when attendance was optional, the courses ran for eight weeks during July and August during which time all schools were ordered to close. Three levels of instruction—elementary, intermediate and bilingual—were offered in this initial year with a new grade of Ard-Teastas ('Higher Certificate') being introduced in 1923. In the following two years, 1924 and 1925, the summer courses ran for a period of four weeks and attendance was made compulsory for teachers under the age of forty-five years, reverting again to voluntary attendance in the period 1926–28.

While established primarily for the benefit of primary school teachers, summer courses were also established for secondary teachers. Conducted by the Association of Secondary Teachers these were primarily located in the university colleges of Dublin, Cork, Galway and Trinity and at Ballinskelligs, Co. Kerry, the Dublin College of Modern Irish holding a further two summer courses in Loreto Convent, Bray and in the Dominican Convent, Eccles Street, Dublin.[8]

In the absence of tangible measures of success, it is necessary to have recourse to contemporary perceptions. By this measure the summer courses were successful in achieving what they were developed for. By 1927 'the great bulk' of teachers had spent their sixth successive year 'mastering the national language in order to be in a position to enable the rising generation to grapple with its difficulties and delight in its mellifluous cadences'.[9] Such contemporary enthusiasm for the achievements of the summer courses was a measure both of their success and their appeal for teachers. In the same year the Department of Education reported that, as a consequence of the courses, Irish in a number of areas was 'becoming the customary school language and Irish literature and tradition are being conserved and reintro-duced into the life of the nation'.[10] By 1929 it was thought teachers had been given ample opportunity to learn the language,[11] and combined with the success up to then and the coming on stream of newly qualified teachers competent in Irish, it was deemed unnecessary to provide summer courses in 1929.

However, over the next decade primary school teachers continued to be provided with opportunities to attend summer courses in the Gaeltacht or to spend periods of time in private study in the Gaeltacht. In any year between twenty and fifty days could be spent learning Irish, with a con-comitant reduction in the number of school days to a minimum of 200.[12]

Following the Second World War, during which there were serious restrictions on internal travel and which was blamed by the Department of Education for the 'laghdú mór le deich mbliana anuas ar líon na ndaoine, idir mhúinteoirí agus scoláirí scoile, a thaithíodh an Ghaeltacht i rith na saoire',[13] it was deemed necessary to reinvigorate the summer colleges. This process began in 1944 when the Minister for Education announced that summer courses were to be organised by the Department for secondary school teachers as the standard of Irish in the secondary schools was considered low. Some teachers still possessed only a limited command of the language,[14] while many teachers as a result of 'the Emergency' had never travelled to the Gaeltacht. By 1951 there were ten colleges in operation, located in An Rinn, An Spidéal, Béal Átha an Ghaorthaidh, Rann na Feirsde, Gaoth Dobhair, Carraig Airt, Cloch Cheann-Fhaolaidh, Teidhlinn, Carraig a' Chobhaltaigh and Garraidhe Boithe.[15] Again in 1959 two courses in Irish were run for secondary school teachers, one in Dublin and one in Cork, the Department of Education claiming that 'bhí éileamh chomh mór san orthu nárbh fhéidir ionad a chur ar fáil do gach iarrthóir'.[16]

Reflecting on the summer courses for teachers, both before and after the establishment of the Free State, and which continued to be organised through the 1960s, Professor Myles Dillon, already noted as a critic of the shortcomings of the revival policy, commented that:

> there were Irish colleges in Ballingeary and Carrigaholt and Spiddal and Tourmakeady and Cloghaneely, where an extra-ordinary mixture of people assembled—priests and laymen, old and young, simple and intellectual. We learned Irish frantically by day; danced and sang, or listened at the fireside, by night … It was a sort of fairyland for city-bred people like myself. Then came freedom … Irish was no longer something you choose to do for love. In many cases it was imposed as a requirement of your profession. Soon the Irish colleges swarmed with unfortunate primary teachers, some of them past middle age, who had been hunted into them during their summer vacation by the fear of loss of increment. The spirit of adventure was gone and there was soon an atmosphere of drudgery.[17]

Nevertheless, they served an essential purpose, given the policy of Gaelicisation of the schools following Independence, and given that for practical reasons courses ran for only a short period in the summer months, they achieved their potential. And of course, the period of 'summer vacation' which teachers spent on courses was well compensated for by the extended and more flexible summer holidays.

Teacher training colleges and Preparatory Colleges

While the summer colleges were a short-term measure designed to deal with an immediate practical difficulty, the reorganisation of teacher training would be crucial if long-term success was to be achieved. In the primary sector, the development of the teacher training colleges, where previously Irish was only an optional subject, would be crucial. By the late 1920s it was clear that the 'Gaelicisation' of the training colleges had taken place. From the 1930s all subjects were taught through Irish in St Patrick's training college, Drumcondra. Irish was also the conversational language of the college, while its student teachers were only sent for practice to schools where all standards were taught through the medium of Irish.

A similar trend emerges from the other teacher training colleges. The majority of work carried on in the de la Salle training college in Waterford was done through Irish while the Department of Education described the atmosphere of Mary Immaculate training college in Limerick as 'thoroughly Gaelic'. Progress in the use of Irish at Our Lady of Mercy training college, Carysfort, was also said to be 'highly satisfactory', with over 90 per cent of lectures in psychology, mathematics, science, nature study, history, geography, drawing and some other subjects being given in Irish. The Department of Education was in little doubt about this new 'marked progress and marked appreciation for the Gaelic tongue, which stands out in bold contrast to the difficulties in this connection which were met with in the past'.[18] This was a comment applied specifically to Carysfort but which could fairly be applied to teacher training in general. A more negative observation, again made in the context of Carysfort but which resonated through all levels of the national linguistic endeavour, is perhaps more revealing of a mindset:

> The lessons, in their selection and preparation failed to reveal any new inspiration, or any high ideal on the part primary schools could and should play in the Ireland of the future. Herein I should say is the greatest weakness in the work of this college from a national standpoint. Even when the language is efficaciously taught, it is somewhat like an electric wire with the current off.[19]

The work of the teacher training colleges and the emphasis on the Irish language was significantly boosted by the establishment of coláistí ullmhúcháin, or preparatory colleges, the idea for which developed in a committee established by the Department of Education which reported in March 1925. The purpose of the committee was to examine the area of teacher training in the context of the Gaelicisation of the schools.[20] A central influence on the direction of the new policy was a seminal article by Timothy Corcoran in *Studies* in 1925. One of the key players in underwriting the applied educational aspects of the nationalist aspiration of reviving the Irish language, Corcoran suggested that the national well-being would be well served if a minimum of 50 per cent of the vacancies in the training colleges were reserved for native Irish speakers, the remaining places being also open on a more favourable basis to native speakers by giving extra marks 'to real spoken Irish'.[21]

It was in this context, and subsequent to the report of the Department's committee, that the Department of Education decided to establish a series of residential preparatory colleges—in essence Irish medium second level schools for pupils who wished to become primary school teachers—in 1926 to ensure an adequate supply of 'well educated Irish-speaking candidates for the training colleges'.[22] This in turn, would increase the pool of teachers in the schools able to teach Irish as a subject and to use it as a medium of instruction. A knock-on result for the training colleges would be the prevalence of Irish both as a medium of instruction and as a day to day language of business and administration. Seven preparatory colleges were provided for: three for Catholic boys, three for Catholic girls, and one mixed college for Protestants, each catering for approximately twenty-five students, although within a decade these numbers had mushroomed to a combined student body of approximately 600, falling to 250 during the war years and rising again to over 500 for the following two years.[23] While students who could afford it were expected to pay a yearly fee of £40, those from the fíor-Ghaeltacht who came from financially disadvantaged backgrounds received, along with full remission of fees, allowances for up to £30 towards the cost of clothes and travel.

Located principally in Gaeltacht regions—partly for the benefit of the students who could come in close contact with the cultural and linguistic

Table 3.1
NUMBER OF STUDENTS ATTENDING SECONDARY SCHOOL

School years 1921–22 to 1963–64

Source: Department of Education annual reports, 1921–22 to 1963–64

Table 3.2(a)

NUMBER OF STUDENTS ATTENDING PREPARATORY COLLEGES
(Source: Department of Education annual reports, 1933–34 to 1963–64)

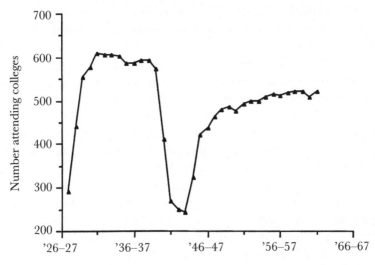

Years in which the Preparatory Colleges were operational

Table 3.2(b)

BREAKDOWN OF STUDENTS ATTENDING PREPARATORY COLLEGES

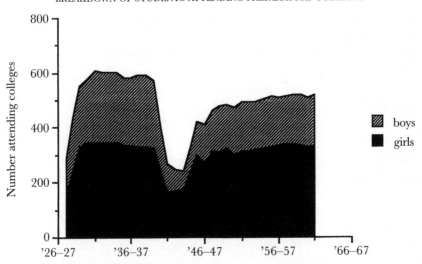

Years in which the Preparatory Colleges were operational

Source: Department of Education annual reports, 1933–34 to 1963–64

life of native Irish speakers and partly to help preserve the Gaeltacht areas both economically and linguistically[24]—the first two preparatory colleges, Coláiste Caoimhín in Glasnevin, Dublin, and Coláiste Íde in Corca Dhuibhne, Co. Kerry, were opened in mid February 1927. In the same year Coláiste Moibhí was opened in Glasnevin for Protestant students. In October of the following year Coláiste Éinde was opened in Na Forbacha, Co. Galway. In 1928 Coláiste na Mumhan was opened in Mallow, Co. Cork, its students being transferred to Coláiste Iosagáin in Ballyvourney in 1940. In 1930 Coláiste Mhuire in Tuar Mhic Eadaigh, Co. Mayo, and Coláiste Bhríde in An Fál Carrach, Co. Donegal, were opened. Following four years in the preparatory colleges (two years to prepare for the Intermediate Certificate examination and two years to prepare for the Leaving Certificate) students spent a further two years in the training colleges before qualifying as primary teachers.

In line with Corcoran's suggestion, half the available places in the preparatory colleges were reserved for candidates who got over 85 per cent in the qualifying oral Irish examination. Of these places, half were allotted to candidates from the fíor-Ghaeltacht. Age of entry was also biased in favour of applicants from the fíor-Ghaeltacht. While the upper age limit was fifteen and a half years on 1 August of the examination year, the upper age limit was raised to sixteen and a half years for fíor-Ghaeltacht candidates. Those who did not qualify for entry but who showed promise received a grant of £5 for their efforts, fifty such grants being paid in 1943 for example. Incentives were also provided for teachers to put students forward for entry: the efforts of principal teachers in national schools whose pupils showed promise in the examination or who qualified for entry received a gratuity.[25] Those who failed the oral tests, first introduced at the end of the 1940–41 school year, were prevented from becoming teachers.[26]

While preparatory colleges achieved what they set out to achieve, namely, the 'flooding' of training colleges with students well acquainted with Irish, with the concomitant effect this would have on the standard and extent of language ability among primary teachers, they were criticised for barring students with an excellent grasp of subjects other than Irish from entering by virtue of the 'undue preference' given to those with a knowledge of the language.[27] Of course, the colleges were largely based on the principle of 'undue preference'. However, existing primary teachers and their union, the INTO, were clearly unhappy with a teacher training policy which placed such emphasis on preparatory colleges. The teachers' magazine, *Irish Schools Weekly*, reported such criticism of them. One issue in 1933 reported a professor of St Andrews University, Scotland, as saying that the policy was 'reactionary, wasteful and unsound' and that entry ought to be based 'on a strictly impartial competitive examination'.[28] Two further criticisms in 1940 carried in the same source provide an insight on the attitude towards and practice within the preparatory colleges. One article reported on a protest by the Geevagh branch of the INTO against 'the unfair regulation governing entrance to the Preparatory Colleges ... Any regulations where-by practically all candidates outside the Gaeltacht are debarred from entering the teaching profession are reactionary and unjust and will ultimately injure Irish in the non-Irish speaking areas.'[29] In the same month and following persistent questioning by the INTO, *Irish Schools Weekly* alluded to the fact that while students attending preparatory colleges scored above average in the Leaving Certificate examination, their performance in the training colleges was average or below:

> We find it difficult to understand why these students, who were so much above the average turned out to be quite ordinary—or possibly less than ordinary—in the training colleges, and it would seem that the complaints of the INTO have been fully justified.[30]

By this time the Department of Education had begun reassessing the role of the colleges in the context of the excess numbers of qualified teachers then available in a period when student numbers were falling.[31] From 1934 there had been a ban on female primary teachers who married remaining in the service, an arbitrary measure to reduce the number of teachers.[32] In 1939 the colleges took in no new students, a situation which remained until the school year 1942–3, by which time the numbers attending the colleges had reached their lowest point.[33] It was during this period that the first hint of closure came. In 1941 Ó Deirg expressed confidence that 'even if they were to be closed down, they have amply justified themselves'.[34] However, it was Jack Lynch who as Minister for Education removed the *raison d'être* of the colleges when he announced the changed rules for entry to the teacher training colleges in 1958. From that year, competition for all places was to be based on Leaving Certificate results with candidates called for interview and oral examination in English and Irish on merit.[35] Nevertheless, it was left to Lynch's successor, Patrick Hillery, to finally announce in May 1960 the Department's intention to close the preparatory colleges and to replace them with a secondary scholarship scheme for Gaeltacht students.[36]

Universities

It is not surprising that the main focus of teacher training in the context of the Irish language should be the primary sector and the preparatory and teacher training colleges. The number of primary schools and the numbers attending primary schools far outweighed the corresponding figures for secondary schools, while one qualified teacher could provide instruction in Irish in the secondary schools, a situation to which the primary school structure did not lend itself. Also, since Irish was necessary for matriculation within the National University of Ireland (NUI) there could be a reasonable assumption of competency of some level among students who qualified as secondary teachers. However, progress in Irish would have to be made in the universities if Irish was to be used as a medium of instruction in secondary schools and also to ensure a continuity in Irish language instruction from second to third level. We have already noted the Council of Education's view that the decline in the number of A schools was in part due to the great lack of facilities to continue education through Irish in the universities.[37]

Within two years of its inception the NUI, the academic ruling body of the Irish university colleges (with the exception of Trinity College, Dublin) established under the Irish University Act, 1908, announced its intention to make Irish language and literature obligatory for matriculation. This regulation came into effect in 1913. It was introduced during the time of the NUI's first chancellor, the Most Revd. William J. Walsh, Catholic Archbishop of Dublin and Primate of Ireland and former president of Maynooth College from 1880–85. Walsh was succeeded by Eamon de Valera thus ensuring continued adherence to what was described as the 'natural cultural principle',[38] which made Irish compulsory for entry to NUI colleges.

While the Free State government interfered little in the structure or requirements of the NUI, it did involve itself in the role of University College, Galway, the only NUI college bordering a Gaeltacht area. With a view to increasing the proportion of instruction given through the medium of Irish—perhaps in time hoping that Irish could be made the compulsory medium of instruction in the college[39]—and making better provision for the study of Irish language and literature, the University College Galway Act, 1929, increased the statutory income of the college (£12,000) by an additional grant of £16,000, while withdrawing a non-statutory grant of £8,800. The central conditions pertaining to the increased funding were: that the college appoint three lecturers to give instruction through the medium of Irish in mathematics, history and economics; that it reduce fees to approximately pre-1914 levels to induce students from Gaeltacht areas to attend UCG in preference to other colleges and that it establish a special scholarship scheme for those from native Irish-speaking districts.[40] In line with these regulations, fees for a course of lectures in Irish were reduced to half the fee for the corresponding course in English, while the fee for Gaeltacht scholars was only half the corresponding cost of lectures for other students. Also, by 1932 the college governing body was offering a number of £60 scholarships each year to Gaeltacht candidates.

From 1930 all students attending courses in UCG had to show that they had a competent knowledge of Irish. No student was permitted to sit a university examination without having attended an Irish conversation class at the college for one hour per week during the preceding session. All students had to then present themselves for an oral examination, which had to be passed before a degree could be awarded.[41] This Act was reinforced by the UCG (Increase of Grant) Order of 1932 which provided for an extra £750 to be granted for the year beginning 1 April 1931 and an additional £1,500 to be paid together with the £28,000 in each subsequent year.[42] Among other initiatives, this allowed UCG establish a demonstration school in Irish as part of the Higher Diploma in Education course. This school, Scoil Brighde, which had two teachers appointed by the college under the Professor of Education, assisted in the training of students. A certificate of capacity to teach through the medium of Irish was awarded to all successful candidates.

A further request from UCG for a £3,000 capital grant and an additional £800 per year, made when a delegation from the college met with Eamon de Valera in April 1933 was turned down. De Valera suggested instead that the fees of those students not doing their work through the medium of Irish be increased, thus meeting the college's financial requirements.[43] A possible reason for the reluctance to supply further funding was a dissatisfaction with what had been achieved following the provision of previous grants. In order to ensure that UCG carried out the objectives outlined in the Act of 1929, a committee was established consisting of the President of the college, the Ministers for Finance and Education and the Attorney General. However, in 1934 MacEntee, the Minister for Finance, expressed dissatisfaction with the college authorities in relation to their obligations under the Act. He was particularly disappointed with the efforts made in relation to the appointment of Irish speakers to posts within the college and the college's commitment to Irish medium courses.[44] Two years later there were teachers in UCG giving instruction wholly through Irish in history, ancient classics, education, mathematics, economics, commerce and accounting, while instruction in physics and chemistry was given partly through Irish.[45]

Further developing the importance of UCG as an Irish medium university, in 1947 the government established a university scholarship scheme for students pursuing degree courses, including examinations, solely through Irish. Although not limited in theory to UCG, in practice it was the only university where a student could pursue a degree course entirely through Irish. Up to fifty scholarships were offered each year. Qualification depended on passing at least three Leaving Certificate examination papers answered through Irish, obtaining honours in Irish itself and performing satisfactorily in a qualifying oral Irish examination. The scholarships, worth £150 annually and renewable each year subject to satisfactory performance in examinations, were split evenly between male and female students and were complemented by similar scholarships limited to students from the fior-Ghaeltacht.[46]

Apart from Galway, University College, Dublin, the largest of the NUI colleges and where Timothy Corcoran was Professor of Education, was also making an induced effort to increase its use of Irish. The lack of facilities for learning Irish in UCD was described in 1923 by William Magennis, Professor of Metaphysics at the college and a Cumann na nGaedhael Deputy:

> When I was a schoolboy, very much against my own interest let me boast, I took as an Intermediate subject the subject of Irish. Afterwards, when I came to the University College, Dublin, it was impossible to carry on and it was necessary to substitute German.[47]

The University Education Act, 1926, changed this situation as it provided for a full-time lectureship in Modern Irish Language and Literature. The Act also stipulated that the teaching of Irish folklore form part of the course of the Modern Irish Department which in 1931, following an assurance of financial assistance from the government of up to £3,000 per year, put forward a number of proposed changes for re-organisation and expansion. The proposals included the replacement of an existing lectureship in Irish with a professorship of Modern Irish Poetry; replacing an assistantship and part-time lectureship in folklore with a full-time lectureship in folklore; the replacement of an existing assistantship in Irish with honours teaching in a special branch such as modern Irish philology or phonetics and dialects with the status of professor; and the creation of a number of new full-time posts, including one lectureship in Modern Irish and five assistantships including one in respect of Medieval and Modern Irish for post-graduate work and one in folklore.[48]

The re-organisation was initiated in 1932, the college authorities agreeing with the government to ensure that no person should be permitted to present for any degree examination unless they had previously passed an oral examination in Irish. There were certain exceptions to this which included foreign students. Mirroring the UCG rules of 1930 this regulation, given effect in 1934 under the University College, Dublin Act of that year, required students of all faculties to attend prescribed Irish conversation classes during their first and second years of study. In return for implementing these regulations the Department of Modern Irish Language and Literature received its promised grant of £3,000 per year.[49]

However, before long, as happened in the case of UCG, questions were raised about UCD's sincerity in promoting the language. In the case of UCD the questioning underlined both the insecurities and at times the paranoia of unswerving revivalists and on the other hand, the extent to which at least in some institutions national idealism was not allowed hinder practical considerations. It was Conradh na Gaeilge which in 1940 raised questions when the college appointed Arthur Conway as president. Conway had been Professor of Mathematical Physics and Registrar of the college from 1909 to 1940 but, apparently, his knowledge of Irish was questionable. Three years later the League was again at logger-heads with UCD over the appointment of W.J. Williams to the college's Chair of Education on the grounds of lack of Irish. Yet, as was the case with Conway, Williams was confirmed in his post.

By the end of the 1940s there was a rethinking regarding the necessity for students from all faculties to undertake Irish language courses followed by examinations. In the academic year 1949–50 the rules were somewhat relaxed, exempting students over twenty-five years of age from the linguistic requirements while students in general were no longer required to attend a prescribed course in Irish, although it was still necessary to pass the oral Irish examination.[50] This was the first breach of the Irish rule in UCD, the age limit being reduced to twenty-four years in the academic year 1960–61,[51] while four years later the requirement was dropped altogether. In its stead optional graded evening classes in Irish open to all registered students of the college and running over three terms were organised, leading to the award of a Certificate in Spoken Irish.[52]

While St Patrick's College, Maynooth, never had the same regulations regarding Irish, although it played an important role in ensuring the status of Irish in the NUI,[53] the position of Irish in University College, Cork, was quite similar to that which prevailed in UCD. By the academic year 1940–41 all first year students not taking Irish as a subject, with the exception of 'genuine' native Irish speakers and missionary religious 'who are definitely going or have been for a period of three years or more, on the foreign missions',[54] had to attend an oral Irish class and subsequently pass an oral Irish examination before graduating. As in UCD, this rule applied to students from all faculties, while pre-medical students had to pass the oral test in Irish before proceeding. The college also provided lectures through the medium of Irish in mathematics, history, geography and chemistry while its *Calendar* from the mid 1950s included a declaration in support of Irish. Like UCD, however, the college's rules regarding Irish began to relax in the 1960s, and from 1967–68 students, while still obliged to attend oral Irish classes were no longer required to take an oral examination before graduating.

The one college outside the NUI structure was Trinity College, Dublin, 'that Elizabethan fortress in College Green' where 'outspoken opponents of Irish … are to be found in great numbers' according to the *Catholic Bulletin*,[55] a description which if anything was reserved in the context of its portrayal as 'un-Irish'. As was the case with the NUI colleges, the question of the language within it was associated with the need to raise finances. Recognising this reality, the college authorities organised special courses in spoken Irish for students who intended becoming secondary teachers in Ireland from 1941–42 onwards. This was prior to the college's application in 1947 to the government, of which Eamon de Valera, Chancellor of the NUI, was Taoiseach, for an annual grant of £35,000 and a once-off capital grant of £75,000. The request followed the publication in December 1946 of a *Memorandum on the needs of Trinity College Dublin*. This set out in detail the financial requirements of the college in order to justify an application for State assistance.[56] The college authorities expected that funding would only be forthcoming on the condition that Irish be made a compulsory subject in its entrance examination.

Following a meeting in February 1947 between the Provost and Registrar of Trinity and de Valera and Frank Aiken, the Minister for Finance, the government agreed to grant the college £35,000. On granting the money, no formal request regarding the position of Irish within TCD was made. However, the perception that de Valera and Aiken agreed to the funding without attaching any linguistic conditions,[57] a perception which rested easily on the shoulders of both the Irish government and the authorities of Trinity, is incorrect. Behind the scenes efforts were made by both sides to be as accommodating as possible on the issue of the Irish language. In

March 1947 E.H. Alton, the Provost of Trinity, wrote to de Valera assuring him that the board of the college would:

> endeavour as soon as possible and at the latest within twelve months, to secure the services of at least two or three scholars capable of teaching appropriate university subjects to full university standard and through the medium of Irish ... The number of such lecturers can be increased later if the new scheme is successful.[58]

Alton also alluded to the board's intention to offer a fee remission of ten guineas per half year to students capable of profiting from lectures given through the medium of Irish and to offer prizes to students achieving high marks in examinations answered through the medium of Irish. Nevertheless, both provisions were theoretical as no lecture course was given through Irish. In July of the same year K.C. Bailey, Registrar of TCD, wrote to Frank Aiken outlining the difficulties the college was having in finding lecturers able and willing to lecture through Irish. Offers had been made to lecturers in mathematics and history but both (unnamed in correspondence) declined the positions. However, the college did arrange for a course of lectures to be delivered through Irish on pre-Christian and Early Christian Art for 1948 and the registrar remained hopeful of arranging a course of lectures through Irish in mathematics.[59]

Meanwhile, the university's calendar for the year 1946–47 played its role in cultivating a perception of interest on the part of Trinity in the language by strongly recommending that students intending to teach in Ireland spend a period of time in the Gaeltacht in addition to attending the special conversation classes in Irish.[60] In the following academic year, lectures through the medium of Irish amounted to four mathematics lectures per week to freshman students and one lecture per week on Pre-Christian and Early Christian Art in Ireland. This remained unchanged until the academic year 1950–51 when the latter lecture series was replaced by one lecture per week on Irish history which was open to the public. In that year, 55 per cent of Trinity's students came from outside the Republic, approximately half of whom came from Great Britain. This was a significant increase on pre-war figures when out of State students accounted for only 34 per cent of the total student body, over two-thirds of whom came from Northern Ireland.[61]

By the academic year 1956–57, ten years after first receiving financial assistance from the Irish government, Trinity's endeavours to provide lectures through the medium of Irish had been quietly abandoned as the necessity of continuing the exercise in window dressing diminished.

Before leaving the subject of the universities it is interesting to note that, by the 1960s, UCG was the only college offering the Higher Diploma in Education—the necessary qualification for students wishing to become secondary teachers—through Irish. Comisiún um Athbheochan na Gaeilge recommended that UCC follow a similar line and that UCD offer the course partly through Irish in the light of the fact that up to 50 per cent of secondary schools at the time taught at least some subjects through Irish. For a few years prior to 1949–50 UCC had offered a Higher Diploma in Education course in Irish parallel to that in English, but from that academic year, with the exception of sporadic intermissions, only teaching practice could be pursued through Irish although students were given the option of answering the examinations in Irish.[62] Interestingly, the Commission, referring specifically to UCG, expressed the view that parallel courses in English and Irish in the Arts and Science faculties were not necessary and wasteful of resources.[63] Its preference was for the continuance of courses through Irish where there was an overlap. The government response to these recommendations, as outlined in the White Paper of 1965, merely stated that they would be 'examined by the appropriate ministers in conjunction with such recommendations as may be made on the same points by the Commission on Higher Education'.[64]

Table 3.3

PERCENTAGE OF PRIMARY TEACHERS WITH VARYING QUALIFICATIONS IN IRISH, SELECTED YEARS [65]

School Year	No Certificate in Irish	Ordinary Certificate	Bilingual Certificate	Ard-Teastas
1928–29	38.1	31.2	24.6	6
1929–30	32.2	33.7	28.2	5.9
1930–31	27.2	33.4	33.4	6
1931–32	25.8	34.2	34.1	5.9
1932–33	23.7	32.8	37.4	6.1
1933–34	22	32.6	39.1	6.2
1934–35	19.8	32.1	41.7	6.4
1935–36	20.5	28.5	47.8	6.6
1936–37	16.3	27.8	49.1	6.7
1937–38	15.1	27.3	51.1	6.5
1940–41	11.1	24.5	57.6	6.8
1944–45	9.5	19.6	64.2	6.7
1949–50	8.3	16.9	68.6	6.2
1954–55	7.3	12.4	74.7	5.6
1960–61	4	6.6	85.1	4.3

Teacher competency in Irish

In 1922, out of 12,000 lay primary teachers, less than one third had any formal qualification in Irish, 1,107 possessed a bilingual certificate which qualified teachers to use Irish as a medium of instruction, and a further 2,845 had the basic ordinary certificate which qualified teachers to teach Irish as a subject.[66] By 1931 only 5.9 per cent of the 14,268 teachers had the Ard-Teastas (the 'Higher Certificate' in Irish) while 34.2 per cent had an ordinary certificate and 34.1 per cent a bilingual certificate, leaving 25.8 per cent of teachers with no formal qualification in the language. Tomás Ó Deirg commented some years later that to be fully qualified in Irish an individual required possession of either the bilingual certificate or the Ard-Teastas.[67] Despite the work of the training colleges and universities it was clear that the new programme of the primary schools, with its emphasis on the Gaelic revival, was introduced ten years before there was a suitably qualified teaching staff to implement it, the number of teachers with no qualification in Irish being only marginally less than the number with the bilingual certificate and Ard-Teastas combined up to the early 1930s (see Table 3.3). Even in 1932 Ernest Blythe, the most senior government minister during the period 1922–32 and Vice-President of the executive council for the latter five years, admitted that:

> it is undoubtedly a fact that a great many—perhaps the major-
> ity of our teachers—are not able to give instruction through
> Irish. We have to do the best that can be done with them, but a
> great many of them are hardly competent even to teach Irish
> satisfactorily.[68]

Neither was this a once-off or intemperate comment. The Department of Education right through the 1920s acknowledged that only 'fírbheagán' teachers had the capacity or competence to teach any subject through Irish,[69] a situation attributed to the fact that 'Níl ár ndóthan múinteoirí cliste againn'.[70] While the Department acknowledged that it was quite difficult to teach Irish or through Irish in infant standards in normal two teacher schools when one teacher was in charge of numerous standards, it observed that even teachers with the bilingual certificate were showing little inclina-tion to use Irish as the ordinary language of the school.[71] Yet, the impli-cations of these observations for students and for the revival policy were not addressed. Indeed the extent to which people were prepared to avoid admitting that the lack of teacher competency was a fundamental obstacle to the revival policy was astounding. One government Deputy, an Irish teacher and active member of the Gaelic League, observed in the mid 1930s that even teachers who did not have a great grasp of Irish should be obliged to use it as a medium of instruction.[72]

Apart from instruction in Irish itself, primary teachers were offered no courses and little advice on bilingual education. Those who possessed the Ard-Teastas, the highest qualification in competency in Irish but held by a minority of teachers from the 1920s to the 1960s, often complained of being disadvantaged in so far as inspectors expected much more exacting work from them.[73]

Having advised teachers and managers in May 1930 of imminent changes, in 1932 the Department of Education set out to clarify and strengthen the requirements for competency in Irish among primary teachers. The new *Rules and Regulations* stipulated that:

(a) In the case of schools situated in a district scheduled as Irish speaking, candidates must have obtained a certificate of competency to give bilingual instruction.

(b) In the case of schools situated in English-speaking districts candidates must have obtained a certificate of competency to teach Irish. Ability to carry out the requirements of the programme with reasonable competency will, however, be regarded as sufficient qualification in Irish in the case of candidates for appointment who on 1 July 1922 were over thirty years of age and under forty years of age and who have served with the sanction of the Department in a permanent capacity. Candidates who on 1 July 1922 were over forty years of age and who have served with the sanction of the Department in a permanent capacity on the staff of a national school but have not the qualification in Irish indicated, may be sanctioned.[74]

Again relying on the fall-back position of financial inducement, the rules specified that, in the case of school principals, assistant teachers and junior assistant mistresses teaching in an official Irish-speaking area, no increment of salary could be granted after 30 June 1932 'unless and until such a teacher obtains a certificate of competency to give bilingual instruction'.[75] In the Galltacht, no increment of salary was to be granted after June 1932 to teachers who did not possess a certificate of competency in Irish and after June 1935 to those who did not possess a certificate of competency in bilingual instruction.[76] However, in 1940 a test case was brought before the High Court by the INTO relating to a teacher who had twice failed to secure the bilingual certificate and who, consequently, had been denied three increments. The court ruled against the plaintiff but on appeal to the Supreme Court it was ruled that the increments had been 'withheld without justification'. The judge stated that the rules which applied when the plaintiff was first appointed could not be lawfully altered to his detriment. As a result of the case the government decided to back pay increments withheld from teachers in similar circumstances.[77]

The awarding of bonuses to teachers with special qualifications was also in future to be conditional on the possession of a certificate of competence to give bilingual instruction.[78] The new rules were in part a response to the annoyance of the Department that:

> There had been ... a number of those well within the age when reasonable fluency in Irish might be attained, who have failed to respond, whether through mere lethargy or indifference to the demands of patriotism, to the appeal which was made to them.[79]

Whether it was due to a 'failure to respond' or not, the lack of competency in Irish among managers and teachers in primary schools was evidenced in a memo of the Department dated 16 September 1932 concerning the issuing of circulars which implicitly admitted that there were many managers and teachers who could not read or understand Irish. While the Department stated that in future all circulars would be issued in Irish only, English translations would be sent to managers and teachers who did not understand Irish.[80]

In secondary schools there were clear difficulties regarding the competency of teachers, mirroring the problems of the primary sector. Apart from the fact that secondary teachers often lacked the fluency of their primary counterparts, due in part to a decreased emphasis on Gaeltacht summer courses, and included a much smaller proportion of native speakers, even those teachers who obtained honours degrees in Irish often lacked conversational skills and fluency in the language according to the Department of Education.[81] While the Department recognised that a result of this was an inability even among qualified teachers to give *effective* instruction through Irish,[82] the consequences for the standard of education or for the revival of the language were never raised.

In order to standardise the Irish competency of secondary teachers, the Department introduced the Teastas Múinteora Gaeilge in 1932. From February 1942 it was expected that applicants for registration as secondary teachers would produce evidence of having a competent knowledge of

Irish. This was defined as the ability to converse with fluency and correctness so as to allow the applicant use it after a period of experience in teaching as a medium of instruction.[83] The regulation was aimed at providing a large pool of teachers competent to give instruction through the medium of Irish.[84] The White Paper on the revival of Irish issued in the 1960s expressed satisfaction that the majority of secondary teachers who were teaching Irish were competent to do so.[85]

Paralleling the Teastas Múinteora Gaeilge was the Ceard-Teastais Ghaeilge, also introduced in 1932 as the formal qualification in Irish for teachers in technical schools, allowing them to use Irish as a medium of instruction in other subjects. The aim of technical education, which was first given a statutory basis in Ireland prior to Independence through the Agricultural and Technical Instruction (Ireland) Act, 1899, was to provide pupils who left primary schools with vocational training before taking up employment and to provide continuation education through night classes for those already in employment. In 1924 the Department of Education took over the responsibility for technical education from the Department of Agriculture and two years later, in 1926, it established a commission to inquire and report on the vocational sector. Reporting in 1927, the commission's main recommendations were included in the Vocational Education Act, 1930. Under this Act, technical and continuation education continued to be organised at local level by statutory committees. Instruction was provided in technical and manual skills required in the agricultural, industrial, commercial and trades sectors to pupils, usually aged between fourteen and sixteen years. Among the night-time courses organised for the adult population were classes in Irish.[86]

In March 1941 the Department of Education introduced the first of a series of courses for whole-time teachers of Irish in technical schools, the Teastas Timire Gaeilge. This was aimed at promoting the Irish revival in the vocational sector. Although it provided serving teachers with a significant opportunity to further their language skills, twenty years later Comisiún um Athbheochan na Gaeilge recommended refresher courses for teachers of Irish and the establishment by each Vocational Education Committee (VEC), the local controlling bodies of vocational schools established under the 1930 Act, of subcommittees with responsibility for promoting Irish language activities.[87]

While teachers in both the primary and secondary sectors were often criticised for their lack of skills in Irish, mostly by the Department of

Education which distanced itself from any of the evident shortcomings, there can be little doubt about the enthusiasm and commitment of the majority of teachers for the language. However, this was soured in many cases by an increasing emphasis on the Gaelicisation of the schools despite inadequate training. There was a tacit political recognition that teachers were 'doing their best'[88] in the circumstances. Even while the Department of Education in the 1930s was castigating them, the Minister, Tomás Ó Deirg, was praising their efforts.[89] By the mid 1940s even the reports of the Department of Education were beginning to praise secondary teachers who were said to be teaching Irish 'le fonn is le dúthracht'.[90] By 1960, when the position of Irish in the secondary schools was coming in for severe and sustained attack, the Department was commenting on the encouragement that teachers were giving their pupils in the speaking of Irish.[91] In general, one feels that the comments published in *Irish Schools Weekly* in 1941 relating to primary teachers may sum up the approach and commitment of teachers in both sectors:

> Irish has long been the nightmare of our profession, and the fact that many of us have not qualified for strait-jackets is a tribute to the solidity of our mental make-up … We could probably all agree, that the language should be brought back and we are willing to grow grey prematurely in the effort.[92]

In conclusion, it may be said that the moulding of teacher training in line with the new emphasis on Irish in the schools was successful from the 1930s. However, in the period 1922–32, a huge weakness of the revival policy was its imposition on the schools before there were teachers qualified to teach Irish, teach through Irish, or on occasion able to speak Irish themselves. The period 1922–32, as has already been suggested, was crucial for the revival, perceptions of the language and its place in the schools. The practical problems resulting from unqualified teachers gave rise to criticisms of the schools-based revival policy at an early stage. Such negative associations arguably damaged the credibility of the revival from the outset. The Gaeltacht courses for teachers were of significant benefit, but even given the enthusiasm for them, they amounted to little more than 'crash courses'.[93] Speaking of his primary school teacher, who was in his late forties when the schools-based revival policy was embarked on, Noel Browne noted that: 'it was impossible for him to learn the language in such a short time, and consequently to teach it to us'.[94] The subsequent measures taken in the training colleges and universities, and the establishment of the preparatory colleges, ensured that new generations of teachers were equipped to carry out the post Independence school programme.

The effectiveness with which the issue of teacher training was addressed stands in contrast to the tardiness with which other practical issues were addressed, or even recognised. This is particularly true in the context of the provision of school text books in Irish, the subject of the following chapter.

CHAPTER FOUR

'Mór-Ghanntanas Leabhar': Irish Language Books

PARALLELING the obstacle of an untrained teaching force was the problem of providing a literature in the Irish language capable of sustaining the schools-based revival policy. While this necessitated in the first instance the provision of Irish language text books, the supply of other material in Irish—general literature, magazines, periodicals and newspapers—would be an essential tool of the revival. Providing a literature in Irish, as distinct from a purely Irish literature, was not a straightforward matter however. Issues ranging from typeface (Roman versus Gaelic) to the complications presented by dialectical, spelling and grammatical variations dogged the provision of standard texts, while the emphasis on translations, mostly of readily available English works, provided a wholly uninspiring corpus of work.

The tradition of publishing in Irish had a chequered history up to 1922. Dating from the collapse of the Gaelic order in the seventeenth century, formal training in the Gaelic literary language ended in Ireland and during the eighteenth century there was scarcely any publishing in Irish aside from some religious works, dictionaries and grammars.[1] However, by the late nineteenth century the Gaelic League had begun the task of recreating a literature in Irish, bringing a significant new vibrancy through the publication of plays, poetry and prose. The League founded *An Claideamh Soluis*, a bilingual newspaper, and promoted and produced Irish language text books such as Fr. Eugene O'Growney's four volume *Simple Lessons in Irish*. Nevertheless, a less *ad hoc* and more focused and government centred effort would be necessary from 1922, particularly if the promotion of Irish as a medium of instruction was to be given the necessary backup of Irish language text books.

Irish language text books

It took the government two years to realise the importance of becoming involved in the provision of Irish language text books and a further two years before it took any practical action based on that delayed realisation. Almost with a sense of surprise the Department of Education in its annual report for the school years 1924–26 commented on the fact that the lack of an adequate supply of Irish language text books acted as a deterrent to many teachers in making more general use of Irish as a teaching medium in the schools.[2] However, acknowledgement of the problem did not provoke action: money provided in the 1925–26 government estimates for the publication of suitable text books in Irish for use in secondary schools was not spent.[3] Again this underpinned the extent to which nationalist idealism rather than practical consideration was the force behind the revival policy. Comisiún na Gaeltachta, in its report of 1926, was the first to advise State support for the production of standard sets of readers in Irish,[4] while *Irish Schools Weekly* was continually vocal in alluding to the absence of Irish texts in primary school. Yet, despite the Department of Education's acknow-ledgement that the lack of text books was 'a deterrent' to promoting Irish as a medium of instruction, the government's initial response to the recommendation of Comisiún na Gaeltachta was that 'while acceptable in principle, [it] presents such serious practical difficulties that it is not feasible at present'.[5] It was the school year 1926–27 before a State sponsored publi-cation agency under the direction of the Department of Education was finally established. Called Coiste na Leabhar ('the Books Committee') it was referred to more commonly as An Gúm ('the scheme' or 'the action plan'). Initially established to publish suitable school text books following demands from teachers for such provision, it was the first sustained govern-ment approach to providing Irish language reading material. While encom-passing a broader brief than the production of school books, its first two years of existence were focused solely on the needs of the education system.

Manuscripts suitable as primary and secondary school texts were sub-mitted to a committee of 'Irish scholars' which decided on suitability for pub-lication. Primary school books were then examined by inspectors before being sanctioned.[6] The initial necessity of producing as many Irish language texts as possible seemed of premier importance, praise of An Gúm usually being couched in terms of the number of books published.[7] Despite this, however, An Gúm was obviously not producing a sufficient volume of texts and by the end of the 1920s the Department of Education was suggesting that teachers in primary schools carry out their work without the use of books:

> Smaoineamh nua a bheadh é na naoidheanáin a mhúineadh
> gan an leabhair. Tá an iomad muinghine ag ár múinteoirí go
> léir as na leabhair—agus as leabhair shuaracha leis—agus is
> deacair leo oibriú gan an leabhar.[8]

By 1931 the situation had worsened, the production of material for primary school children being almost non-existent. This fact was recognised by the Department of Education which reached agreement with the Department of Finance to offer special bonuses to authors and translators producing reading material for the seven to eleven years age group in an attempt to encourage a greater volume of publications.[9]

While the lack of volume perhaps negates an argument about quantity taking precedence over quality, there were concerns raised from an early stage about the standard, content, quality of Irish and cultural emphasis of An Gúm publications. Although there was no question of producing anything 'unsuitable for discussion in the convent school',[10] Frank Fahy, a Fianna Fáil Deputy for Galway and a qualified secondary school teacher, claimed that not only were some school texts wholly lacking in nationalism, but that a number were 'contabhartach do spiorad na náisiúntachta',[11] while the standard of Irish was poor. On the other hand, the Board of Education of the Church of Ireland was pointing to the 'markedly sectarian character of many of the Irish phrase and reading books'.[12] This partly emanated from the fact that 'almost every series of Irish lessons contained a lesson on the priest and the Mass'.[13] Perhaps the greatest problem was that, in the words of a government Deputy, 'everything in Irish that comes out from a publisher is regularly put on the programme when it comes out, whether it is good, bad or indifferent'.[14]

Whatever about the national emphasis of early publications—it is arguable that the Church of Ireland view rather than Fahy's is nearer the fact—within ten years it was clear that many Irish language books were stiflingly nationalist in content, with any conciliatory attitude towards Protestant concerns all but evaporating.[15] In 1939 *The Leader*, itself a deeply nationalist newspaper founded by D.P. Moran in 1900, pointed out that young people were being turned off reading Irish because too many texts discussed Irish itself and the saving of Irish,[16] while in 1947 the INTO complained that many Irish texts were irrelevant to students:

> We would point out that such subjects as the Penal Laws, the
> Island of Saints and Scholars, the Suffering of Ireland, appeals
> to speak Irish, the beauties of the countryside, etc., unfortun-
> ately have little interest for most children.[17]

These issues continued to be raised up to the 1960s—the Labour Party used terms like 'thoroughly old-fashioned', 'unattractively produced' and 'nothing less than a disgrace' in a report of 1963 to describe text books in Irish [18]—as was the appropriateness of the standard of book being produced for its target school audience. De Valera, while Taoiseach in the mid 1940s, claimed to have been disturbed by 'complaints which he has heard from persons of knowledge and experience in education matters to the effect that the text books in Irish for both the primary and secondary schools are in many cases of so high a standard of difficulty as to be beyond the children's capacity' [19] and requested that the matter be examined. However, the problem persisted and through the 1950s the issue was raised at annual congresses of the INTO which passed resolutions asking that:

> a permanent series of Irish text books with vocabularies and glossaries be prepared for use in primary schools and that in the interests of the revival of the Irish language the standard of Irish in these text books be considerably lower than at present obtaining. [20]

The response of the Department of Education was to merely acknowledge that such issues had been raised. [21]

The provision of Irish language text books for secondary schools was marginally more successful than for the primary sector. From the period 1924–26 the Department of Education provided £4,000 for the production of suitable Irish language text books at minimum cost for secondary schools. The authors received special bonuses with the rights to the books reverting to them once the costs of publication had been recouped. [22] With the coming on stream of An Gúm the provision of secondary texts was accelerated, although by 1927 of seventy-one manuscripts submitted to An Gúm for publication only thirteen had been accepted and only three were available in the schools with a further three in print. As in the case of primary school texts, adjudication of manuscripts submitted for publication was carried out by a 'committee of experts'. [23]

The Department of Education recognised the fact that despite the work of An Gúm there was a serious shortage of Irish books available for secondary schools and acknowledged this as one of the 'two greatest obstacles' facing the schools-based revival policy. [24] As in the case of primary teachers, the Department immediately proceeded to blame the secondary school teachers, many of whom it claimed were not up to the job of teaching through Irish despite 'ard-cháilíochta léighinn'. [25] By the mid 1940s, at which time de Valera was lauding the quality and quantity of Irish language books in general,[26] An Gúm had published 102 secondary school text books, rising to123 by 1958, an average of less than two new titles per year. This lack of sufficient achievement in providing secondary texts prompted Comhdháil Náisiúnta na Gaeilge, the umbrella body of organisations promoting the language founded in 1943, to write to the Department of Education in the mid 1950s to express anxiety about the 'mór-ghanntanas téascanna i nGaeilge' and to call on the Department to implement an emergency plan to provide the essential books as quickly as possible.[27]

From the mid 1940s the work of An Gúm was augmented by Foilsiúcháin Náisiúnta Teoranta (FNT) and Sáirséal agus Dill, an independent Irish language publishing house founded in 1945 which hoped to do 'rud fiúntach'[28] in the provision of Irish text books in particular. However, to an extent such enterprises, dependent on government grants provided through Bord na Leabhar Gaeilge which was established in 1952 in order to pay subsidies to private publishers, was hampered by official bureaucracy which provided grants only after books had been published. As a result, according to Sáirséal agus Dill:

> new texts written in Irish are not being produced and old ones are not being reprinted when stocks become exhausted. As books become unobtainable classes are changing from Irish to English as a medium of instruction.[29]

Table 4.1
AN GÚM PUBLICATIONS UP TO JULY 1951

Category	Original	Translations	Total
Fiction	91	136	227
Biography	31	16	47
Travel	15	8	23
Plays	91	108	199
Poetry	43	1	44
Essays	27	3	30
Books for young people	48	89	137
Secondary school text books	50	27	77
Books of terms	8	–	8
Miscellaneous	44	19	63
Others (incl. music and reference books)	151	–	151
Total	599	407	1,006

Source: An Gúm Publications (N.A., D/T, Publications in Irish: An Gúm, S 9538 (A & B).

The *Report of the Council of Education: Curriculum of Secondary Schools*, published in 1962, reinforced the Sáirséal agus Dill analysis, describing the situation as 'critical'[30] and partially ascribing the decline in the number of A schools to the difficulty in obtaining suitable Irish language text books to facilitate teaching through the medium of Irish. At this time there was 'no subject on the curriculum for which a full range of text books is available and even standard works are not available for some subjects'.[31]

That such a situation might prevail in the initial years of the policy was understandable; yet, the fact that such a lack of texts was allowed continue into the 1960s, forty years into the revival policy, despite the recognition by the Department of the centrality of good quality school texts to the revival effort, raises a number of questions. The Labour Party document of 1963, *Challenge and Change in Education*, rightly summed up the strange situation when it castigated the government's hypocrisy in urging schools to teach through the medium of Irish while not ensuring that the same schools had sufficient, good quality Irish language text books.[32]

Complications in publishing: some technical issues

One of the difficulties in producing books in Irish which contributed to the inconsistency in government policy was the absence of a standardised Irish spelling and grammar. The issue of standardisation became a significant debating point, as did the issue of 'an chló-Rómhánach' [Roman type]. Any 'capricious experimentation'[33] with the technical side of the language was utterly rejected by the purists.

On the issue of typestyle, it was the Department of Education's belief that both primary and secondary teachers were happiest with the 'cló-Gaelach' [Irish type] and that any change to 'an chló-Rómhánach', which was used well before the founding of the Free State[34] and towards which there was a leaning in the Department, would have to be introduced in stages. It was decided that for the school year 1927–28 Irish books for secondary schools could be printed in Gaelic type provided that one book in every six together with all translations were issued in Roman type,[35] a regulation which caused some dissatisfaction:

> When the regulations of the Department regarding the type to
> be adopted for the publication of commissioned translations
> into Irish were made known, one writer declined to undertake
> a translation and two other writers refused to compete for publi-
> cation of books on whose translation they were engaged.[36]

In a letter to the Department of Education in December 1930 the Department of Finance made it clear that from March 1931:

> the rule will be that all books accepted for publication by your Department, whether under the scheme for secondary school texts or under the scheme for works of general literature in Irish, must be printed in Roman type.[37]

Meanwhile, and somewhat at odds with the Department of Finance regulation, an advisory committee to the Department of Education of 1931 recommended that authors be allowed choose the typeface and that the 'sean-chló' [old type] should not be abandoned. It reiterated the earlier departmental decision that all translations should be in Roman type[38] although it was decided that Fr. Patrick Dineen's translation of Virgil's *Aeneid I* should be published in Gaelic type.[39] Within the Civil Service, where the head of each department could designate the type used, Roman type predominated on the basis that provision of an equal number of Gaelic script typewriters would be too costly,[40] although in April 1937 the Irish version of the draft Constitution was published in Gaelic type, a symbolic gesture more than anything else.

By the 1950s the official bias towards Roman type was being more strongly pursued and following agreement between the Irish Publishers' Association and departmental inspectors in April 1953 that the introduction of some pages in Roman type into text books would not be a problem,[41] the Department sent a letter to teachers and school managers requesting children to be taught how to read Irish in the 'cló Romhánach'.

Another obstacle in the production of sufficient Irish language text books from an early stage was the lack of a standardised—or indeed any— terminology for some subjects. This was a particular problem in the teaching of science and technical subjects. To overcome it a Coiste Téarmaíochta was established under the Department of Education which by the school year 1928–29 had published two books of terms, one relevant to the teaching of history and geography and the other to the teaching of grammar and literature. By 1939 books of terms had been published for history, geography, science, music, business and games. Again, the period of time which elapsed between problem recognition and problem solution seemed unnecessarily protracted, but once addressed the problem was adequately solved. The 1968 progress report of the *An Páipéar Bán um Athbheochan na Gaeilge* outlined the extent of the progress which had been made.[42]

A more serious problem was that of 'standard Irish'. Dr Johanna Pollak was asked by the government to give her opinions on the subject and in May 1943 she incorporated her views in the document 'On Teaching Irish'. It was her opinion that, 'if an agreement could be attained regarding a standard Irish, a great amount of difficulties would probably be overcome'.[43] The INTO report of the previous year had urged that a body be established to look objectively at the standardisation of spelling and the simplification and standardisation of Irish grammatical forms, the implementation of which would significantly benefit both the student and teacher. Some examples of the consequences of the lack of standardisation in school editions of prose texts sanctioned by the Department of Education were given in the INTO report to illustrate the extent of the problem:

1. Varieties of spellings:
   Gaodhluinn, Gaoluinn, Gaedhilg, Gaedhilige.
   amárach, amáireach, imbárach, imbáirerach.
2. Irregular verbs:
   níor chuaidh, ní dheachaidh.
   chuala, chualaidh.
3. Other verb forms:
   ag fágáil, ag fágaint.
   le cloisint, le cluinstin.
4. Aspirations and eclipses:
   ar an gcapall/ar an chapall.
   gan chuardach/gan cuardach.[44]

In response to the request of the INTO, the Department of Education, which later acknowledged that 'cuireadh bac ar dhul chun cinn agus forbairt na Gaeilge tré shean-fhoirmeacha agus foirmeacha éagsúla litrithe bheith in úsáid',[45] established a committee to examine the standardisation of both spelling and grammar. Reporting in 1943, its recommendations were contained in *Litriú na Gaeilge: An Caighdeán Oifigiúil*, the new standard spelling being imposed on publishers of school texts from 1946. Following the issuing of a circular to all primary school teachers in February 1948,[46] there was to be a concerted effort to teach each standard the new 'litriú caighdeánach'. Starting with first and second classes in 1948–49, it was envisaged that all classes in primary schools would be familiar with the standard spelling by the school year 1951–52.[47] While examination papers for the primary certificate and for secondary and vocational scholarships could be answered in 'the old spelling' up to 1951, thereafter 'the official standard spelling will be followed in all question papers set in the Irish language and candidates will be expected to use that spelling in their answers'.[48]

However, directives regarding standard spelling were limited to school texts. This led to the problem even after standardisation of children learning to spell one way at school but encountering numerous alternative spellings in non-school texts which resulted in the child not knowing 'cead atá ceart agus céard atá mícheart'.[49] This problem was never fully resolved: in 1961 a debate emerged over the signposting of the President's residence as 'Árus an Uachtaráin' rather than the standard spelling, 'Áras an Uachtaráin'.

Following publication of *Litriú na Gaeilge: An Caighdeán Oifigiúil*, demands increased for a similar volume setting out a standard grammar in Irish. The lack of standardisation resulted in many problems and increased the difficulty associated with teaching and learning Irish. For example, a pupil could learn one set of grammatical forms from one teacher only to be taught a different set from subsequent teachers, while school texts often varied in terms of grammatical usage. The first step towards establishing strandardised grammatical forms was taken in 1953 with the publication of *Gramadach na Gaeilge—Caighdeán Rannóg an Aistriúcháin*. The intention of this publication was to get ideas and suggestions from the public on the forms it contained so that a common standard could be arrived at. In 1957, the 1953 publication together with the submissions received on the standard it set out were re-evaluated and a new draft standard was prepared with input from native Irish speakers, teachers and others familiar with the language. It was subsequently agreed with the Department of Education that the revised version should be published as the standard in Irish grammar in terms of official usage and as a guide for teachers, although it was made clear that this official standard published in 1958 'did not invalidate other correct forms or prevent their usage'.[50]

All of these issues—typeface, standardisation of grammar and spelling and the initial lack of terminology—could only have had the effect of adversely affecting students' progress in Irish and of making the revival of the language more difficult. While many would argue that the regional variations in such matters as grammar and spelling added to the richness of the language—'that the beauty of the language lies to some extent in its complexity'[51]—it also undoubtedly complicated its learning to an unjustifiable extent. The haphazard approach to dealing with these issues and the long delays in officially recognising them as potentially serious impediments to the revival of the language, played their role in creating the gulf which emerged between the aims and achievements of the schools-based language revival policy.

General publications: a library of books or a literature?

In a lecture to the Secondary Teachers Congress in 1936, Prionsias O'Kennedy expressed teachers' anger at the spate of translations being offered to readers and students of Irish, concluding that: 'this translation venture has certainly provided a library of books in Irish, but there is a vast difference between a library and a literature'.[52] Facilitated by the Industrial and Commercial Property (Protection) Act, 1927, which legislated that if a work did not appear in Irish translation within ten years of publication then copyright in Irish translation lapsed, translations were seen as serving the dual purpose of making up the shortfall in Irish books available in the short-term while giving prospective original writers a sense of the mechanics of writing.[53] However, it was often the 'futile and trivial, if not actually harmful, things like the translation into Irish of English detective stories'[54] which became the focus of the translation effort. By 1936, the year of O'Kennedy's lecture, forty-seven original novels in Irish had been published since the establishment of An Gúm (including the highly censored version of *Fánaí* by Seán Óg Ó Caomhánaigh—see Table 4.2) while 200 books had been approved for translation with ninety-eight novels in translation already published. This figure was buoyed by successive translation competitions organised by An Gúm and awards for the best work in this genre.[55] While they included more than detective stories, the majority of translations were of books readily available in English such as *Dr Jekyll agus Mr Hyde*, translated by Conall Cearnach; *Dracula* translated by Seán Ó Cuirrin; *Scéal Fá Dhá Chathair* translated by Seán MacMaoláin; *Ben Hur* translated by Seosamh MacGrianna; *Arda Wuthering* translated by Seán Ó Cíosáin and *Cú na mBaskerville* translated by Nioclas Tóibín, rendering much of the effort and work futile. It was only in the 1950s, by which time the output of An Gúm had declined, that there was evidence of a greater emphasis on the translation of books from languages other than English. De Valera in 1945 had declared himself very much in favour of the publication of translations from the continental languages, 'particularly recent works likely to be of interest to Irish readers and not already available in English'.[56]

The list of Irish books published for young people reflected the emphasis on translations, mostly of works readily available in English like *Pinocchio* and *Róibín Huid*, some of which, such as *David Copperfield*, were likely to appear on the English literature and language course of the school curriculum. However, translations were cheap and expedient and therefore received official support. An initiative in the mid 1930s by the Department of Education to produce an eight page bi-monthly paper for young people was not supported by the Department of Finance largely on the grounds that it would be loss making to the tune of £500–£600 per year.[57]

Table 4.2

PAGE 74 OF THE 1927 EDITION OF *FÁNAÍ* WITH THE CENSORED PARTS HIGHLIGHTED*

'Coimeád í, coimeád í,' ar seisean go tochtach. 'Ná scar coíche léi. Gach uair a bhraithfidh mé uaim í cuimhneoidh mé ort.' **Dhruid sí níos giorra dó. D'ardaigh a ghlac is an chros chun a beola. Chaith sé a ghéaga ina timpeall. Ghéill sí dó agus neadaigh ina bhaclainn, a haghaidh iompaithe in airde chuige. Shír dó agus neadaigh ina bhaclainn, a haghaidh iompaithe in airde chuige. Shír a bheola a beola agus dhlúthaíodar.**

'Tá grá agam duit', mhúch sé ar a béal lena phóg. **Thugadar póg ar phóg dá chéile. Phóg sí arís agus arís é, an chéad fhear riamh. Milseacht dochoimsithe ina póg agus idir osna agus póg di chogair sí**.

'Mo ghrá tú, mo ghrá tú.'

D'fháisc sé leis í. Ar seisean:

'Lá éigin tá súil agam gur fiú mé do phóg.'

'Is fiú cheana: is tú mo chéadshearc.'

'Agus is tusa mo mhaoineach,' chogair sé ina cluais agus chuimil a bhas dá leiceann is dá ghealbhráid. 'Dar an chros sin i do láimh gur tú mo mhaointeach.'

'Agus ní thréigfidh tú go deo mé?'

'Go brách na breithe,' d'fhreagair sé.

Neadaigh sí ní ba ghiorra do agus leag an ceann i gcoinne a uchta, a láimh á sá aige trína gruaig álainn is á basadh go héadrom ar a haghaidh. Bhí an uain go haoibhinn, brothallach, na billiúin creagar go glórach i bpáirceanna na cruithneachta, na mílte leamhan, cuil is peidhleacán ag foluain is ag sugradh i solas an ghluaisteáin. Sceamh faolchú i mothar crann uathu agus d'fhreagair criún tamall ó bhaile í. **Ghabh fonn suain Peig de Róiste; ní mór thit sí ina codladh ar an aiste sin ina bharróg. B'shin é an chéad uair riamh d'fhreagair sí bréagadh fir. B'é an rud a b'iontaí ar domhan é agus bhí áthas uirthi gurbh é an chéad fhear é.**

'Ó, a Sheáin, is tú an chéad fhear a phóg riamh mé agus choíche ní phógfaidh éinne eile mé.'

Chaith sí a géaga ina thimpeall. Theann sí leis. D'fháisc sé chuige í. Phóg sé a béal is a bráid is a súil agus chogair sé:

'A Pheig, a Pheig.'

'Ná lig uait mé,' d'osnaigh sí agus d'imigh an lúth as a géaga. Leag sí a leaca lena leaca. Tháinig néal uirthi gur luigh a súile ...

*Taken from Tadhg Ó Dúshláine (ed.), Seán Óg Ó Caomhánaigh, *Fánaí* (Maynooth, 1989).

Recognising that 'nobody was writing for the nine to sixteen age group',[58] the Department proposed instead the further provision of translations from English and French. Following an appeal by Ó Deirg to Sean MacEntee, the Minister for Finance,[59] in July 1937 the Department agreed to subsidise *An Gaedheal Óg*, a ten page insert in Irish which from February 1937 formed part of the fortnightly *Our Boys* published by the Christian Brothers. In 1945 *An Gaedheal Óg* was succeeded by *Tír na nÓg*.[60] Prior to 1937 the only such material produced for young people was in the pages of *An t-Éireannach*, a weekly Irish language newspaper first published in June 1934 and dealing with national and international affairs. For the government *An Gaedheal Óg* was an easy solution but one which was not entirely adequate. In 1947 the INTO called for two 'simple, well-written, well-illustrated, children's comic papers' for junior and senior pupils, for issue fortnightly through the schools.[61]

There is little doubt that the focus on translations was not only limiting but, combined with a serious lack of financing which was castigated by Ernest Blythe in 1936 and which resulted in unpublished manuscripts piling up in the Department of Education,[62] detracted from the publication of original works in Irish.[63] The case of Seosamh MacGrianna, a leading author in the Irish language from Co. Donegal who spent some time translating works into Irish is exemplary. His manuscript of *Mo Bhealach Féin* which was submitted to An Gúm in 1935 remained there for five years before being published. Described when published as an omen in the progression of Irish literature, *Mo Bhealach Féin* 'extended the scope of Irish writing and brought a new quality of introspection'.[64] *An Druma Mór*, the manuscript of which was submitted by MacGrianna to An Gúm in 1933 was only published in 1969, winning the Irish-American prize for literature in Irish. In 1936 Blythe raised this inefficiency which was leading to 'the grave shortage, amounting in many directions to complete absence, of reading matter in Irish,'[65] and suggested the appointment of an independent Irish publications board which:

> would have the advantage of enabling the government and the public to fix responsibility and of cutting out the elaborate procedure which must always hold up progress when work outside the normal course of administration is undertaken by a Department of State.[66]

However, given the subsequent long delays in the publication of MacGrianna's work, it is clear that neither the letter nor the spirit of

Blythe's suggestion were implemented. Oifig an tSoláthair placed the blame for the weaknesses identified by Blythe firmly with the Department of Education.[67]

A further issue, of course, was the extent to which the Censorship of Publications Act, 1929, purged original literature of its uniquely Irish flavour. Alongside English authors like Somerset Maugham and Dylan Thomas many Irish authors fell foul of the censorship board, the body charged with implementing the legislation, which was, according to Francis McManus:

> The most consistent and permanent contact between the Irish State and Irish writers … [It] could ban works with a savagery that seemed pathological.[68]

The effect on literary fiction in particular was profound: 'censorship … has never been simply the banning of books: the paternalism that perpetuates Irish censorship succeeded for many years in blocking the interchange of ideas between Irish society and its writers'.[69]

By the 1950s there was a decline in the number of manuscripts being sent to An Gúm for publication partly as a result of the long delays which authors could expect between the time of submission for publication to the actual date of publication. In the early decade the suggestion was made by Cumann na Scríbhneoirí that a subsidy be paid to each private publisher of Irish books. In 1952, with the support of Comhdháil Náisiúnta na Gaeilge which was of the opinion that the structure of An Gúm did not allow for the provision of general reading material in Irish,[70] it made a submission to the Taoiseach outlining its proposal. In response, Bord na Leabhar Gaeilge was set up and the Department of Finance agreed to provide £5,000 towards its establishment. In his address to the inaugural meeting of the Bord, Sean Moylan, the Minister for Education, stressed the importance of providing the more 'popular type of reading matter'. His fear was that Irish writers and publishers catered too much for the highbrow reader.[71] A grant of £2,500 could be availed of by private publishers once a book had been published—a condition which, as already noted, led to its own problems—providing that 1,000 copies had been printed and at least 500 had been sold, except in the case of specialist university books. No grant was payable 'i leith leabhair a foilsíodh d'aon ghnó mar théasc-leabhar scoile'.[72] It was expected that all books published would be of a high standard 'agus gurbh fhiú iad do chur a fáil mar chuid do nua-litríocht Gaeilge'.[73] The grant went some way towards remedying the problem which publishers like Sáirséal agus Dill had in competing with An Gúm and, more importantly, towards making up for the shortfall both in the brief and work of An Gúm.

By the 1950s the fruits of the original revival literature could be seen in the form of *Nuabhéarsaíocht, Nuafhilí* and *Nuascéaltaíocht. Nuabhéarsaíocht,* published by Sáirséal agus Dill in 1950 in Gaelic type and edited by Seán Ó Tuama, contained the work of twenty-one poets including Séamus Ó Céilleachair, Máirtín Ó Díreáin and Máire Mhac an tSaoi. The collection was followed by *Nuafhilí,* published by Oifig an tSoláthair in 1956 and edited by Séamus Ó Céilleachair. It included works by Tomás Ó Díreáin, a brother of Máirtín, and Séan Ó Ríordáin. The first collection of modern Irish prose was published in 1952 by Sáirséal agus Dill under the title *Nuascéalaíocht.* Edited by Tomás de Bhaldraithe it included works by Máirtín Ó Cadhain who won many prizes for his literature, Síle Ní Chéileachair, and Mícheál MacLiamóir, a world-famous actor and first director of the Taidhbhearc theatre in Galway.[74] The publication of these volumes of hugely important literature was a significant achievement and underpinned the weaknesses of the official concentration on translations. The volumes were also to prove the forerunners of a new vibrancy which would see a flourishing of original publications in Irish by a myriad of authors over the following decades.

Financial incentives to authors

As already noted, the lack of finance had a crippling effect on publications in Irish from the establishment of An Gúm, although there were financial incentives offered to stimulate both translations and original literary endeavours. The maximum payment for a book in Irish initially stood at £50. This was raised to £120 in 1928 and in 1930 the cap was removed in favour of rates based on the number of words in the book, ranging from £1 to £1.10.0. per 1,000 words. Also introduced in 1930 was the payment of a royalty on the sale price, while maximum rates were later raised to £3 per 1,000 words for original works. Special rates of £3 per 1,000 words were paid to authors of local histories submitted in Irish.[75] Two prizes of £150 were awarded in 1930 for the best original work. In the same year sixty-eight people were paid grants for books, while in 1931, eighty-seven people received grants.[76]

Books specifically geared towards a young readership were awarded a higher rate to encourage translators and original writers to produce material for this age group. From 1931, rates of between £2 and £4 were offered for books between 1,600 and 2,100 words suitable for the seven to nine age group, and £3–£5 for books catering for the nine to eleven age group.[77] However, the amount allocated for grants was reduced as time went on, a fact alluded to by Comisiún um Athbheochan na Gaeilge in its report of 1963:

> the net expenditure on both An Gúm and Bord na Leabhar Gaeilge equals the net expenditure on An Gúm alone in 1937–38.[78]

Grants up to a maximum of £28 per month were also made available to newspapers circulating in Gaeltacht areas which contained at least two columns of Irish per week that related to local news. By the late 1950s *The Derry People*, *The People's Press*, *The Connacht Tribune* and *The Connacht Sentinel* were benefiting from this scheme.[79]

In conclusion, it may be said that despite the availability of grants, there was never a satisfactory number of Irish language books produced to facilitate the language revival. This was partly the result of the language's more recent history rather than solely the responsibility of post-Independence governments: the 'technical' difficulties with Irish would most likely not have arisen were it not for the language shift of the nineteenth century. Had Irish continued to be the majority language in Ireland it would most probably have undergone the standard development associated with language, including 'considerable simplification'.[80] This would have ensured that issues of grammar, spelling and terminology did not hinder the production of reading material. The lack of books was particularly evident in the education system where Irish was compulsory as a subject and where there was active encouragement of Irish as a medium of instruction. Despite the schools-based revival policy, successive governments consistently refused to recognise that there was a shortage of Irish language text books, resulting in even enthusiastic schools having to revert to English as a medium of instruction. Neither can the history of the language be blamed for the shortcomings evident in the work of An Gúm, almost from its inception. This government agency, under the Department of Education, never succeeded during this period in providing an adequate supply of ordinary reading matter in Irish. Neither did it fulfil the demand for Irish language school text books—its primary focus of operation. Apart from quantity, the quality of text books in Irish was another issue in the provision of Irish material for schools, the Department of Education itself admitting as late as the 1960s that there were numerous problems with the content and standard of primary school readers.[81] Mirroring the problems in the secondary school and general categories, this begged the question why it was taking so long to sort out the provision of Irish medium reading material. While it would be questionable to argue that had the problem been sorted out the revival might have been more acceptable and successful, there is little doubt that the failure to address the adequate provision of reading material in Irish very much hampered the official revival policy.

CHAPTER FIVE

'An Atmosphere Gallda':
Irish outside the Schools

THE NEAR absence of opportunities to use Irish outside the schools and the failure to promote Irish outside the schools to anything like the extent to which it was promoted within them, placed the schools in the position of being a unique Gaelic and Gaelicising institution within an overwhelmingly English-speaking society. The inaction in promoting Irish outside the schools was not so much the result of inertia as of policy. There was a feeling that the schools alone could revive the language, as it was felt the schools alone had been responsible for displacing Irish with English in the nineteenth century. It was a genuine belief. The problem was that schoolchildren and their parents realised there were limited opportunities to use Irish in the broader society, while teachers became disillusioned that they were the only group charged with effecting the revival. Indeed, the lack of opportunities to use Irish outside the schools discredited the emphasis on it within them, particularly its use as a medium of instruction. It was only from the 1950s that there was general acceptance that 'the school and the teacher' should not 'stand alone in the effort to revive Irish'; that, in the words of the Council of Education report, the revival 'demands from each citizen and each organ of society untiring aid for its success'.[1]

Paralleling the near absence of opportunities to use Irish outside the schools was the near absence of opportunities for the majority of the population to learn or improve its Irish. This failure to provide classes on an organised national level was striking. While it reflected the prevailing attitude that the schools alone could revive the language, W.T. Cosgrave, President of the executive council and Minister for Finance, did express concern in 1923 at the absence of opportunities for the majority of the population to learn Irish, promising the development of structured, nationwide, Irish classes. However, despite examination of some possible approaches, one revolving around the payment of old people to teach their grandchildren to speak Irish,[2] there was no further development until 1939 when discussion of the provision of Irish classes for adults was included in the report of the Comisiún i dtaobh na Gaedhilge san Stát-Sheirbhís. The report recommended the establishment of clubs on similar lines to Cumann Lúthchlas Gael (GAA) and Conradh na Gaeilge to provide an opportunity for people to socialise and to speak and learn Irish. The proposed clubs would cater mostly for young people but formal classes in Irish would also be organised for those who had left school for some years as 'is ar éigean a bheadh dóthain Gaedhilge acu chun í do labhairt go líofa'. Apart from teaching Irish it was recommended the clubs' activities should include singing, drama, local history, dancing and 'siamsa do gach saghas'. While the Department of the Taoiseach was supportive and announced its intention to provide financial aid to implement the recommendation, there is no evidence of the provision of Irish classes for adults on a nationwide basis. Neither is there evidence of a widespread demand for classes among the adult population, sufficient measure, perhaps, of their lack of interest in becoming part of the revival movement.[3]

This chapter focuses on the position and status of the language outside the schools, the opportunities to use the language in the wider society and the significance attached to it by individuals and institutions outside the education system. While a thorough synthesis of contemporary views and efforts, both official and unofficial, is not attempted, some exemplary evidence is provided, with a focus on Irish in the Civil Service, the attitude of political parties and the Catholic Church to the language, the use of Irish in the media and the promotion of Irish in the Gaeltachtaí.

Irish in the Civil Service

Compulsory Irish was introduced as a condition of entry into the Civil Service as a means of extending the use of Irish outside the classroom. De Valera later described the role of the service as 'treoir do thabhairt don phobal i gcoitchinne in obair na Gaedhilde'.[4] Described as a natural corollary to the acquisition of self-government,[5] to some extent it justified the learning of Irish in the schools by providing a *raison d'être*, or as Dr Thomas Hennessy, a Cumann na nGaedheal T.D. who won the by-election following the death of Countess Markievicz in 1927, said, by coercing pupils into learning Irish with the bribe that they could not get a Civil Service appointment without knowledge of it.[6] However, such an interpretation was too narrow and ignored the desirability of having people in the service competent to serve the Irish-speaking population in their native language.

From the establishment of the Free State, Irish became compulsory for entry to the Civil Service except in the case of temporary staff serving before 1922 who were given the opportunity to become permanent. In this latter case Irish was an optional subject only for the transitional examination. From 1926 successful candidates for the Civil Service, in addition to securing the requisite qualifying percentage in the Irish examination, were obliged before the end of their probationary period (usually two years) to pass a further oral test in Irish of a standard higher than that imposed on entry.[7] The examination could be attempted up to three times, failure on the third occasion resulting in expulsion from the service.[8] Yet, this requirement clearly posed no stumbling block to establishment. In the period from April 1924 to December 1934 lack of proficiency in oral Irish was cited in only three of the twenty-nine cases where Civil Servants failed to become established.[9] It may be noted that the emphasis on an oral examination stood in contrast to the strong emphasis on written examinations in the primary and secondary schools.

To assist Civil Servants in retaining, improving and cultivating the language, Cumann Gaodhalach na Stát Sheirbhíse was established in 1926. Officially recognised by the Department of Finance, it organised classes, lectures and social events in Irish.[10] Reinforcing the position and status of Irish within the service was the offering of positions to Gaeltacht applicants in the late 1920s, something seen as 'very good evidence of zeal on the part of the authorities in fostering the Irish language'.[11] However, the business of the Civil Service was carried out almost entirely through English.

The work of the Cumann Gaodhalach was augmented by a decision of the Department of Finance in 1933 to provide one week of unpaid leave per year for Civil Servants willing to spend a minimum of two weeks in the Gaeltacht on a recognised Irish course. H.P. Boland, one of the assistant secretaries of the Department of Finance under Ernest Blythe, had raised such a possibility under the Cumann na nGaedheal government. Nevertheless, at that time the idea of Civil Servants staying in army camps in Gaeltacht areas did not appeal to Blythe:

> If Civil Servants assemble or are assembled in great numbers
> in the Gaeltacht, they should be dispersed, if necessary, by
> machine guns.[12]

Blythe's fear was that Civil Service officers, rather than learning Irish, would spread the use of English in the contracting Gaeltachtaí. The 1933 decision was a watered-down version of a recommendation made by the

Gaeltacht committee of the Cabinet which advised that Civil Servants be allowed an extra seven days paid leave in the year, provided that two weeks of their total annual leave was spent in a Gaeltacht area.[13]

As was the case in the education system, the trade off between objective standards—among Civil Servants and in work carried out—and fluency in and promotion of Irish became a significant issue. In 1935 the Commission of Inquiry into the Civil Service observed that the emphasis on ability in Irish 'militated against obtaining an adequate supply of good candidates', particularly at higher levels in the Civil Service and the report of the Commission recommended that Irish should not form a compulsory part of the competitive examination.[14]

The compulsory Irish examination for entry to the Civil Service certainly increased the likelihood of fluent Irish speakers, who were not necessarily otherwise well qualified, being appointed while it also caused a certain level of bitterness among highly qualified applicants with a weak command of Irish. The former had been the main complaint against the preparatory colleges, namely, that many of the students proceeding to the training colleges had an excellent command of Irish on completion of teacher training but were decidedly weak in other subjects. Not surprisingly, the recommendation of the Commission of Inquiry into the Civil Service that Irish should not form a compulsory part of the competitive examination was ignored, only to be brought to the fore in a further commission of inquiry thirty years later. Instead a commission was established to plan and supervise the extension of the use of Irish in the Civil Service as a result of investigations by an inter-departmental committee which sat from 1934–36, although 'before it could have any permanent results', its work was interrupted by 'the Emergency', subsequent to which it was never re-established.[15] By this time, Eamon de Valera, while urging civil and public service employees to be an example to the general public in their efforts to revive the language,[16] acknowledged that the more competent people were losing out to the fluent Irish speakers who were on occasion less competent. However, again reflecting developments in the schools where the retardation of educational achievement was acknowledged but excused on the grounds of the overriding importance of reviving the language, de Valera, a great believer in sacrifice, argued that this settling for 'the second best' was part of the sacrifice necessary to restore the language. In May 1939 he told the Dáil:

> You cannot do it without making sacrifices ... You have
> frequently to take the second best. We have, in regard to certain

appointments that have been made, appointments of a technical character, said that where a person had a competent knowledge of Irish, if he is otherwise qualified, he had to take precedence over those who may have even better technical knowledge. If you do not do that, you make no progress.[17]

However, as Donal O'Sullivan pointed out in his book *The Irish Free State and its Senate* (1940):

if the poor are ill, it is small consolation to them to know that their 'second best' dispensary doctor had 'a competent knowledge of Irish'.[18]

While ensuring a capacity within the State sector to provide service through Irish to the Gaeltacht population was an issue often overlooked by critics of compulsory Irish for entry and establishment within the services, it was the weighting given to linguistic ability above technical qualification, supported by de Valera, which came in for most criticism. James Dillon saw this 'fraud and compulsion' as having 'reduced Irish to a deplorable state':

I declare now that to hear people talking Irish in Dublin one is inclined to ask oneself what are they after, what are they up to or in whose eye are they trying to put a finger now. If you meet two Civil Servants talking Irish in government buildings it is a pretty good indication that there is a job on.[19]

Expanding on what he found irksome, Dillon gave an example from his first term as Minister for Agriculture (February 1948–June 1951). During that time a vacancy arose for the position of professor at the veterinary college, responsibility for the filling of which was given to the Appointments Commission. Several people applied:

One candidate was a research lecturer in Cambridge; another was a veterinary graduate who had graduated about three months before and who was assistant to a veterinary surgeon ... in rural Ireland. On the technical examination ... the research graduate from Cambridge sailed out in front and we counted ourselves lucky that he had applied ... We were delighted when we were told that on the first round he was away out on his own.

There was a second round. The man out in front, a Cambridge graduate but an Irishman, had a competent knowledge of Irish, whatever that may be, but the other chap who had

graduated months before was a native speaker. Before I knew
where I was I was presented with the fact that the man who had
graduated in general veterinary medicine three months before
was to be a professor. I refused to appoint him. At this stage I
stuck my heels in and said 'I will not participate in this farce ...'
The battle was still going on when I left office. That happened
in 1951 and I heard rumblings afterwards that there was blue
murder ... That happens regularly in the public service.[20]

The position of Irish in the Garda Síochána may be taken as a further
example of the policy of accepting linguistic ability over technical skills.
The increasing number of Gaeltacht recruits from the 1920s to the mid
1930s reflected a desire to promote the language among the force. Eoin
O'Duffy commented that hundreds of Gardaí 'would not have the remotest
chance of admission were it not for their knowledge of Irish'.[21] Irish was
made a compulsory subject in the entrance examination for the force from
1937. More significant than the official requirements were the voluntary
efforts made by Gardaí themselves in the promotion and learning of Irish
and many local stations organised language classes for members at their
own expense. Significantly, most officers at headquarters were competent
Irish speakers, in contrast to 'the majority of Civil Servants who worked
there [and] had no Irish'.[22] However, there was evidence of growing dis-
enchantment with the language revival among Gardaí by the late 1930s.
Those with a good knowledge of Irish were susceptible to postings in rural
Gaeltacht areas—'bog stations'[23]—while O'Duffy's warning that members
of the force not fluent in Irish by December 1938[24] would be dismissed was
detrimental to the perception of the language and the revival effort.

By the 1960s the Civil Service was the only major area in which there
was active—though not always genuine according to some retrospective
analyses[25]—promotion of the Irish language outside the schools. On the
eve of the decade, which saw a number of commissions making recommendations regarding Irish in the Civil Service, approximately 4,000 or 14 per
cent of the total number of public service employees were fluent Irish
speakers, while a further 14,000, or 50 per cent, had a reading and writing
knowledge of it.[26] While those who used this knowledge on a daily or even
weekly basis was more than likely minimal, it did mean that at least some
members were in a position to offer services through Irish to the Irish-
speaking population, a right which that population was entitled to but, one
feels, only spasmodically enjoyed. The first commission to report in the
1960s was Comisiún um Athbheochan na Gaeilge which recommended

that the Irish test at probation level in the service be dropped. This was followed by the report of the Public Services Organisation Review Group (1966–1969) which was established by Seán Lemass with the aim of suggesting improved decision making processes within the Civil Service. Commonly referred to as the Devlin Report, it was far more significant and focused than Comisiún um Athbheochan na Gaeilge as its remit did not concern the position of the language *per se* but rather the productivity of the service. While describing the national revival policy as outside their mandate for investigation the review group identified the requirement of a knowledge of Irish as one of the weaknesses in the recruitment system which was leading to 'a failure to attract sufficient candidates of top quality'.[27] The report of the review group stated that:

> the use of the Civil Service alone as a means of promoting the Irish language diverts the service from its other tasks. A realistic language policy should be nationwide in its application and if the Civil Service alone is required to make a knowledge of Irish a requirement on recruitment it will be restricted in competition with other employers.[28]

The perception that the Civil Service alone was actively pursuing the revival is interesting: teachers were far more heavily burdened and the schools were far more focused on it. Nevertheless, this does not take from the problem of balancing the needs of the revival with productivity, an issue raised in the course of the 1932–35 inquiry but which had not been addressed.[29]

The official response of the National Coalition government to the issues raised by the commissions of inquiry was in line with Fine Gael's promise to change the language policy both inside and outside the schools. At the same time that the requirement to pass Irish in order to be awarded the secondary school Leaving Certificate was dropped, the government, in 1974, dropped the obligatory Irish examination for entry to the Civil Service. The 'absolute preference' given to candidates with a knowledge of Irish in professional and technical competitions was superseded by an equal weighting being given to proficiency in Irish and English while candidates proficient in both now received 'credit for this in determining order of merit'.[30] The relevant circular outlined the intention—implemented on 1 April 1976[31]—that knowledge of Irish would no longer be obligatory for promotion within the service, although ability in Irish would be taken into account, while the work of Gaeleagras na Seirbhíse Poiblí, the internal Irish language promotion unit which organised courses and classes for Civil

Servants, was to be expanded. The probationary Irish tests were abolished from 11 November 1974 while those on probation who had increments withheld due to failure in the probationary Irish test were to be paid them from 11 November 1974, although retrospective payment from the time of deferment was ruled out.

The new provisions governing linguistic ability for Civil Servants, elaborated on in a Department of the Public Service circular of November 1975 and implemented in the period November 1974 to April 1976, were more equitable and realistic than those which formerly applied. In essence they ensured that talent and competency were no longer sacrificed on the altar of the language revival while credit continued to be given for competency in both Irish and English.[32]

The main political parties and Irish

In the 1960s, following the report of the commission on the revival of Irish, the Dáil and Seanad Committee on Procedure and Privileges set up a joint sub-committee to examine possible measures which might be taken to facilitate the greater use of Irish in both houses of the Oireachtas. The problem was that while Irish became a 'highly political subject in independent Ireland',[33] politicians, the legislators and implementers of the language revival policy, never took an active or leading role in ensuring that Irish was restored as a vernacular. Example never came from the top. Policy, formulated from above, was always geared in the direction of the bottom up. The policies pursued by Eoin MacNeill, the first Minister for Education, were geared specifically towards the young generation of people who had the least political, or indeed any, influence. Compulsion was never imposed on the majority electorate.

The status accorded the Irish language in the Cumann na nGaedheal administrations of 1922–32 was predictable: many of the founders of the Gaelic League were to be found among the Cabinet ministers.[34] Perhaps the most committed language revivalist of Cosgrave's four successive administrations from December 1922 to March 1932 was Ernest Blythe. An Ulster Protestant, Blythe was first elected as a Sinn Féin MP for North Monaghan in 1918. He became Minister for Local Government in the first executive council and in September 1923 was appointed Minister for Finance, a position he held until 1932. Described by his private secretary, Joseph Brennan, as 'a dead loss as a Finance Minister',[35] he spent much time and energy pursuing the language revival. Among his ideas was an attempt to ensure that all forms used between departmental divisions were in Irish only. He also suggested that all teaching jobs in national schools should go to native Irish speakers. Neither idea was pursued. However, Blythe was the main force behind establishing the preparatory colleges. Such an active interest in the language, often to the detriment of financial matters, led to the charge by people like Brennan that Blythe was more a Minister for Irish than a Minister for Finance:

> He was certainly less inclined to accept criticisms of language projects which, for the most part, he had himself generated, than of the multitude of proposals and expenditure that were submitted for Finance sanction.[36]

With the foundation of the Fianna Fáil Party in 1926 the continued pursuance of the language revival policy was confirmed. Eamon de Valera, the party's leader, became more and more closely associated with the revival, James Dillon accusing him of encouraging the cry 'Dev Irish: Irish Dev' implying that 'unless you are a "Dev" man you are no good to the language movement'.[37] A month before the official launch of the new Fianna Fáil Party, de Valera issued a circular outlining its five aims, the second of which was the restoration of the Irish language and the development of a native Irish culture. With the entry of Fianna Fáil deputies to the Dáil in August 1927 there was a noticeable increase in the number of speeches delivered in Irish.[38] For example, in 1927 alone there were four volumes of official reports of Dáil proceedings, representing over 8,000 columns of debate. In that year the first three volumes, covering the period 25 January to 16 August 1927, contained almost no debate in Irish, Richard Mulcahy's parliamentary question to the Minister for Defence being the solitary exception. Yet, in the final volume for that year, volume 21, which covered the period 11 October to 24 November 1927, twenty-five parliamentary questions were tabled in Irish, covering subjects as diverse as road improvement works and the division of lands, while Irish was used in general debates on a number of occasions on issues such as estimates for relief schemes, relief of unemployment and local government.[39] In relation to education, a situation developed where questions posed in Irish by Fianna Fáil Deputies to John O'Sullivan, the Minister, were responded to in English,[40] while on another occasion the Parliamentary Secretary to the Minister for Post and Telegraphs, Michael Heffernan, refused to answer a supplementary question posed in Irish by Seán T. O'Kelly until such time as he asked it in English: 'when he puts the supplementary question in that language I will answer him'.[41] When Fianna Fáil came to power in 1932, Tomás Ó Deirg, the new Minister for Education, gave the majority of replies in Irish, regardless of the language in which the questions were asked.[42]

One of the eight commitments included in the Fianna Fáil election manifesto of February 1932 was the promise:

> to endeavour by systematic effort to preserve the Irish language and make it again the spoken language of the people; to save the native speaker from the emigrant ship, to provide employment for him in the Gaeltacht and make it possible for the language to spread out naturally from the Gaeltacht to the surrounding areas.[43]

Having succeeded in forming a government with the support of Labour following the election, de Valera re-affirmed his commitment to progressively increasing the use of the Irish language in the schools in a radio broadcast on St Patrick's Day, 1932.

The language always formed the cornerstone of de Valera's concept of nationality, even to the extent that political unification of the island of Ireland was only second in importance to him.[44] At the Fianna Fáil Ard-Fheis of November 1932 he spoke about an 'Irish-Ireland nation', appealing in particular to the younger generation 'to make up for the mistakes in regards to the language' thus ensuring its revival.[45] Echoing article 4 of the 1922 Constitution which stated that the national language of the Irish Free State was Irish, the Constitution drafted by de Valera in 1937 declared in article 8.1 that 'the Irish language as the national language is the first official language'. At the Ard-Fheis in October 1937 he exhorted the people of Ireland to use the language as the only definite implement which could ensure the separateness of Ireland as a nation:

> If we want to stand as a really distinctive nation, we must preserve that one great attribute of nationhood that is our language. For that we have to depend upon the schools and the grown-up people and we have to depend upon other organisations in Irish life.[46]

The appeal to the 'grown-up people' seemed timely as the previous April in the Seanad election, the electorate for which was composed of Dáil deputies and local authority members, only one of the six candidates identified in particular with the Irish language on the cultural panel (one of the five vocational panels) was elected, namely, the headmaster of a secondary school located in a Gaeltacht area where Irish was used as a medium of instruction. Among the defeated candidates were the president of the Gaelic League and the director of the Irish Folklore Commission.[47]

Seemingly forgetful of the wider public, de Valera's revival policy was actively geared towards the education system. Encouragement of the general public took second place to compulsion in the schools. Under Tomás Ó Deirg the revival of the language came to rely more and more on the schools while the Gaeltachts continued to dwindle in size. No effort was made to popularise the use of Irish outside the schools or provide an opportunity for those leaving school with a fluent command of the language to use it subsequently. Playing his own part in the revival, Ó Deirg delivered most of his speeches in the Dáil through Irish, leaving himself open to the accusation that only 10 per cent of the Dáil actually understood what was being said.[48] It was a situation which, not surprisingly, incurred the wrath of James Dillon. After one such speech in 1936 Dillon reacted by saying:

> I suppose the minister expects congratulations ... But is there any legislative assembly in the world, and I do not exclude darkest Africa, in which a minister would get up and address the house for two hours in the certain knowledge that not three deputies out of the whole house understood a word that he said? In my respectful submission to this house such a procedure is reducing the legislative assembly of this country to a complete and howling farce.[49]

Ó Deirg, like his successor Patrick Hillery who on occasion answered parliamentary questions tabled in English through Irish,[50] was genuinely supportive of the language revival, was a fluent Irish speaker and was perhaps more comfortable with Irish than English. However, there were occasions when this natural tendency to use Irish coincided with the desirability of using it as a political tool, something Fianna Fáil Deputies were particularly susceptible to doing. Gerald Bartley, a Fianna Fáil Deputy from Connemara, submitted a question in Irish to Noel Browne aware it was later claimed that Browne, the Minister for Health, had no Irish, in order to show him up as 'an uncaring anglophile and West Briton'. Browne, in his autobiography, vividly recalls the incident:

> Mr Kennedy [Secretary of the Department of Health], a fluent Gaelic speaker, translated the parliamentary question for me

into English, and then translated my reply into Irish. He kindly tutored me in the phonetic version of the reply. On the day, miserable with fear, I presented myself in the Dáil chamber. Having replied to a number of questions in English and difficult enough in themselves, I came to Gerald Bartley's question in Irish. Collecting whatever nerve is conjured up by us on these occasions I spoke my reply in phonetic Irish to a silent and surprised Dáil chamber.[51]

The attitude and actions of Bartley on this occasion were detrimental to the language movement. As in the schools, the forcing of the language on people who had an insufficient grasp of it to enable them understand it, might well have served to alienate people from Irish and the revival.

In June 1959 Seán Lemass replaced Eamon de Valera as leader of Fianna Fáil and as Taoiseach. Although not a fluent Irish speaker, to describe him as Ronan Fanning does, as not as ardent an advocate of the revival as de Valera, is somewhat misleading.[52] Lemass's advocacy of the language revival was as strong as de Valera's. It was only his own personal lack of competence in Irish and lack of enthusiasm for learning it that set him apart from his predecessor. In 1960 Fianna Fáil published a brief propagandist history of its organisation, recalling that 'Ón gcéad lá riamh, d'aithin Fianna Fáil tábhacht an Gaeilge i saol an náisiún. Níorbh rosc gan bhrí acu "Éire shaor, Éire Ghaelach".'[53] Lemass insisted during the 1961 election campaign that the national aspiration of restoring the language could not be diluted 'by even a fraction'.[54]

In the same election Fine Gael included in its election manifesto a proposal to abolish compulsory Irish in the schools. Described by the *Irish Times* as a 'sensible and courageous attitude'[55] the issue of compulsion was to form a large part in an otherwise unremarkable election campaign. Speaking at Portarlington, T.F. O'Higgins said that the foremost element of the Fine Gael programme was the provision of better education opportunities for all the Irish people, together with a more realistic Irish language policy, 'based on inducement rather than compulsion'.[56] Lemass criticised this 'policy of retreat' and expressed the continuing commitment of Fianna Fáil to the aim of restoring the language to common usage in Ireland.[57]

Some of the provincial and national newspapers supported the Fine Gael stance on compulsory Irish, seeing it as one which would almost certainly increase the party's vote in the election.[58] While Fianna Fáil was again returned to power, Fine Gael's campaign to end compulsory Irish was, if anything, intensified. In 1966 the party published the *Just Society* policy document which talked about preservation of the language by realistic means while removing compulsion. Fine Gael had now moved from a policy of revival to a policy of preservation in the year in which de Valera, as President of Ireland, called on the people to rededicate themselves to the national aim of language revival, 1966 being the fiftieth anniversary of the Easter Rising.

Fine Gael was provided with the opportunity to realise its objectives with regards to Irish in March 1973 when, together with the Labour Party, it formed the National Coalition government. Standing by its rhetoric, Richard Burke, the new Minister for Education and a former secondary school teacher, ended the necessity of passing Irish in order to be awarded the Intermediate and Leaving Certificate examinations, although Irish as a subject remained compulsory with the government only paying capitation to schools in respect of students registered for it. The following year, circular 9/74 of the Department of the Public Service heralded the end of the Irish examination in the probation tests for the Civil Service.[59]

Irish in the Gaeltachtaí

With the foundation of the Free State, the revival of the Irish language focused on two areas of development—the schools and the Irish-speaking districts. There is little doubt that while attempts were being made to revive the Irish language in the Galltacht through the education system, the Gaeltacht areas, both geographically and demographically, were contracting on a constant and steady basis. Between 1891 and 1926 alone, arguably including the period of greatest activity by the Gaelic League, the Irish-speaking population declined by 18 per cent.[60] The decline in the use of Irish in Gaeltacht areas was paralleled by an increase in the use of English. The work of the Congested Districts Board between 1891 and 1923, for example, led to an increased exposure to English in the Gaeltachtaí by virtue of its work in improving communications, agricultural methods and cottage and fishing industries.[61] The trend of Anglicisation of Gaeltacht areas continued through Independence.

Before discussing the implications of a geographically and demographically contracting Gaeltacht, it is necessary to define what officially constituted a Gaeltacht area. The report of Comisiún na Gaeltachta (1926) defined the Gaeltacht as areas in which 80 per cent or more of the population spoke Irish and defined the breac-Ghaeltacht as areas in which at least 25 per cent of the population spoke Irish. It defined an Irish speaker as a person possessing 'an ordinary conversational knowledge of Irish'.[62]

The area comprising the Gaeltacht was further defined in the Housing (Gaeltacht) Act, 1929, which listed the areas deemed to be part of the Gaeltacht, and the School Meals (Gaeltacht) Act, 1930. The definitions provided in these Acts proved inadequate, however, on practical grounds. For example, Rath Cairn, County Meath, was excluded from receiving the £2 deontas introduced in 1934 as it did not officially come within a Gaeltacht area, even though many of its inhabitants were native Irish speakers transplanted from other officially recognised Gaeltacht areas. In 1935 it was agreed to pay the deontas to the people of Rath Cairn 'but this ruling is regarded as a concession and does not apply to future years' as 'the area in which the settlement is situated is not regarded as part of the Gaeltacht'.[63] It was only in 1936 that the situation was remedied, with the official recognition of Rath Cairn as a Gaeltacht.

Perhaps the best definition of the Gaeltacht is to be found in the 'Scoláireachta Iolscoile do mhic léinn on bhFíor-Ghealtacht' (1953 edn).[64] Its fluid interpretation of what exactly constituted the Gaeltacht appears more reasonable than applying the status of Gaeltacht to a set of townlands and villages:

> Fé láthair, tá an fhíor-Ghaeltacht … suite sna líomatáistí seo leanas: (1) Corca Dhuibhne ar an taobh thiar agus thiar-thuaidh de Dhaingean Uí Chúis; (2) Oileáin Árann agus Conamara ó imeall chathair na Gaillimhe go Caiseal; (3) An líomatáiste lár-iartharach de Dún na nGall, agus fós roinnt cheantar ar an taobh den líne ó Ard na Ráthta go dtí na Cealla Beaga.[65]

For the purposes of the present work it is this broad definition which is used in discussing government policy regarding the Gaeltacht, which as can be noted from the above definition was not a geographically contiguous area.

The report of Comisiún na Gaeltachta (1926) painted a gloomy picture of the position of Irish in the Gaeltachtaí. After years of neglect, the prestige and position of the language was low and children picked up more Irish at school than from their parents who were reluctant to pass it on.[66] The position of the language in Gaeltacht schools was particularly disturbing. Many primary school teachers had themselves received instruction in an English-speaking environment. The lack of native Irish teachers was one of the strongest arguments put forward for the establishment of preparatory colleges. According to Comisiún na Gaeltachta many teachers working in Gaeltacht districts who held the Ard Teastas or the bilingual certificate were not capable of using Irish as a medium of instruction. In the partly Irish-speaking areas only 30 per cent of teachers were officially qualified to give instruction through Irish, 701 teachers had no qualifications in Irish and a further 471 were only qualified to teach it as a subject.[67] These were alarming figures which would have a direct bearing on the geographical extent of the fíor-Ghaeltacht. To address the lack of qualifications in Irish among teachers the Commission recommended the removal from Gaeltacht schools of all teachers unlikely to become qualified to give instruction through Irish in a reasonable time. In addition, it recommended the improvement in the teaching capacity of those working in Gaeltacht areas as a matter of urgency.[68]

In the Gaeltacht, schooling for the most part meant primary schooling as post-primary education was to a great extent non-existent. This had ramifications for primary education which, rather than leading to higher education, seemed to lead nowhere. As already described, there existed from the school year 1924–25 three classes of secondary schools reflecting the levels of Irish used, from A schools where Irish was used as a sole medium of instruction to C schools where it was taught as a subject only. The one secondary school in a Gaeltacht area, located in Dingle, County Kerry, belonged to class C. The Commission was equally unimpressed by the efforts of the technical schools, where only a very small number of instructors were competent to give instruction through Irish.[69]

The poor state of Irish found by the Commission in Gaeltacht areas was supported by evidence provided by Frank Fahy, a qualified secondary teacher and Fianna Fáil Deputy for Galway, a constituency which included a substantial Gaeltacht area:

> An ceanntar ina bhfuil Clanna Caoilte agus An Sciobairín tá sé sa Ghaedhltachta agus tá dá scoil déag ann ar a laighead nach bhfuil dá-theangach, agus ní ró-mhaith a múintear an Ghaedhilg mar ádhbhar léighinn féin ina leath acu sin. Tá an Ghaedhilg dá lot i scoileanna na limistéireachta san.[70]

In its concluding recommendations the Commission stressed the necessity of making Irish:

> forthwith, the sole language of instruction in education, English being taught effectively as a second language … and to provide general higher educational facilities not less than those available to persons in English-speaking districts, together with certain other necessary and suitable educational facilities.[71]

In partly Irish-speaking areas it recommended the introduction of Irish as a medium of instruction in all schools 'in such subjects as will most assist in the development of the language as a vernacular'.[72] The extent to which such recommendations were taken seriously by the government is questionable. Frank Fahy's comments were made three years after the presentation of the Commission's report while five years after the publication of the report, 50 per cent of Gaeltacht children were being taught either wholly or partly through English in standards above the infant classes.[73] This figure, emanating from the Department of Education, underpinned the remarkable contradiction in government policy. On the one hand Irish was being promoted as a medium of instruction in the Galltacht to an extent which was unacceptable to many, while in the Gaeltacht, the natural constituency for Irish medium education, up to 50 per cent of children were being taught through English.

Regarding the provision of secondary schools within Gaeltacht areas, the government said that 'owing to the poverty of the vast majority of people in the Gaeltacht', there would be little demand for secondary schooling 'which does not produce immediate wage-earning results' making provision not 'commensurate with the cost'.[74] In 1932, the new Fianna Fáil administration, through *Rules and Regulations for National Schools*, promised the erection of special schools in Gaeltacht areas to facilitate the use of Irish as a medium of instruction where the existing school mainly used English but where there was a population of children whose first language was Irish.[75]

Fianna Fáil also proposed making Galway an Irish-speaking town, chiefly through the development of the university, a belated government initiative in response to Comisiún na Gaeltachta's recommendation that higher education facilities be provided through Irish for Irish-speaking areas to the same standard as those available to English speakers. Supported by Coiste na bPáistí and the Departments of Posts and Telegraphs and Justice, the idea was to create 'within the limitations of our resources, an Irish speaking Oxford'.[76] As outlined in an earlier chapter, by 1936, a substantial amount of progress had been made in the Gaelicising of University College, Galway, with certain lecturers giving instruction wholly through Irish in history, ancient classics, education, mathematics, economics, commerce and accounting. Provision was also made for the award of a number of scholarships for fíor-Ghaeltacht students to the value of £110 per year.[77] The efforts of the government were lauded by the *Irish Press* which was of the opinion that there was no other place in Ireland 'chomh Gaedhealach leis an mbaile mhór seo'.[78]

By 1942, when *Teagasc trí Ghaeilge* was published, all new full-time teachers in technical schools located in the Gaeltacht had to be competent to give instruction through Irish. However, it was clear from the Council of Education (1955) that the position of Irish in Gaeltacht primary schools was still not adequate. Its report stated that the continuing criticism of the standard of Irish in the Gaeltacht schools 'can only be interpreted as the failure of the school to provide a link between the child and the traditions of his locality and environment'.[79] Over ten years later John McNamara in his book *Bilingualism and Primary Education* (1966) claimed that the accomplishment of children in Irish-speaking areas in English and mathematics was 'poorest of all' in the context of national trends, while 'their attainment in Irish as measured by a very simple test of written Irish affords little grounds for complacency'. He continued: 'for many of these children, the adult world in Ireland and England, will be an English-speaking one; and they appear to be ill-equipped indeed for life in it.'[80] It was a stark assessment, coming over forty years after the schools-based language revival campaign was introduced. It is hardly surprising that a policy which proved so incapable of meeting the demands of what should have been its primary constituency ran into so many difficulties on a national basis.

Aside from the education system the three most significant measures taken by the government in its Gaeltacht preservation policy were, first of all, the introduction in 1934 of the deontas, a yearly subsidy payable to every Gaeltacht family in respect of each child between the ages of six and fourteen years capable of speaking Irish naturally and fluently and attending primary school; secondly, the belated establishment of a ministry with special responsibility for the Gaeltacht in 1956; and thirdly, the setting up of Radio na Gaeltachta in 1972. The deontas was perceived as going some way towards rectifying the position described by the *Irish Times*:

> Níor chuir muintir na Gaeltachta mórán spéise i gcainnt na ndaoine a bhíodh ag tabhairt comhairle dóbhtha; bhí a fhios aca go maith gurbh' éigean dóbhtha a mbeatha féin a shaothrú comh maith agus thiocfadh leo le Gaedhilge nó gan Gaedhilge. Bhí an teanga aca; ach ní raibh sí ag an gcuid is mó de na daoine a raibh na postanna is fearr sa tír aca ... an dream a raibh an chumhacht aca shíl siad gur leor don Ghaeltacht an beagán.[81]

It was hoped the deontas would ensure the use of Irish in Gaeltacht and breac-Ghaeltacht areas and provide an incentive for those living on the verges of the Gaeltacht to use Irish more often in the hope that some day they too might qualify for it.[82] Very much welcomed by school inspectors,[83] its success in both the above areas was apparent to the officials of the Department of Education:

> De réir tuairiscí tá feabhas tagaithe ar staid na Gaedhilge san bhfíor-Ghaedhealtacht, agus san mbreac-Ghaedhealtacht le blian anuas, agus tá deontas an dá phunt ag cuidiú go mór leis an nGaedhilg. Deirtear go bhfuiltear in áiteacha ar theorainn na Gaedhealtachta ag iarraidh an béarla a choinneáil siar chun an dá phunt a thuilleadh.[84]

While it may indeed have been a factor in converting bilingual communities on the edge of Gaeltachtaí towards integration with their all-Irish speaking neighbours, it is also clear that the deontas alienated those among the Galltacht population who were raising their families through Irish. No matter how good individual efforts in the Galltacht were, the deontas could still not be received.[85] Indeed, as already alluded to, many native Irish speakers found themselves denied the deontas when transplanted by the land commission to more viable properties in Galltacht areas and letters were sent to the government pleading their cases and outlining their efforts in keeping Irish alive 'i gcorp lár na Galltachta'.[86]

While the Department of Education was anxious not to have any qualifying examination for receipt of the deontas,[87] inspectors were advised that where they doubted the competency of children, the youngest person in the household should be spoken to in Irish to assess their fluency. Failing this the Gardaí or the school principal were to be contacted.

In 1946 the grant was increased to £5 while the upper age limit was set at sixteen years, although a move in the 1950s by inspectors to reduce the lower age to four years was rejected. The raising of the age limit meant that children attending secondary and vocational schools in the Gaeltacht or breac-Ghaeltacht qualified for the grant. The reason for the increase in the grant was twofold: there was more money available because the numbers getting the £2 grant had dropped and the extra money was seen as an added incentive to Gaeltacht and breac-Ghaeltacht people to use the language to the greatest possible extent.[88]

The second and potentially most promising initiative undertaken by a government in relation to native Irish speakers was the establishment of the Department of the Gaeltacht by the Second Inter-Party government. The idea of establishing an independent ministry with specific responsibility for the Gaeltacht was first mooted by 'many witnesses' interviewed by

Table 5.1
NUMBER OF STUDENTS RECEIVING THE DEONTAS*

School Year	No. of pupils
1948–49	2,244
1949–50	3,317
1950–51	2,974
1951–52	3,079
1952–53	2,818
1953–54	2,130
1954–55	5,932
1955–56	6,425
1956–57	5,362
1957–58	4,807

*Taken from N.A., R/Gael., An Deontas £5: Foireann agus Modha Oibre, R 5.

Comisiún na Gaeltachta. However, the Commission itself was of the view 'that the setting up of any such special administrative authority would be neither desirable nor practicable, under the changed conditions of government in the country',[89] a position it did not elaborate on or explain. As late as 1953 the Inter-Departmental Committee of Oifig na Gaeltachta agus na gCeantar gCúng, in response to a submission from Comhdháil Náisiúnta na Gaeilge, claimed that no convincing case had been made for the establishment of an autonomous board dealing with the development of the Gaeltacht.[90] The main argument of the Comhdháil submission of October 1953 was based on the increase in the number of writers in Irish. Seeing this increase as integral to a positive result in the language revival campaign, the fear was that 'these writers will write no more in Irish if they become convinced that the Gaeltacht will not be saved'. The establishment of a board for the Gaeltacht would be seen as a positive gesture, proving that 'the battle for the Gaeltacht can be won'.[91] At this time the greatest demand for an autonomous board dealing with the Gaeltacht was coming from Muintir na Gaeltachta, 'a left-wing break away from Comhdháil' made up mostly of teachers. The group received much support during a debate in the Seanad in November 1955 on 'Forbairt agus Caomhnú na Gaeltachta' when senators called for a 'bord neamhspleách' to examine and develop the Gaeltacht. Otherwise, one senator warned: 'long before the end of the present century, at the present rate of decline, it seems certain that, as an Irish-speaking area, it will have finished altogether'.[92]

Seeing flexibility as being the most important attribute of a board, it was feared that a special government department would get bound up in too much bureaucracy. However, Richard Mulcahy, the Minister for Education, who was advised by his Civil Servants that the call for a board 'cannot be taken as representative of a spontaneous demand within the Gaeltacht',[93] made clear his opposition to an autonomous board outside the direct control of government. Instead he declared in favour of a special Cabinet ministry with responsibility for Gaeltacht areas:

> Is léir go mbeidh buntáistí agus neart ag an Aireacht. Beidh cúram daingean agus doimhin ag an Aire; beidh sé istigh i measc na nAirí eile, beidh a ghuth ann agus a chluas ann agus comhcheangal leis na hAirí eile …[94]

In 1956 the Ministers and Secretaries (Amendment) Act was passed providing for the establishment of a Department of the Gaeltacht and Mulcahy took on the new portfolio in addition to Education. It was the first ministry dedicated to the Irish language since Seán T. Ó Ceallaigh was appointed to the short-lived Department of Irish in the First Dáil of 1919. The functions of the new department were:

> to promote the cultural, social and economic welfare of the Gaeltacht; to encourage the preservation and extension of the use of Irish as a vernacular language; and, to such extent as may be necessary or appropriate, to consult and advise with other departments of State in respect of services administered by such departments which affect the cultural, social or economic welfare of the Gaeltacht or which concern the national aim of restoring the Irish language.[95]

The establishment of the new ministry came at a time when criticism of government policy regarding the Gaeltacht was reaching a crescendo. The INTO was calling for the reservation of places for native Irish speakers in the Civil Service, Aer Lingus, the Electricity Supply Board (ESB) and other semi-state bodies in order that school goers in Gaeltacht areas could be provided with an incentive to receive an education and to preserve the language.[96] The *Pictorial*, a weekly Dublin newspaper, was scathing of government policy in relation to the Gaeltacht, quoting a teacher from Rossport as saying that Irish had become the badge of the second-class citizen:

> We're fed up being living inhabitants in a folklore museum. Preserve the people first—not the language.[97]

It was hoped that the new ministry which was broadly welcomed would not prove to be too little too late: 'time is not on the side to the Gaeltacht'.[98] There was a perception that the economic and social decline of the Gaeltacht had been allowed proceed unchecked to such an extent that 'the road back may not be easy'.[99] Concerning the linguistic decline, integrally linked with the economic and social decline, Peadar O'Donnell outlined the pressures on Irish among the native Irish-speaking population:

> The English language fed itself into their lives through their schools, the Sunday sermons, missionary retreats, political meetings. The young ... who went into exile wrote home in it.[100]

Whether the new ministry was capable of turning the economic, social and linguistic fortunes of the Gaeltacht around was called into question at an early stage. Soon after its establishment, there were calls for the replacement of the department with an independent board. Sean Treacy, a newly elected Labour Deputy and education spokesman for the party from 1961–65, asked the Taoiseach in 1961, by means of a Dáil question:

> If in view of the widespread dissatisfaction with the Department of the Gaeltacht he will consider abolishing this Department, and setting up a State board to look after the Gaeltacht.[101]

The Taoiseach disagreed that there was widespread dissatisfaction with the Department which continued in its original form despite the criticisms. This controversy helped ensure, however, that the Irish language came to the forefront as an issue in the 1961 General Election, into which the three main political parties went with new leaders.

Comisiún um Athbheochan na Gaeilge (1965), which regarded the preservation and strengthening of the Gaeltacht areas as essential to the restoration of the language, recommended that the government establish a co-ordinated and structured State language policy, while the first detailed evaluation of the Department of the Gaeltacht in the form of the Devlin Report (1969) recommended its abolition, saying 'many of its activities might be performed more economically by other departments'. It was a harsh judgement which perhaps missed the point of the new department which had to place linguistic development above economic issues. However, the review group did admit that the existence of the department helped 'foster a sense of unity' among those living in the geographically scattered Gaeltacht areas.[102] Responding to the recommendation of Comisiún um

Athbheochan na Gaeilge, the government gave responsibility to the Department of Finance for ensuring that 'State policy on the language will, in future, be put into effect systematically on all fronts'.[103]

The Catholic Church and Irish

The interaction between what were promoted as the pillars of Irish nationhood, namely, the Irish language and the Roman Catholic religion, is an area deserving of a dedicated study in itself. Here, an attempt is made in outline to examine the extent to which the institutional Catholic Church was supportive of its parallel pillar of nationhood, the Irish language. Its attitude towards the language would be important, Comisiún na Gaeltachta placing the securing of the 'co-operation of the Clergy' as 'an immediate objective' in strengthening the position of Irish in the Gaeltachts.[104]

Interaction between the Christian churches and the fortunes of the language had a significant history prior to Independence. From the early 1800s many Church of Ireland ministers studied Irish with some Protestant clergy and missionaries making strenuous efforts to convert Irish speakers by distributing Irish language versions of the Bible and other religious texts. Numerous Bible societies began writing and publishing Protestant texts in Irish, the London Hibernian Society, founded in 1806, being the first of its kind.[105] The Irish College at Stackallen in County Meath which trained clerics for the Church of Ireland was a response to the difficulty experienced in providing clergy with the linguistic capability of ministering to the native Irish people. In 1832 the Protestant archbishop of Tuam announced that he would not ordain anyone who could not speak the Irish language. The by-product of the effort to save souls was the continued use of Irish. However, much of the Protestant enthusiasm had cooled long before the establishment of the Free State, as they found it difficult to adapt to the narrow concept of nationalism which was cultivated around the language and which saw the language being presented as an exclusively Catholic-nationalist appendage. There was a deep irony in this association: from the early 1800s until the 1870s it could be strongly argued that the Protestant churches had done more in cultivating and acknowledging the language than the Roman Catholic Church. With the establishment of Maynooth College in 1795 the important languages of the Catholic Church in Ireland were Latin and English. The development of the Church's missionary activity overseas militated against the use of Irish in the education of clerics, English being more useful in the missionary fields. At home in Ireland, the

Catholic Church's following of the popular nineteenth-century trend of embracing English was seen as a factor in the language shift of the period, the church's view being that it was 'more important to save souls than to save Irish'.[106]

From the establishment of the Gaelic League in the 1890s the Catholic Church did, of course, genuflect in the general direction of the language revival. In June 1900 the Catholic bishops passed two favourable, though far from significantly progressive resolutions, regarding the teaching of Irish in national schools (most of which were under the authority of the local parish priest):

1. We strongly recommend that in the primary schools in all Irish-speaking districts the instruction should be bilingual, English being taught through the medium of Irish.

2. We also regard it as most desirable that in the primary schools in other districts the Irish language should be taught to children of the third and higher classes wherever the manager of the school deems it advisable and the parents make no objection.

Cultivating the link between the pillars of nationalism the resolutions, reproduced on several occasions in *An Claidheamh Soluis*, were welcomed by the Gaelic League as 'an excellent embodiment' of the reforms required for the teaching of Irish in the national schools.[107] There was never any doubt but that priests, both in their religious ministry and as managers of schools, could 'give more help than any other class in the community towards the language revival'.[108]

By 1918 Father M.P. O'Hickey (Father Eugene O'Growney's successor as Professor of Celtic Literature and Languages at Maynooth College who was subsequently dismissed from the post in 1909 by the bishops for his public questioning of their stance on the introduction of compulsory Irish for matriculation in the NUI) was criticising the part being played by the clergy in the revival of Irish. The fact was that little attention was paid by the Irish Church to the Irish language. Asking 'what have the priests of Ireland being doing' for the language, O'Hickey, who argued that priests 'alone could never inaugurate a powerful and widespread movement for the recognition of the claims of our national language', questioned in particular the contribution of Maynooth College to the language, saying that it:

has undoubtedly sent forth men who have achieved eminence
in the field of Irish historical and antiquarian research, but to

purely Gaelic scholarship, however, it has given very few names and scarcely one, it must I fear be admitted, of the first rank.[109]

An ideal confluence of language and religion came with the opening of Scoil Mhuire in the grounds of the Department of Education in Marlboro Street in January 1927 when John O'Sullivan was Minister for Education. Reported as a 'union of Church and State',[110] the new school was to provide education solely through Irish. Richard Mulcahy saw the development, the result of requests by parents for all-Irish education for their children, as a symbol 'that foreign rule was over'.[111] However, Scoil Mhuire, rather than becoming a prototype for other schools, became an exception in the clerical dominated Irish education system. The Irish language and the Catholic religion may well have been the badges of a separate national identity, but little interaction was to take place between them.

The Gaelic League very much cherished the open support of some of the Catholic hierarchy for the language revival, tending to quote such support at length in various publications. An example may be found in the Gaelic League pamphlet *The Case for Irish* published in the 1930s. On the back cover Most Revd. Dr McRory, Primate and Archbishop of Armagh, Most Revd. Dr Harty, Archbishop of Cashel, Most Revd. Dr Dignan, Bishop of Clonfert, and Most Revd. Dr MacGaoithin, Bishop of Down and Conor, were quoted for their support of the language movement and the Gaelic League. The Archbishop of Tuam, Dr Gilmartin, was also a supporter of the language revival, urging in December 1932 the students of St Jarlath's College, Tuam, to 'cultivate our own games, our own amusements, our own language and our own music'.[112] In 1937, Eamon de Valera called for the co-operation of the Catholic Church in reviving the language. In his Ard-Fheis speech of that year he asked for the full support of the Church which he believed was 'due to the Irish nation' and was 'essential if we are to save the language', while recognising at the same time that such support would entail necessary sacrifices.[113] Two years later, when an effort was made to provide for classes and activities in Irish outside the schools, the support of the Church was seen as imperative for success:

> Baineann an scéim go dlúth le cuid de ghnó na hEaglaise, taobh amuigh den teangain ar fad—na daoine óga do choimead ins na dtuaith agus caitheamh aimsire a chur ar fáil dóibh a thiocfaidh isteach le tuairimí na hEaglaise.[114]

Comisiún um Athbheochan na Gaeilge (1963) also alluded to the 'outstanding position enjoyed by the clergy' and reminded them that their response to the language revival would be of great importance.[115] Three years later de Valera claimed that:

> Tá cléir de gach eaglais ar thaobh na Gaeilge—easpaig, sagairt agus ministrí. Tá formhór na múinteoirí, na mbráithre agus na mban rialta ar a taobh.[116]

A telling practical indication of the Church's attitude to the revival could be seen in its approach to the teaching of religion in schools. Most schools in the Galltacht, on the orders of the local clergy, were using English as the medium for religious instruction. The use of the vernacular in religious instruction was enshrined in the Catholic Church by the Maynooth Statutes of 1927[117] and the *Programme of Religious Instruction in the Catholic Colleges and Secondary Schools* for 1928–29 duly recommended that pupils be taught the liturgy programme in the vernacular, irrespective of the language of instruction used in the school.

The clergy did have their own Irish language revival organisation, Cumann na Sagart Gaelach, established in 1916. In 1961 Glór na nGael was established by the Cumann following the receipt of a letter by Fr. Tomás Ó Fiaich from Revd. Dr Sean MagRiabhaigh, a Columban Father teaching theology in the Columban College, Navan suggesting the establishment of a competition between the towns and villages of Ireland for their efforts in promoting Irish. The idea was that prizes would be awarded to the areas which did most to bring about the revival of Irish. In 1961 the Chairperson of Cumann na Sagart, Tomás Ó Fiaich, wrote to the President, Eamon de Valera, asking him to become a patron of the competition for the 'Most Irish town in Ireland'. De Valera agreed and with Cardinal John Dalton became co-patron of Glór na nGael, the name harkening back to the *vox Hiberionacum*, the voice of the Irish, which inspired St Patrick to return to Ireland. The first competition period was 1962, the anniversary of St Patrick's return to Ireland as a missionary. In Galltacht areas, Glór na nGael offered three prizes of £200, £100 and £50 for those towns and villages judged to have done most to promote the language while in Gaeltacht areas there were two prizes of £100 and £50.[118]

Despite such efforts and the qualified statements of support, the institutional Catholic Church, anxious to be seen as a defining mark of Irish nationality, was never concerned with the fate of the Irish language. The huge contributions of individual clergy and bishops, on occasion at the expense of their own position within the Church, served to highlight the extent to which the institutional Church ignored the language movement. Use of Irish in the teaching of religion or in religious ceremonies was actively resisted. Peadar O'Donnell commented that 'Sunday sermons' were one of the Anglicising forces in Irish-speaking areas. Gearóid Ó Tuathaigh's comment about the Church, like other elements of the 'Establishment', being 'indifferent where it is not actually hostile' is perhaps the most positive comment that could be made.[119]

Irish in cinema and radio

The use of Irish in the electronic media had the potential to give the language a functional and modern status which in many people's perception it did not have. In the period under discussion, the media in question are the cinema and the radio, a national television service only being established in 1961. While there was a clear recognition of the importance of the radio and cinema as vehicles of the revival, practical issues such as audience demand dictated that for the most part they could not be and were not exploited for the purposes of the language revival. Unlike the schools, cinemas which had developed in Ireland from the beginning of the twentieth century could not be compelled to show a certain number of films in Irish, despite promptings from some quarters to introduce such a quota system.[120] The first Irish sound film, a centenary commemoration of Catholic emancipation screened in 1929, was narrated entirely through English. An attempt to accompany the successful *Man of Aran* with an Irish language short also produced by Robert Flaherty entitled *Oidche Sheanchais* fizzled out. One of the first films recommended by the Department of Education for showing in primary schools—dealing with health and hygiene practices—was narrated through English.[121]

However, there were efforts made by groups such as Compántas Amharclainne na Gaeilge to introduce Irish into the world of cinema by producing bilingual variety shows. Gael Linn, the Irish language and culture group founded in 1953, was an important source of Irish language films from the 1950s to the 1970s. Apart from *Amharc Éireann*, the first regular Irish newsreel since the demise of 'Irish events' in 1920, its most famous films were *Mise Éire*, premièred at the Cork Film Festival in September 1959, and *Saoirse?* premièred two years later. Both were feature length Irish language productions. In 1962 the Department of Education encouraged primary school teachers to provide an opportunity for fifth and sixth class pupils to see this latter film during school hours.[122]

Table 5.2
RADIO LICENCES PER HEAD OF POPULATION, 1937 AND 1946

County/ Provence	No. of licences (31 Dec. 1937)	Population (1936 census)	Licences: pop. (Ratio, 1937)	Licences: pop. (Ratio, 1946)
Dublin	43,578	587,000	1:14	
Meath	2,129	61,327	1:29	
LEINSTER	66,085	1,219,501	1:19	1:12
Cork	13,007	355,496	1:28	
Clare	1,407	89,764	1:64	
Kerry	2,260	139,775	1:62	
Waterford	3,920	77,599	1:19	
MUNSTER	31,208	941,392	1:31	1:18
Galway	3,306	168,134	1:51	
Mayo	2,620	161,064	1:62	
CONNACHT	9,611	524,847	1:55	1:30
Donegal	3,041	142,192	1:47	
ULSTER*	5,289	280,114	1:53	1:29
ÉIRE	112,192	2,965,854	1:27	1:17

*Ulster only refers to counties in Free State/Republic.
Source: Radio Éireann: Report on Broadcasting, 1937, p. 1 and Radio Éireann Annual Report, 1946, p. 23.

Comparatively, radio was of far greater significance than cinema in the promotion of Irish. However, as in the case of cinema, popular demand left little room for Irish language broadcasting. Also, the significance of whether Irish was broadcast on 2RN/Radio Éireann must be seen in the light of the number of radio sets throughout the country in the period up to the 1950s. As Table 5.2 illustrates, in 1937 there were a total of 112,192 radio licences in the country, an average ratio of licence to population of 1:27. Significantly, there were far fewer licences in Gaeltacht areas, with equivalent ratios of licence to population of 1:51 in Galway and 1:62 in Mayo, the counties with the greatest number of native Irish speakers.[123] Of course these figures do not take into account unlicenced sets, the discovery of 25,000 such sets in 1938[124] by the authorities indicating the prevalence of unlicenced sets. Nevertheless, even if there were as many licenced as unlicenced sets, the ratio of sets to population in Gaeltacht areas was still extremely low and compared very unfavourably with the number of sets in many other parts of the country.

The national radio station, 2RN, was launched in January 1926 by Douglas Hyde whose inaugural address was delivered mostly through

Irish. From an early stage Conradh na Gaeilge became actively interested in using radio as a means of supporting the Irish revival. In 1936, by which time the national service had changed its name to Radio Éireann, the radio sub-committee of Conradh na Gaeilge published a pamphlet *An Gaedheal agus an Radio*, subtitled 'leabhrán do thabhairt eolas do Ghead-healaibh ar an fheidhm is acfainn a bhaint as an radio, agus ar an gcéardachas is riachtanach chuige sin'. Referring to the station as 'stáisiún Baile Átha Cliath', the pamphlet was critical of Radio Éireann for copying the programme format and content from other European radio stations while ignoring programmes which dealt specifically with Irish culture and heritage.[125]

By the late 1930s Radio Éireann, then on the air for seven hours per day, was broadcasting up to 172 talks and discussions in Irish per year, each averaging fifteen minutes. Among the programmes was 'Nuacht an Lae' ('News of the Day') which replaced Scathán na nGaedheal in July 1938 and which, according to the Radio Éireann report for 1939, gathered people in 'groups around the wireless sets' especially in Gaeltacht areas where fluent speakers 'find the news more interesting when heard in Irish'.[126] However, the image of native Irish speakers sitting around the wireless listening to the Nuacht was somewhat misleading with the literal translation of the English news into Irish making it easier for those living in the Gaeltacht to understand the English rather than the Irish version.[127] This situation arose directly from the difficulty encountered by Radio Éireann in finding staff both proficient in Irish and professionally qualified for the news division of its service,[128] a reflection on the competency in Irish of those leaving the education system. A further difficulty was the proliferation of oral dialects in place of standard oral Irish, each Gaeltacht area having its own dialect and finding other dialects difficult to understand.

There was a strong emphasis on programming in Irish for young, school-going listeners and on educational programmes for adults anxious to improve their Irish such as 'Bhfuil an Abairt seo Agat?', a fifteen minute programme broadcast every Friday in the early 1940s and followed later by 'Is Your Irish Rusty?', 'Listen and Learn' and 'Noda Eolais'.

While it is impossible to judge with any accuracy the demand for Irish programming among the general population or the listenership levels to Irish programmes, Chomhdháil Náisiúnta na Gaeilge was clearly unhappy with levels of Irish on national radio, calling for more Irish in a meeting with the Taoiseach in 1952.[129] A few years later the INTO joined the call for more Irish on radio, especially for children 'a lasfaidh ina gcroí grá don

Ghaeilge',[130] while Comisiún um Athbheochan na Gaeilge (1963) expressed concern at the failure to use the service to any significant degree in the language revival effort.[131] In response, the Broadcasting Authority (Amendment) Act, 1966, directed the authorities of the renamed Radio Teilifís Éireann to be mindful of the national aim of reviving Irish. By this time the number of Irish language broadcasts had fallen from an earlier peak in the mid 1940s and 1950s when there were a substantial number of Irish language programmes being broadcast.[132]

The White Paper which followed the report of the language revival commission disclosed that RTÉ had been directed to examine the feasibility of setting up a broadcasting station to cater specifically for native speakers and which would be based in the Galway Gaeltacht. It was an idea first mooted in the Dáil in November 1926 by the then Minister for Posts and Telegraphs, J.J. Walsh, who said he was expecting the development of a dedicated radio station for native Irish speakers. The idea faded into the background until the late 1930s[133] and in 1943 the Secretary of the Department of Posts and Telegraphs, P.S. O'Hegarty, set up a committee to examine the possibility of an Irish station under the ministry of P.J. Little. Little, a solicitor and journalist, had been editor of *New Ireland, Éire, Sinn Féin* and *An Phoblacht*. The report of the committee, published in 1945, listed numerous and seemingly insurmountable problems. Again, the idea of a radio service for the Gaeltacht faded.

It was April 1972 before Radio na Gaeltachta as a branch of RTÉ finally began broadcasting. It catered specifically for the Gaeltacht population. By this time the national television station was completing its first decade in existence, having been judged by Comisiún um Athbheochan na Gaeilge within its first year of existence to be failing to contribute 'to any significant degree'[134] to the language revival. By the late 1960s approximately four hours of Irish language programming was being broadcast on a weekly basis.[135] By the mid 1970s some were convinced that 'the State television service is working steadily against the language'.[136] While too trenchant a view, the electronic media and in particular television, has the greatest potential for usurping native culture and linguistic patterns. If the national broadcaster had a responsibility for leading rather than following popular demands, then this assessment, put forward by Gearóid Ó Tuathaigh, becomes more sharply focused.

In conclusion, it may be said that the 'atmosphere Gallda' which prevailed outside of the classroom made the revival of the Irish language through the schools an almost impossible task. Very little room was afforded the Irish language in any of the key areas or institutions of Irish life. At best, the attitude towards the Irish language among bureaucrats, politicians, the Catholic Church and the national broadcasting network can be described as tokenism. By the early 1960s it was clear that the majority of the people had dismissed the idea of reviving the language, while many saw it as a mere 'ábhar breise ar chlár na scol, gléas chun teipithe ag scrúdaithe, nó chun mion-phostanna faoin Stát d'fháil'.[137]

An Saol Nua: Another Damnosa Hereditas?

THE IMPORTANT issues in concluding are the extent to which the language revival policy was successful, the effect the policy had on perceptions of the language and the impact of the policy as a central defining issue on the education system. There is little doubt that the dignity[1] of the language suffered from 1922 due to the failure of the revival and the at times ham-fisted way in which it was approached. According to James Dillon, successive Irish governments did more to injure the Irish language than 'the British government were able to do in the previous hundred years'.[2] In particular, the policy of compulsion in the schools and elsewhere alienated some people from the language or at least turned enthusiasm for the revival into apathy.[3] Such contemporary sentiments continued to be expressed by a variety of people throughout the period under discussion. In 1956, during the Second Inter-Party government, Declan Costello, a Fine Gael Deputy who subsequently became a High Court judge, expressed the view that far from reviving the language the schools-based revival policy hindered the development of the revival.[4] Two years later, when Fianna Fáil was again in power, Dr Noel Browne spoke of the hostility and indifference towards the language among children and parents created by the school revival policy.[5]

In the context of achievement, it must be observed that the schools-based revival policy failed in its aim of making Ireland an Irish-speaking nation. The revival partly failed because it was based on the idea that it was 'a matter of history' that the national school system had been established to 'oust the Irish language, and to spread and make secure the position of English'.[6] As discussed in the opening chapter, this analysis of history failed to take account of the decline in the use of Irish prior to 1831, the year the national school system was established; the evidence that parents supported the 'Anglicising' influence of the schools; and the other social and economic realities of nineteenth-century Ireland which impinged on the status of

Irish. The premise that the schools had sole responsibility for the decline of the language served the nationalist agenda of the first decades of Independence. Serving the agenda was understandable—history is still written to various, including nationalist or anti-nationalist, agendas—but does not lessen either the ultimate failure of the policy or the social, economic and financial costs of pursuing it.

The result of the officially unquestioned nationalist assumption was that the post Independence revival effort impacted hugely, almost exclusively and certainly most profoundly on the schools. The unwarranted forcefulness of the schools-based revival policy undoubtedly damaged perceptions of the language while the policy of compulsion—in the education system and elsewhere—did not sit easily on the shoulders of the people. The schools-based revival was at the very least disruptive of the standard of education in the primary and secondary sectors, and the failure to acknowledge and address this together with the castigation of those raising concerns in this context damaged the status of the language. The failure to recognise the contemporary concerns expressed from 1922 was not the result of ignorance. There was knowledge in political and academic circles of both the criticisms and the scientific research which called into question the emphasis of the schools-based revival. For example, a file in the Department of the Taoiseach with material dating from the early 1930s to the mid 1950s included a copy of Harold Palmer's *The Scientific Study and Teaching of Languages* (1917) together with an academic assessment of it as it applied to Ireland dating from 1936.[7] There was a simple 'decision' to ignore the criticism and evidence and when questioned about it to assert that experience elsewhere or pedagogic studies in general could not be applied to Ireland. Even research commissioned by the government in the 1940s was rejected and remained unpublished when it criticised the policy being pursued.[8] As outlined in the central chapters, when a large amount of specifically Irish scientific research became available in the 1960s, reinforcing much of the criticism of the policy, the initial reaction was again framed within the traditional two-pronged approach: criticism of the research and castigation of its authors. However, the research of the 1960s was to hold significant sway in a reassessment of the revival, marking the beginning of a new era in language policy.

Apart from pedagogic and scientific evidence, public concern over the policy was acknowledged but ignored. In particular, successive governments chose to turn a deaf ear to criticisms of compulsion. While arguments for and against Irish being a compulsory subject and a compulsory examination subject in the secondary school State examinations can be made, it was thoroughly unjust to establish Irish as a subject which had to be passed in order to pass certificate examinations. It gave Irish a status it did not deserve either in practical or cultural terms. Its only effect was to foster cynicism towards and occasionally passionate dislike for the national language. This three-way compulsion in the schools, where Irish had to be studied as a subject, taken in examinations and passed in order to be awarded a school leaving certificate examination—irrespective of how well one performed in other subjects—discredited the revival policy. It established the language as a tradable commodity in the context of education, careers and lifestyles. Those who did not have it were disadvantaged in comparison to those who had, resulting in Irish being a divisive factor. Irish became increasingly associated with the word 'scrúdú'[9] and it is perhaps reasonable to assume that interest in it was stimulated by parents' hope that their children would pass the compulsory Irish test necessary to get their examinations and possibly lead to a post in the Civil Service,[10] one of the most respected and secure employments throughout the period. The ending of the necessity to pass Irish in secondary school examinations in order to pass overall in the early 1970s was too little, given too grudgingly.

The failure to listen to criticism, particularly of compulsion, may have turned opposition to the status of Irish as a necessary subject for the award of the Intermediate and Leaving Certificate examinations into opposition to the language's position on the school curriculum in general. Also, one wonders about students' lasting perceptions of the language on leaving the education system. The INTO stated in 1942 that the use of Irish as a medium of instruction could easily lead to 'a positive dislike for the language' and its association with 'what is unpleasant and distasteful'.[11]

The vilification of critics served the language and the revival badly. Opposition to the method of revival was neatly equated with opposition to the language, and it was claimed that 'opposition to the Irish language is an opposition to the very idea of an Irish nation'.[12] Critics of the methods used to revive the language were labelled 'anti-Irish, anti-Gaelic and anti-everything else'.[13] As James Dillon stated: 'the curse of the language movement ... are the intolerant, narrow-minded egotists who imagine that anyone who differs with them in the smallest matter of detail must be a traitor and a West Briton'.[14] Of course it is important to note that criticism was often drowned by the silence of many (the majority?) and the vocal strength of the political, academic and cultural elite who promoted compulsion.

While compulsion was dogmatically pursued, the schools-based revival policy failed because of the failure to focus on practical as distinct from ideological issues. From the outset there was a lack of teachers qualified to teach Irish or through Irish; of sufficient or suitable Irish language text books and general reading material in Irish; of a standardised spelling and grammar and of suitable terminology for many subjects. These problems, particularly the lack of suitable text books, led to some schools, which had been using Irish as a medium of instruction, reverting to English for practical purposes. The fact that these issues were only addressed after the introduction of the policy of Gaelicising the schools, and then with significant delay, underpinned the extent to which, as outlined below, ideology was notably outpacing pragmatism. Equally, the emphasis on written Irish in the schools, despite the stated aim of giving students a command of the spoken tongue, led to a situation whereby students were leaving primary and secondary school with a very limited command of spoken Irish. In such circumstances the policy could never have achieved its aim.

The practical difficulties which undermined the success of the policy extended to Gaeltacht areas, the natural constituency for Irish medium instruction which was not adequately catered for. Many teachers in Gaeltacht areas were incapable of teaching through Irish and 50 per cent of Gaeltacht children were still being taught either wholly or partly through English by 1931.[15] Thirty-five years later, in 1966, it was claimed that the standard of education in primary schools in Gaeltacht areas was poor in comparison to the rest of the country, while attainment among students in Irish 'afford[ed] little grounds for complacency'.[16] It is significant that successive governments took no remedial action either in the Gaeltacht or the Galltacht to address the obvious shortcomings of the policy.

After the first decade of teaching Irish as a subject and teaching other subjects through Irish in the schools, little had been achieved. The policy, taken up and pursued with vigour by the new Fianna Fáil government in 1932 was very far from making Ireland an Irish-speaking nation. The Department of Education put this down to the period 1922–32 being one of preparation when the necessary foundations were laid on which the revival could be achieved. It was a 'tréimhse trialach d'oidí' which would be followed by a flowering of the language in the schools and elsewhere.[17] However, the flowering never occurred, either in the schools or anywhere else. Rather it was officially recognised that students quickly lost whatever fluency they gained in Irish within some years of leaving school. The report of Comisiún i dtaobh na Gaedhilge san Stát-Sheirbhís (c.1939), which included recommendations on Irish classes for adults, suggested the establishment of formal classes in Irish for those aged eighteen years or over and those who had just left primary school as both groups 'would hardly have sufficient Irish for conversation purposes':[18]

> Bheadh roinnt daoine go mbeadh a hocht déag bliain nó breis slán acu ag teacht isteach ionnta agus is ar éigean a bheadh dóthain taithí acu ar labhairt na Gaeilge ... toisc go mbeadh a cheathair nó níos mó de bliadhna curtha isteach acu ó fhágadar an scoil. Fiú amháin na daoine a bheadh díreach tar éis bun scoil d'fhágaint, is ar éigean a bheadh dóthain Gaedhilge acu chun í do labhairt go líofa.[19]

It is clear from the Department of the Taoiseach file which contains this report that the lack of ability in Irish among school leavers and the loss of any competency gained within 'four or more years' of leaving school caused neither surprise nor panic. The file simply contains two departmental responses: first of all, that the Department was 'happy to help with the endeavour' suggested and secondly, that it supported the idea of evening classes as 'too many young men ... pass their evenings in idleness leading sometimes to mischief or to demoralising pursuits'.[20] A decade later Tomás Ó Deirg was expressing concern that pupils on leaving school tended to forget the Irish they learned[21] while in 1962 the *Report of the Council of Education: Curriculum of the Secondary School* spoke of the 'great intellectual and educational wastage when students who leave school with a good command of Irish lose that accomplishment through lack of opportunity for its use'.[22]

There was intellectual and educational wastage in another respect too, such as the extent to which the position which was afforded the language weakened pupils' achievement in other subjects, limited the scope of the curriculum and took the focus from other developments in the education system. The contemporary evidence of pupils' achievement and the curriculum being limited due to the position given the language was acknowledged and justified. The extent to which the focus was taken off other developments in the field of education is more difficult to appraise, although it was raised as an issue by Fine Gael in its *Just Society* policy document of 1966:

> Educational research has not received in Ireland the attention that it requires if we are to have a sound education system. The Department of Education has been extraordinarily deficient in this respect, failing to sponsor research by educationalists.[23]

J.J. Lee raises a further issue in this regard—the extent to which the revival policy, particularly the teaching of young children through Irish, 'did not … sacrifice all the children of the nation equally':

> Children from more affluent homes, whose parents could repair some of the damage done in the schools, naturally enjoyed an advantage over poorer children whose parents would not or could not take a comparable interest in their education. Teaching infants through Irish provided one further bulwark for the existing social structure in that it inevitably discriminated against already deprived children.[24]

Of course to paint the language as the sole or even most dominant negative influence on the education of pupils would be unbalanced. Other issues such as large class size (which made the teaching of a non-vernacular language particularly difficult[25]), the number of one teacher schools with individual teachers in charge of multiple levels, pupil absenteeism, early school leaving and inadequate and unequal access to secondary education were all matters of concern. However, it is in the context of these issues that the standard of education received in primary schools in particular became more crucial for the life chances of those who would not, primarily for financial reasons, proceed to secondary school or university. The restricting of the curriculum, even to the extent of reducing the scope of the mathematics and English courses, the emphasis on teaching remaining subjects through a non-vernacular and the dominating focus on Irish as a subject only served to narrow an already restricted personal education.

Perhaps of greatest influence on the success or otherwise of the schools-based revival policy was the extent to which Irish was used outside the education system. The fact that Irish could not be successfully revived through the schools alone was recognised by many politicians and commentators from the 1920s and the Department of Education in time admitted as much. As early as 1925 one of the members of the Commission of Inquiry into the Preservation of the Gaeltacht, Michael Tierney, expressed doubts about using the schools as the sole element of the language revival campaign.[26] Towards the end of the 1920s Séamas Ó Grianna, brother of Seosamh MacGrianna and author of many critically acclaimed Irish language novels including *Mo Dhá Róisín* and *Caisleán Óir*, speaking at the 1929 annual congress of the Gaelic Teachers' Organisation in Dublin, was emphatic in his view that 'the language would die if it were left to the schools'.[27] In the same year J.J. Byrne, a Cumann na nGaedheal

Deputy for Dublin North, expressed similar sentiments when he underlined the fact that children could not be expected to become Irish speakers after seven years in school without the co-operation of their parents at home.[28] This point was echoed by Shán Ó Cuív in 1936 when he stated: 'that the schools alone cannot save the language'.[29]

Successive governments were aware of the problem that existed. Even the Department of Education admitted in the mid 1930s that Irish was merely an academic subject 'sa gcuid is mó de na scoltacha go fóill i n-áit a bheith á labhairt ag an aos óg taobh amuigh den scoil'.[30] In 1940 Tomás Ó Deirg, then Minister for Education, spoke of the problem as the most significant force in preventing the language revival from making progress, asking: 'Cad í an eochair osclóchas an glas sin?'[31] Absolving the government from responsibility for producing the key, Ó Deirg saw it as the duty of the 'náisiún go h-iomlán' to provide the key to the revival by using the Irish language in their everyday lives. He blamed teachers for the growing association of Irish with the education system, accusing them 'do bheith ag dearcadh ar an nGaedhilg go fóill mar nach mbeadh innti ach gnáth-adhbhar léighinn'.[32] By the late 1940s it was clear to at least some teachers that 'at present, the survival of spoken Irish is … very unlikely'.[33] It is interesting to note that by this time the word 'revival' had been replaced by the word 'survival'.

Little was done—or perhaps could be done—to address the lack of opportunity to use Irish outside the schools. *Comisiún um Athbheochan na Gaeilge* (1963) acknowledged that much school effort in teaching and learning Irish was wasted and agreed with the Council of Education that 'the schools alone cannot restore Irish as the language of the people'.[34] The Council, reporting a year before the Commission, had blamed the decline in the number of A schools (those which used Irish as a sole medium of instruction) and the more general waning of interest in the language on the fact that English was the sole language of business and commerce.[35] Forty years into the revival the Commission was of the opinion that 'the time has now come' for 'the second stage' of the revival, namely, 'putting the great amount of Irish now known throughout the community to general use'.[36] The reality is, however, that schools tend to follow society rather than vice versa,[37] that any such move in the 1960s would have been an eleventh hour action and, as argued above, would probably have been as unsuccessful if attempted at any previous time. Compulsion of use could not be extended to society at large in the same way in which it had been copper-fastened in the education system. In such circumstances, society would largely remain English-speaking and the opportunities to use Irish outside the classroom would remain minimal. The people, who apparently did not want to see the language die but who were unprepared to willingly sacrifice much in its revival, as much as the government ensured this, something implicit in the 1968 progress report on the White Paper on the revival of Irish which again urged the wider public to use Irish more often in order that the efforts in the schools could produce results.[38]

The shift in the politicisation of the language in the 1960s, which saw the nationalist focus of the revival being increasingly balanced by an emphasis on realism and practicality, marked the beginning of a new assessment of the language which in turn led to the setting of more realistic targets. The new assessment was the result of two significant developments. These were the mobilisation of the Gaeltacht population and its demand for rights and recognition, resulting in the establishment of the Roinn na Gaeltachta in 1956, and the growing and vocal opposition to many facets of the schools-based revival policy in the Galltacht, including compulsion, an issue which was politicised through Fine Gael's qualified anti-compulsion stance. The changing climate is indicated by the fact that Irish became an issue in the General Election of 1961.

The new balance and move towards pragmatism in the policy was not brought about without significant rancour between those who persisted in the political-nationalist view of the language to the exclusion of other considerations and those who sought recognition of the failure of the policy to date and who wanted it considerably amended. The status of the language, the disillusionment of the revivalists and the convictions of those who wanted an end to compulsion were well summarised by the events at a Language Freedom Movement meeting in the Mansion House on 21 September 1966, attended by some 2,000 people. The aim of the Language Freedom Movement, established in Autumn 1965, was to have compulsory Irish abolished at all levels. The year of the Mansion House meeting was a significant one, 1966 being the fiftieth anniversary of the Easter Rising. During the year, Misneach, a radical group of people including well-known Irish authors, went on a seven day hunger-strike in an attempt to focus attention on the plight of the language. The report of the LFM meeting reproduced in the *Irish Times* speaks for itself:

> As John B. Keane rose to speak, a man in the front of the audience jumped on the stage and seized the tri-colour, shouting that it should not be displayed at a meeting of this kind ... A struggle ensued ... Jeers from hecklers, bursts of applause and derisive shouts continued to interrupt the speakers. Dawson

> Street was lined with Gardaí … Small Union Jacks were waved
> in confusing profusion and at one point, as if at a given signal,
> a large Union Jack surrounded by smaller duplicates was raised
> with derisive shouts of 'Judas', 'Speak Irish', 'The Irish Red
> Guards are here', and 'Blue shirts'… The crowd cheered wildly
> as An tAthair Ó Fiaich stood up from his seat in the middle of
> the auditorium. He stretched his hand forward imploringly,
> supporting the demand [that opponents of the LFM be given a
> voice from the platform] but he could not be heard in the din
> …[39]

The meeting concluded with Irish revivalists being allowed speak from the platform alongside LFM members.

The episode admirably illustrates how polarised views on the Irish language had become. Although it had been a common thread of nationality during the hey day of the Gaelic League, by the 1960s the revival policy, if not the language, had become a divisive element in the concept of nationhood. The divisiveness is tribute enough to the ham-fisted policies of successive governments which, it could be argued, by the late 1960s had destroyed the possibility of reviving the Irish language, at least in the medium term. The attempted revival through the education system illustrated the dangers of allowing ideology win over pragmatism in the formulation of policy. Had realism been the guiding force behind the language revival policy in the schools, then some degree of success could well have been attained. However, idealism far outran practical consider-ations and by the 1960s the schools-based revival policy had become discredited. At most, the generality of students received a passing oral knowledge of Irish and a more indepth written knowledge of it. Yet, this could have been achieved through the simple teaching of Irish as a subject, and with a hugely reduced educational and financial cost to the State and the students.

Notes

Notes on Introduction

1 *Saorstát Éireann Official Handbook* (Dublin, 1932), p. 180.
2 Donald Akenson, *The Irish education experiment: the national system of education in the nineteenth century* (London and Toronto, 1970), p. 390. See also John Coolahan, *Irish Education: History and Structure* (Dublin, 1981), pp. 18–19.
3 Timothy Sheehy (Fianna Fáil), DD vol. 38, 27 May 1931, col. 1868–9.
4 Quoted in Pádraig Ó Loinsigh, 'The Irish Language in the Nineteenth Century', *Oideas*, Earrach (1975), p. 11.
5 P.H. Pearse, *The Murder Machine and Other Stories* (Dublin, 1976), p. 5.
6 See Donald Akenson, *The Irish Education Experiment: The National System of Education in the Nineteenth Century*, p. 381.
7 Michel Peillon, *Contemporary Irish Society: An Introduction* (Dublin, 1982), p. 101.
8 See for example Caoimhín Ó Donachair, 'The Irish Language in Co. Clare in the Nineteenth Century', *North Munster Antiquarian Journal*, xiii (1970).
9 Michael Hartnett, 'A Farewell to English', *A Farewell to English* (Dublin, 1978).
10 Muiris Ó Droighneáin, *Taighde i gcomhair Stair Litridheachta na Nua-Ghaedhilge* (Dublin, 1936), p. 9 [the winter time of Irish].
11 *An Claidheamh Solais*, 25 March 1899.
12 Quoted in Donnchadh Ó Súilleabháin, *An Piarsach agus Conradh na Gaeilge* (Dublin, 1981), p. 177 [what is the aim of the Gaelic League? ... To have Irish people speaking Irish].
13 Eugene O'Growney, 'Preface', *Simple Lessons in Irish: Parts 1, 2, 3 and 4* (Dublin, 1919).
14 Resolution passed at meeting of Sligo branch of the Gaelic League, 24 April 1899, in *An Claidheamh Solais*, 6 Bealtaine 1899.
15 From *Waterford News*, Sept. 1899. Quoted in Shán Ó Cuív, *The Problem of Irish in the Schools* (Dublin, 1936), p. 7.
16 See Patrick J. Corish, *Maynooth College, 1795–1995* (Maynooth, 1995). Also, Gearóid Ó Tuathaigh, 'Maigh Nuad agus Stair na Gaeilge' in Etáin Ó Síocháin (eag.), *Maigh Nuad: Saothrú na Gaeilge* (Maigh Nuad, 1995).
17 *Comisiún na Gaeltachta* (Dublin, 1926), p. 12.
18 Ibid., p. 13.
19 Ibid.
20 Micheál Ó Síothcháin quoted in Peadar Ó Loingsigh (ed.), *A Call to Ireland* (Ireland, 1911, 1944).
21 *Comisiún um Athbheochan na Gaeilge: Summary in English of Final Report*, p. 10.
22 The constitution of Sinn Féin is quoted in Dorothy MacArdle, *The Irish Republic*, 4th edn. (Dublin, 1951), pp. 915–16.
23 M.P. O'Hickey, *Language and Nationality* (Waterford, 1918), p. 4.

24 William Magennis, DD vol. 1, 1 Dec. 1922, col. 2591.
25 National Programme Conference, *National Programme of Primary Instruction* (Dublin, 1922).
26 Ibid., p. 4.
27 Letter published in *Irish Schools Weekly*, 21 March 1922.
28 Irish Language: Development in the Schools, N.A., D/T S 7801c.
29 DD vol. 1, 1 Dec. 1922, col. 2571–72.
30 DD vol. 2, 20 March 1923, col. 2330.
31 Ibid., col. 2325 [let us not betray the cause].
32 'Commission on Secondary Education', Library, D/Ed., RF 373.5 (417). See T.A. O'Donoghue, 'The Dáil Commission on Secondary Education, 1921–2', *Oideas*, (Samhradh, 1989), pp. 61–74.
33 D.A. Gleeson, 'Fr. T. Corcoran, S.J.: An Appreciation', *Studies*, xxxii (1943), pp. 157–8.
34 Timothy Corcoran, 'The Irish Language in the Irish Schools', *Studies*, xiv (1925), pp. 377–88.
35 Ibid., p. 387.
36 *Comisiún um Athbheochan na Gaeilge: Summary in English of Final Report* (Dublin, 1963), p. 9.
37 Intermediate Education Commissioners, *Rules and Programme 1924–25*, pp. 8, 12.
38 *Second National Programme Conference (1925–6) Report*, p. 22.
39 Ibid.
40 Ibid., pp. 28, 29.
41 Ibid., p. 11.

Notes on Chapter One

1   Department of Education, *Notes for Teachers, Primary School: Irish* (1933), p. 55.
2   Michael Kitt, DD vol. 115, 4 May 1949, col. 593. [Let it not be said that we would neglect the language of Patrick, Brigid and Colmcille, Brian Boru and Eoghan Rua, Eoghan Ó Gramhnaigh and Patrick Pearse.]
3   Bridget Rice, DD vol. 115, 4 May 1949, col. 574.
4   Conchubhar Ó Liatháin, DD vol. 120, 25 April 1950, col. 1010. [Not only do we wish to save Irish because it is our own language, but because if we lose it we will not be able to save our nation.]
5   *Notes for Teachers: Irish*, p. 54.
6   DD vol. 51, 21 March 1934, col. 1603.
7   DD vol. 24, 6 June 1928, col. 98.
8   See also *Report of Department of Education, 1943–44*, p. 16.
9   *Notes for teachers: Irish*, p. 2.
10 DD vol. 29, 17 April 1929, col. 462–63.
11 *Notes for teachers: Irish*, pp. 53, 54.
12 Tomás Ó Deirg, DD vol. 29, 17 April 1929, col. 392 [and not only that, but that they should be written by true Irish people].
13 Ibid. [the work of the country].
14 Daniel Buckley, DD vol. 38, 21 May 1931, col. 1826.
15 Sean O'Connor, *A Troubled Sky: Reflections on the Irish Educational Scene, 1957–1968* (Dublin, 1986), p. 7.
16 *An Páipéar Bán um Athbheochan na Gaeilge* (Dublin, 1965), p. 112.

17   Thomas O'Connell, DD vol. 8, 3 July 1924, col. 414.
18   *Report of Department of Education, 1930–31*, p. 18.
19   *Report of Department of Education, 1933–34*, p. 21.
20   *Report of Department of Education, 1959–60*, p. 9. [It is also thought that there should be a greater effort made to explain to pupils the reason they should have respect for Irish, that it is our language and that of the Irish nation, and that a national language is the fundamental indication of nationhood.]
21   *Report of the Council of Education: Curriculum in Secondary Schools* (Dublin, 1962), e.g. p. 126.
22   Shán Ó Cuív, *The problem of Irish in the Schools* (Dublin, 1936), p. 17.
23   Frank Fahy, DD vol. 34, 21 May 1930, col. 2150–52.
24   T.F. O'Higgins, DD vol. 110, 19 May 1948, col. 1747–48.
25   Department of Education, *Regulations Regarding Curricula, Certificates, Examinations and Scholarships, with Programme for the Year 1927–28*, p. 10.
26   John O'Sullivan, DD vol. 26, 31 Oct. 1928, col. 938.
27   Department of Education, *Regulations ... with Programme for the Year 1927–28*, p. 7.
28   Department of Education, *Secondary Schools Programme, 1933–34*, p. 13.
29   National Programme Conference, *National Programme of Primary Instruction* (Dublin, 1922), p. 4.
30   *Irish Schools Weekly*, 6 Dec. 1924.
31   DD vol. 59, 10 Dec. 1935, col. 2197.
32   Vincent White, DD vol. 2, 31 March 1923, col. 1350–1406.
33   Memo dated 20 Dec. 1948 (N.A., D/T, Irish Language: Development in the Schools, S 7801).
34   DD vol. 8, 7 July 1924, col. 595.
35   Ibid. col. 609.
36   DD vol. 44, 28 Oct. 1932, col. 746.
37   *Irish Schools Weekly*, 25 Dec. 1926.
38   *Irish Times*, 18 Jan. 1927.
39   DD vol. 61, 24 March 1936, col. 119.
40   DD vol. 96, 27 April 1945, col. 2667.
41   Thomas Coll, 'Are We Reviving Irish', *The Bell*, no. 1, xvii (1951), p. 54.
42   *Sunday Independent*, 1 March 1953.
43   For a discussion of Irish in local authorities see Mary E. Daly, *The Buffer State: The Historical Roots of the Department of the Environment* (Dublin, 1997), pp. 167–71.
44   Letter from Cahirciveen Farmers' Association, 11 Samhain 1958 (N.A., D/T, Advancement of Irish: Misc. suggestions 1942–58, S 12953a).
45   DD vol. 182, 25 May 1960, col. 193.
46   *Irish Press*, 16 Sept. 1957.
47   *Notes for Teachers: Irish*, p. 4.
48   Ibid., p. 8.
49   Ibid., p. 28.
50   *Report of Department of Education, 1940–41*, p. 16 [question and answer].
51   Ibid. [they are happy with any answer which is correct without bothering with accuracy or fluency].
52   *Notes for Teachers: Irish*, p. 42.
53   See Ó Cuív, *The Problem of Irish in the Schools*, p. 16.
54   Eugene O'Growney, *Simple Lessons in Irish* (Dublin, 1918), p. 5.
55   National Programme Conference, *National Programme of Primary Instruction*, pp. 6–7.
56   Circular to managers, teachers and inspectors on teaching through Irish, 11/31

(N.A., D/T, Irish Language: Development in the Schools, S 7801).

57 Typescript of lecture (N.A., D/T, Irish language: Development in the Schools, S 7801). [1. Understanding the new language as it is spoken by native speakers; 2. Understanding the new language as it is written by native speakers; 3. Speaking the new language as it is spoken by native speakers; 4. Writing the new language as it is written by native speakers.]

58 Department of Education, Circular to Inspectors, 4/36.

59 Department of Education, *Revised Programme of Primary Instruction* (1934), p. 5.

60 *Report of Department of Education, 1930–31*, p. 17 [the speaking of Irish … the ordinary language of home and street].

61 *Report of Department of Education, 1927–28*, p. 49. [In many schools, particularly in day schools, the written exercises are not properly supervised.]

62 *Report of Department of Education, 1929–30*, p. 31. [We do not have enough intelligent teachers and teachers do not have the correct methods.]

63 Eamon Ó Ciosáin, DD vol. 61, 25 March 1936, col. 194.

64 DD vol. 83, 27 May 1941, col. 992. [The departmental inspectors have noticed some progress in the speaking of Irish.]

65 *Report of Department of Education, 1940–41*, p. 15.

66 *Report of Department of Education, 1944–45*, p. 18.

67 *Report of the Council of Education (1954)*, p. 138.

68 Ibid., p. 150.

69 Ibid., p. 152.

70 *Irish Press*, 6 Sept. 1952.

71 E.g., letter dated July 1951 from a teacher in Thurles (N.A., D/T, Advancement in Irish: misc. suggestions, 1942–58, 12953a).

72 *Report of Department of Education, 1955–56*, p. 9 [twice that amount].

73 DD vol. 161, 2 May 1957, col. 685.

74 DD vol. 174, 24 May 1960, col. 75.

75 Department of Education, Circular on the teaching of Irish, 11/60.

76 INTO, *Official Congress Programme* (1965), p. 44.

77 Fine Gael, *Just Society: Education* (Dublin, 1966), p. 13.

78 Micheál Ó Síoradáin, 'Na Scoileanna agus an Teanga: Cigire ag Féachaint Siar', typescript, 1986 (Department of Education and Science, Library). [I was able to write essays and had perfect grammar; however, neither I not my teachers could speak Irish.]

79 Maurice Moynihan (ed.), *Speeches and Statements by Eamon de Valera, 1917–73* (Dublin, 1980), p. 525.

80 DD vol. 120, 20 April 1950, col. 840 [the main aim … to improve spoken Irish].

81 INTO, *Congress Programme* (1956), p. 38.

82 INTO, *Congress Programme* (1963), p. 42.

83 *Comisiún um Athbheochan na Gaeilge: summary in English of final report* (1963), p. 61.

84 Commission on Secondary Education: letter to headmasters and teachers with draft programme (D/Ed. Library, RF 373.5 (417)).

85 Intermediate Education Commissioners, *Rules and Regulations, 1924–25*, p. 6. [When starting out it is best not to use books with the students and not to direct them towards reading until they are able to speak Irish fairly well.]

86 Letter from Department of Education to Minister for Finance, 13 November 1935 (N.A., D/T, Galway: Development as an Irish Speaking Centre, S 9303).

87 DD vol. 65, 17 February 1937, col. 431–2.

88 Daniel O'Rourke, DD vol. 83, 27 May 1941, col. 1060.

89   DD vol. 115, 3 May 1949, col. 332.
90   *Irish Times*, 19 March 1953.
91   Letter dated 8 Oct. 1952 (N.A., D/T, Irish Language: Development in the Schools, S 7801) [such an exam would not be workable and introducing such an exam would neither be to the benefit or otherwise of Irish].
92   Notes on meeting of 1 Aug. 1952 (N.A., D/T, Irish Language: Development in the Schools, S 7801).
93   General considerations on the question of a test in oral Irish in the Intermediate and Leaving Certificate examinations, 23 June 1953 (N.A., D/T, Irish Language: Development in the Schools, S 7801b).
94   *Irish Times*, 16 Nov. 1926.
95   *The Catholic Bulletin*, 1, xvii (1927), p. 12.
96   Ibid., p. 15.
97   *Irish Schools Weekly*, 1 Jan. 1938.
98   General considerations on the questions of a test in oral Irish in the Intermediate and Leaving Certificate examinations, 23 June 1953 (N.A., D/T, Irish Language: Development in the Schools, S 7801b).
99   Ibid.
100 Ibid.
101 Ibid.
102 DD vol. 161, 2 May 1957, col. 697.
103 *Report of the Council of Education: Curriculum of the Secondary School*, p. 118.
104 DD vol. 168, 22 May 1958, col. 644 [an oral Irish exam].
105 *Report of Department of Education, 1958–59*, p. 11.
106 *Report of the Council of Education: Curriculum of the Secondary School*, p. 114.
107 Ibid., p. 118.
108 Irish Labour Party, *Challenge and Change in Education* (Dublin, 1963), p. 32.
109 *Comisiún um Athbheochan na Gaeilge: Summary in English of Final Report*, p. 65.
110 Ibid., p. 69.
111 *An Páipéar Bán um Athbheochan na Gaeilge*, p. 110.
112 *Comisiún um Athbheochan na Gaeilge*, p. 8.
113 *Investment in Education: A Report of the Survey Team Appointed by the Minister for Education in October 1962* (Dublin, 1966), p. 240.
114 Irish Labour Party, *Challenge and Change in Education*, p. 31.
115 Fine Gael, *Just Society*, p. 63.
116 *Páipéar Bán um Athbheochan na Gaeilge: Progress Report for the Period Ended 31 March 1966* (Dublin, 1966), p. 36.
117 Micheál Ó Síoradáin, 'Cigire ag Féachaint Siar', p. 8 [believe it or not Irish was taught through English].
118 Páistí sgoile a chur go dtí na Ghaeltacht: sgéimeanna le n-a aghaidh seo, 22 June 1936 (N.A., R/Gael., Grants for Children: Scholarships to the Gaeltacht, F 7/7/36).
119 N.A., D/T, Irish Language: Summer Courses for Children, S 9280.
120 Ibid.
121 Letter from Department of Education to Department of Finance, 13 Dec. 1937 (N.A., D/T, Irish Language: Summer Courses for Children, S 9280) [nothing would more assist in the revival of Irish than the provision of opportunities for English speaking children to spend time in Irish speaking areas].
122 Ibid. [national work].
123 Scéim Chun Páistí Scoile as an nGalltacht a Chur Chun na Gaeltachtaí (N.A.,

R/Gael., Coiste na pPáistí, C 1/9).

124   *Irish Press*, 5 March 1952.
125   *An Páipéar Bán um Athbheochan na Gaeilge*, p. 180.
126   Coiste na bPáistí, *Tuarascbháil Bliadhna*, 1950.
127   Scéim na bPáistí i mBaile Átha Cliath: Scolairí a Cuireadh chuig Gaeltacht an Chnoc, Conemara, 1955: Thuairisc ar an Scéim (N.A., R/Gael., Coiste na Gaeltachta: Agenda and Minutes 1937, F 1/2/37). [I need not say I was disappointed ... I thought many of those aged between 11 and 14 years were weak enough and had got no great benefit in terms of Irish from having spent time in an Irish speaking area ... Their pronunciation was poor and their vocabulary very narrow.]
128   *Irish Times*, 22 April 1977.
129   *An Páipéar Bán um Athbheochan na Gaeilge*, p. 12.
130   N.A., D/T, Irish Language Policy, S 13180 D/61.
131   Ibid.
132   See Nollaig Ó Gadhra, 'Gaelic Ireland', in *Terence MacSwiney Memorial Lectures* (London, 1986), p. 87.
133   Ibid., p. 87.
134   *Comisiún um Athbheochan na Gaeilge: Summary in English of Final Report*, p. 17.
135   *Secondary School Rules*, 1972–73, p. 25.
136   *Secondary School Rules*, 1974–75, p. 25.
137   *Secondary School Rules*, 1972–73, p. 29.
138   *Secondary School Rules*, 1973–74, p. 29.

Notes on Chapter Two

1   DD vol. 89, 5 May 1943, col. 2377. [If all we want is to keep Irish alive as a second 'ornate' language among the people, similar to the position of Latin and French among the educated people in the 1800s, then we can achieve that by teaching Irish for one hour per day in every school, using English the rest of the time ... I am not happy to accept that situation and neither, I think, is the government.]
2   Memo, Roinn na Taoiseach, 20 Nollaig 1948 (N.A., D/T, Irish Language: Development in Schools, S 7801).
3   Padraig Pearse, 'Murder machine' in *Murder Machine and Other Stories* (Dublin, 1976), p. 26.
4   Shán Ó Cuív, *The Problem of Irish in Schools* (Dublin, 1936), p. 11.
5   *Report of the Department of Education, 1951–52*, p. 7.
6   Thomas O'Connell, DD vol. 16, 4 June 1926, col. 405.
7   Report of the opening of the Gaelic League in Derry by Revd. M. Bradley, Vice-President, St Columbus' College, in *Irish Schools Weekly*, 6 Oct. 1938.
8   See for example, *Notes for Teachers: Irish* (Dublin, 1933), p. 54 and *Report of the Department of Education, 1930–31*, p. 18.
9   DD vol. 22 May 1931, col. 1823–4.
10   Shán Ó Cuív, *The Problem of Irish in the Schools*, p. 12.
11   Fianna Fáil Árd-Fheis, 12 October 1937, in Maurice Moynihan (ed.), *Speeches and Statements by Eamon de Valera* (Dublin, 1980), pp. 342–3.
12   *Irish Press*, 22 Nov. 1944.
13   *Report of the Department of Education, 1934–35*, p. 25.

14   For example, Report of Dr Johanna Pollak, 26 May 1943 (N.A., D/T, Irish Language: Development in the Schools, S 7801).
15   Bridget Rice, DD vol. 115, 4 May 1949, col. 573–4.
16   *Report of the Council of Education: Curriculum of the Secondary School* (Dublin, 1962), p. 116.
17   *An Páipéar Bán um Athbheochan na Gaeilge: Progress Report for the Period Ended 31 March 1966* (Dublin, 1966), p. 36.
18   Ó Cuív, *The Problem of Irish in the Schools*, p. 13.
19   Shán Ó Cuív, *Irish Schools Weekly*, 14 July 1923. Richard Whately, the Protestant Archbishop of Dublin from 1831–63, was one of the Commissioners of National Education who expressed the wish of making every pupil 'a happy English child'.
20   Joseph MacBride, DD vol.8, 3 July 1924, col. 422.
21   Pádraig Ó Cuinneáin, DD vol. 110, 19 May 1948, col. 1766. [We all know that when a child aged four or five years goes to school they have knowledge of no language. The child does not care what language they are taught in.]
22   Dr J.J. O'Connell, secretary of the First Programme Conference in a statement to the Second Programme Conference, in INTO, *Report of Commission of Inquiry into Use of Irish as a Teaching Medium to Children whose Home Language is English* (Dublin, 1942), p. 5.
23   National Programme Conference, *Report of the Second National Programme Conference* (Dublin, 1926), pp. 22, 23, 28, 29.
24   Michael Heffernan, DD vol. 8, 7 July 1924, col. 562.
25   INTO, *Inquiry*, p. 10.
26   DD vol. 26, 28 Oct. 1928, col. 8373–4.
27   *Second National Programme Conference*, Section 6, pp. 27–8.
28   *Irish Schools Weekly*, 19 June 1943.
29   Ibid.
30   John O'Sullivan, DD vol. 26, 31 Oct. 1928, col. 1131–2.
31   Circular to managers, teachers and inspectors on teaching through the medium of Irish, 11/31 (Library, D/Ed.).
32   INTO, *Inquiry*, p. 10.
33   Department of Education, *Rules and Regulations for National Schools* (Dublin, 1932), p. 44.
34   Ibid., p. 15.
35   Maurice Moynihan, *Speeches and Statements*, p. 195.
36   DD vol. 51, 21 March 1934, col. 1346.
37   INTO, *Inquiry*, p. 12.
38   Department of Education, *Revised Programme of Primary Instruction* (Sept. 1934).
39   Ibid., p. 3.
40   *Report of the Department of Education, 1934-35*, p. 27.
41   Department of Education, *Revised Programme of Primary Instruction*, p. 3.
42   *Report of the Department of Education, 1934-35*, p. 21 [the time saved in doing this can be used by teachers to teach Irish].
43   See Áine Hyland and Kenneth Milne, Irish Educational Documents, vol. II (Naas, 1992), p. 113.
44   Department of Education, *Revised Programme of Primary Instruction*, p. 3.
45   DD vol. 44, 28 Oct. 1932, col. 766. [It is an injustice not to speak English to children in junior schools in English speaking areas, and to not teach them English when English is their only language and when it is only English they speak and hear outside school. While this situation pertains in English speaking areas,

teachers in Irish speaking areas are breaking their hearts trying to teach English to Irish speaking children.]

46 E.g. James Hughes, DD vol. 83, 26 May 1941, col. 1181.
47 *Report of the Department of Education, 1934-35*, p. 24 [a good step forward].
48 Ibid., p. 25.
49 DD vol. 61, 24 March 1936, col. 92 [now Irish is frequently used as the ordinary language in many homes].
50 John O'Sullivan, DD vol. 90, 12 May 1943, col. 108.
51 Michael Tierney, DD vol. 34, 21 May 1930, col. 2181–2; J.A. Costello, DD vol. 55, 4 April 1935, col. 1979; James Dillon, DD vol. 66, 31 March 1937, col. 154.
52 DD vol. 51, 21 March 1934, col. 1577–8.
53 DD vol. 61, 24 March 1936, col. 115.
54 For example, Michael Tierney, DD vol. 34, 21 May 1930, col. 2181-2 and Bridget Redmond, DD vol. 83, 26 May 1941, col. 1214.
55 Frank MacDermot, DD vol. 65, 17 Feb. 1937, col. 434.
56 *Irish Schools Weekly*, 17 Feb. 1923.
57 *Irish Schools Weekly*, 19 April 1930.
58 DD vol. 38, 21 May 1931, col. 1685–6.
59 Shán Ó Cuív, *The Problem of Irish in the Schools*, p. 17.
60 DD vol. 8, 7 July 1924, col. 584.
61 John Costello, DD vol. 55, 4 April 1935, col. 1979.
62 DD vol. 74, 23 March 1939, col. 2391. See also INTO, *Inquiry*, p. 36.
63 Department of Education, Circular to inspectors, 4/36.
64 See Appendix for copy of questionnaire.
65 INTO, *Inquiry*, p. 57.
66 *Notes for Teachers: Irish*, p. 53.
67 INTO, *Inquiry*, pp. 22, 25–9.
68 Ibid., pp. 30, 32.
69 Ibid., pp. 4, 5, 18, 19, 20.
70 Ibid., pp. 45, 52.
71 Ibid., p. 24.
72 Ibid., p. 57
73 Ibid., pp. 65, 67.
74 Conradh na Gaeilge (Choiste Gnótha), *Teagasc tré Ghaeilge* (Dublin, 1942).
75 The ban remained in place until 1958. See Adrian Kelly, 'Women in Twentieth-Century Ireland: Activism and Change' in Ilka Kangas (ed.), *The Situation of Elderly Women: Four Lifestories of Grandmothers on the Fringes of the European Union* (Finland, 1997), p. 150.
76 Report of INTO: Chief Inspector's Observations (N.A., D/T, Irish Language: Development in Schools, S 7801).
77 INTO, *Inquiry*, pp. 24, 34.
78 Report of INTO: Chief Inspector's Observations (N.A., D/T, Irish Language: Development in Schools, S 7801).
79 Ibid.
80 The failure to resolve the salaries issue resulted in strike action being taken by teachers in Spring 1946. The action was described by Ó Deirg as a 'definite challenge to the authority of the State' (SD vol. 31, 21 March 1946, col. 1047).
81 *Irish Press*, 3 Nov. 1944.
82 Dr Johanna Pollak, 'On Teaching Irish', 1943 (N.A., D/T, Irish Language: Development in Schools, S 7801).

83   DD vol. 83, 27 May 1941, col. 992.
84   DD vol. 97, 15 May 1945, col. 446.
85   DD vol. 24, 6 June 1928, col. 101.
86   Shán Ó Cuív, *The Problem of Irish in the Schools*, p. 17.
87   Richard Mulcahy, DD vol. 113, 14 Dec. 1948, col. 1370. [All work is to be carried out through Irish in the infant classes where the teacher is sufficiently qualified … In every school teachers, where sufficiently qualified, should aim to reach the point as soon as possible in infant classes where Irish is used as the language of instruction and communication.]
88   *Report of the Council of Education on the Future of the Primary School* (Dublin, 1954), p. 156.
89   Ibid., pp. 140, 142, 144.
90   Ibid., p. 144.
91   E.F. O'Doherty, 'Bilingualism: Educational Aspects', *Advancement of Science*, no. 56, vol. xiv (1958), p. 286.
92   *Report of the Council of Education: Primary School*, p. 162.
93   Ibid., p. 164.
94   *Irish Times*, 13 Oct. 1955.
95   INTO, *Official Programme of Annual Congress, 1955*, pp. 26-7.
96   *Irish Independent*, 11 May 1950.
97   Canon W.N. Harvey, 'Report on the Diocesan Synods of Dublin, Glendalough and Kildare', *Irish Times*, 13 Oct. 1955.
98   INTO, *Inquiry*, p. 56.
99   *Report of the Council of Education: Primary School*, pp. 158–60.
100 DD vol. 171, 25 Nov. 1958, col. 801.
101 *Irish Times*, 13 Oct. 1955.
102 *Irish Schools Weekly*, 24 Feb. 1923 [a lack of knowledge and investigation of bilingual education].
103 John O'Meara, *Reform in Education* (Dublin, 1957).
104 E.F. O'Doherty, 'Bilingualism: Educational Aspects', *Advancement of Science*, no. 56, vol. xiv (1958), p. 282.
105 Ibid.
106 Ibid., p. 287.
107 J.R. Morrison, 'Bilingualism: Some Psychological Aspects', *Advancement of Science*, no. 56, vol. xiv (1958).
108 Ibid., p. 288.
109 See Sean O'Connor, *A Troubled Sky: Reflections on the Irish Educational Scene, 1957–1968* (Dublin, 1986), p. 23.
110 Ibid., p. 24.
111 DD vol. 178, 26 Nov. 1959, col. 604.
112 Sean O'Connor, *A Troubled Sky*, p. 44.
113 *Investment in Education* (Dublin, 1966), p. 240.
114 John MacNamara, 'The Use of Irish in Teaching Children from English-Speaking Homes: A Survey of Irish National Schools' (Ph.D. thesis, University of Edinburgh, 1963).
115 John MacNamara, *Bilingualism and Primary Education* (Britain, 1966), p. 24.
116 Ibid., pp. 42, 136.
117 *Notes for Teachers: Irish*, p. 53.
118 John MacNamara, *Bilingualism and Primary Education*, p. 138.
119 INTO, *Congress Programme: 1965*, pp. 42–4.

120 John Coolahan, *The History of Irish Education*, p. 131.
121 Garret Fitzgerald, *All in a Life: An Autobiography* (Dublin, 1992), pp. 79, 305.
122 Fine Gael, *Just Society*, pp. 9, 10.
123 Department of Education, *Reports*, 1922-70.
124 *Report of the Council of Education: Curriculum of the Secondary School*, p. 130.
125 *Irish Times*, 13 Oct. 1961.
126 *Report of the Department of Education, 1924–26*, p. 52.
127 John O'Sullivan, DD vol. 38, 21 May 1931, col. 1691.
128 John O'Sullivan, DD vol. 21, 23 Nov. 1927, col. 1723.
129 Sean O'Connor, *A Troubled Sky*, p. 7.
130 Intermediate Education Commissioners, *Rules and Regulations, 1924–25*, p. 6.
131 Mícheál Ó Síoradáin, 'Na Scoileanna agus an Teanga: Cigire ag Féachaint Siar', typescript, 1986 (Department of Education and Science, Library), p. 7. [Not only were the ordinary subjects taught through Irish, but English was taught through Irish. One of Shakespeare's plays was on the course … It was read in English, but the commentary and explanation was all through Irish. No wonder de Valera said …]
132 Intermediate Education Commissioners, *Rules and Regulations, 1924–25*, p. 6.
133 DD vol. 51, 21 March 1934, col. 1348.
134 Ibid.
135 DD vol. 51, 11 April 1934, col. 1571.
136 *Report of the Department of Education, 1927–28*, p. 49 [the increase and widening].
137 DD vol. 101, 22 May 1946, col. 544 [there is a constant expansion in the use of Irish as a medium of instruction].
138 Tomás Ó Deirg, DD vol. 101, 22 May 1946, col. 544.
139 Richard Mulcahy, DD vol. 115, 3 May 1949, col. 331.
140 *Report of the Department of Education, 1927–28*, p. 49 [greatest obstacles].
141 DD vol. 3, 31 May 1923, col. 1369–72.
142 *Report of the Council of Education: Curriculum of the Secondary School*, p. 128.
143 N.A., D/T, Irish in the Secondary Schools: Reduction of grants 1941,S 12467. [It greatly surprises us that the solution proposed by the Government is to reduce the grant to A schools. We wish to state that Irish does not have a sufficiently strong foothold in the schools to allow a reduction in the financial assistance offered to them to promote it and we ask the Government to reconsider its decision given the objective before us, namely, the revival of Irish as the national language.]
144 Table taken from N.A., D/T, Advancement of Irish: State Support, S 11193.
145 *Irish Schools Weekly*, 19 Feb. 1927.
146 *Rules and Regulations*, pp. 81, 87.
147 N.A., D/T, Advancement of Irish: State Support, S 11193.
148 Intermediate Education Commissioners, *Rules and Programme, 1924–25*, p. 8.

Notes on Chapter Three

1 T.J. O'Connell, DD vol. 8, 3 July 1924, col. 415.
2 *Report of the Department of Education, 1927–28*, p. 15.
3 *An Comisiún um Athbheochan na Gaeilge: An Tuarascáil Dheiridh* (Dublin, 1963), p. 18.
4 Donncha Ó Súilleabháin, *Cath na Gaeilge sa Chóras Oideachais, 1893–1911* (Dublin, 1987), p. 3.

5   *Irish Times*, 22 Feb. 1922.
6   Ibid.
7   *Report of the Department of Education, 1927–28*, p. 47.
8   Ibid., p. 54.
9   *Irish Schools Weekly*, 24 Dec. 1927.
10 *Report of the Department of Education, 1927–28*, p. 18.
11 *Report of the Department of Education, 1928–29*, p. 18.
12 Department of Education, Circular regarding extra personal vacation for teachers attending special summer courses of instruction or study, 9/36 (D/Ed. Library).
13 *Report of the Department of Education, 1947–48*, p. 12 [the significant reduction over the past ten years in the number of teachers and students visiting Irish speaking areas during the holidays].
14 DD vol. 94, 13 June 1944, col. 256.
15 N.A., R/Gael., Coláistí Gaeilge i Gcoitine, C2/5.
16 *Report of the Department of Education, 1958–59*, p. 11 [demand was such that a place could not be found for every applicant].
17 *Sunday Independent*, 1 March 1953.
18 Irish and Teaching of Irish in Training Colleges (D/Ed. Library, Position of Irish in Training Colleges, File 38290).
19 Ibid.
20 DD vol. 12, 11 June 1925, col. 815.
21 Timothy Corcoran, 'The Irish Language in the Irish Schools', *Studies*, xiv (1925), p. 383.
22 *Statement of Government Policy on Recommendation of the Commissioners* (Dublin, n.d.), p. 4.
23 These are approximate figures. See Tables 3.1, 3.2(a) and 3.2(b).
24 *Report of the Department of Education, 1928–29*, p. 13.
25 *Rules and Regulations for National Schools under the Department of Education* (Dublin, 1932), pp. 89–91.
26 *Report of the Department of Education, 1939–40*, pp. 13–14.
27 J.J. Byrne, DD vol. 38, 21 May 1931, col. 1725.
28 *Irish Schools Weekly*, 5 Aug. 1933.
29 *Irish Schools Weekly*, 12 Aug. 1940.
30 *Irish Schools Weekly*, 31 Aug. 1940.
31 *Report of the Department of Education, 1936–37*, p. 8.
32 See Adrian Kelly, 'Women in Twentieth-Century Ireland: Activism and Change' in Ilka Kangas (ed.), *The Situation of Elderly Women: Finland, Greece, Ireland and Portugal* (Helsinki, 1997), p. 150.
33 See Tables 3.2(a) and (b) for a statistical analysis of the numbers attending preparatory colleges.
34 DD vol. 83, 26 May 1941, col. 1231.
35 DD vol. 168, 31 May 1958, col. 640–41.
36 DD vol. 182, 24 May 1960, col. 72–3.
37 *Report of the Council of Education: Curriculum of Secondary Schools* (Dublin, 1962), p. 128
38 NUI, *The National University of Ireland 1932–39* (Dublin, 1939), p. 22.
39 Letter from Department of Education to Minister for Finance, 13 Samhain 1935 (N.A., D/T, Galway: Development as an Irish Speaking Centre, S 9303).
40 University College Galway Act, 1929.

41   NUI, *The National University Handbook 1908–1932*, pp. 135–8.
42   UCG (Increase of Grant) Order, 1932.
43   Report of meeting with deputation from UCG, Leinster House, 27 April 1933 (N.A., D/T, Gaelic Examining University, S 9497).
44   Memo for the executive council re UCG prepared by Minister for Finance, 9 Jan. 1934 (N.A., D/T, UCG: Extension of Use of Irish, S 2407).
45   N.A, D/T, Galway: Development as Irish Speaking Centre, S 9303.
46   N.A., D/T, University Courses in Irish: Scholarships and Prizes, S 14109.
47   DD vol. 3, 31 May 1923, col. 1359–60.
48   Proposed changes at UCD (N.A., D/T, UCD: Teaching of Modern Irish, 6240).
49   University College, Dublin, Act 1934, Section 1(2).
50   UCD, *Calendar 1956–57*, pp. 28–9.
51   UCD, *Calendar 1960–61*, p. 33.
52   UCD, *Calendar 1964–65*, p. 53.
53   Tomás Ó Fiaich, *Má Nuad* (Maynooth, 1972), p. 66.
54   UCC, *Calendar, 1947–48*, p. 17.
55   *Catholic Bulletin*, 4, xiv (1942), pp. 268–9.
56   The booklet can be found in N.A., D/T, University Education: Financial Assistance, S 14018a. See also R.B. McDowell and D.A. Webb, *Trinity College Dublin, 1592–1952* (London and New York, 1982), pp. 474–5.
57   Jack White, *Minority Report: The Protestant Community in the Irish Republic* (Dublin, 1975), p. 155.
58   Letter dated 1 March 1947 (N.A., D/T, TCD: Financial Position 1946–47, 13962a).
59   Letter dated 4 July 1947 (N.A., D/T, TCD: Financial Position, 1946–47, 13962a).
60   TCD, *Calendar 1946–47*, p. 422.
61   N.A, D/T, University Education: Financial Assistance, S 14018c.
62   UCC, *Calendar, 1949–50*.
63   *Páipéar Bán um Athbheochan na Gaeilge* (Dublin, 1965), pp. 132, 134, 136.
64   Ibid., p. 136.
65   *Reports of Department of Education, 1928–29 to 1960–61*. Percentages have been rounded to nearest first place of decimal.
66   *Report of the Department of Education, 1940–41*, p. 16. The report only provided figures for lay teachers.
67   DD vol. 66, 31 March 1937, col. 127. The figures refer to lay and religious teachers.
68   DD vol. 44, 28 Oct. 1932, col. 750.
69   *Report of the Department of Education, 1927–28*, p. 50.
70   *Report of the Department of Education, 1929–30*, p. 31 [very few … We do not have enough clever teachers].
71   Ibid., pp. 31, 35.
72   Donnchadh Ó Briain, DD vol. 55, 4 April 1935, col. 1982.
73   *Irish Schools Weekly*, 19 Feb. 1927.
74   *Rules and Regulations for National Schools* (Dublin, 1932), pp. 47–8.
75   Ibid., p. 52.
76   Ibid.
77   T.J. O'Connell, *A History of the INTO: 100 Years of Progress* (Dublin, 1968), pp. 383–4.
78   *Rules and Regulations for National Schools*, p. 53.
79   *Report of the Department of Education, 1931–32*, p. 20.

80   Issue of circulars in Irish (D/Ed. Library, File 32124).
81   *Report of the Department of Education, 1930–31*, p. 41.
82   *Report of the Department of Education, 1929–30*, p. 65.
83   N.A., D/T, Advancement of Irish: State Support, S 11193.
84   *Report of the Department of Education, 1944–45*, p. 24.
85   *An Páipéar Bán um Athbheochan na Gaeilge*, p. 118.
86   For a brief history of the vocational sector see, for example, John Coolahan, *Irish Education: History and Structure* (Dublin, 1981).
87   *An Páipéar Bán um athbheochan na Gaeilge*, pp. 120, 124, 126.
88   James Dillon, DD vol. 44, 28 Oct. 1932, col. 743–4.
89   For example, DD vol. 44, 28 Oct. 1932, col. 714.
90   *Report of the Department of Education, 1944–45*, p. 24 [with diligence].
91   *Report of the Department of Education, 1960–61*, p. 10.
92   *Irish Schools Weekly*, 24 May 1941.
93   Noel Browne, *Against the Tide* (Dublin, 1986), p. 9.
94   Ibid.

Notes on Chapter Four

1   Brian Ó Cuív 'Irish Language and Literature, 1691–1845', in T.W. Moody and W.E. Vaughan (eds), *N.H.I.* vol. iv (Oxford, 1986), pp. 388, 390.
2   *Report of the Department of Education, 1924–26*, p. 93.
3   An Gúm: Beginnings (N.A., D/T, Publications in Irish: An Gúm, S 9538).
4   *Comisiún na Gaeltachta* (Dublin, 1926), p. 18.
5   *Statement of Government Policy on Recommendations of the Commissioners* (Dublin, n.d.), p. 7.
6   J.M. O'Sullivan, DD vol. 21, 19 Oct. 1927, col. 169–70.
7   Tomás Ó Deirg, DD vol. 61, 24 March 1936, col. 109.
8   *Report of the Department of Education, 1929–30*, p. 31. [A new idea would be to teach infants without the use of books. Teachers have too much faith in books, some of which are of little merit, and they find it difficult to work without them.]
9   Publication of books (N.A., D/Fin., Irish: Production of Short Stories Suitable for Children, S 18/4/31).
10   David Greene, 'Fifty Years of Writing in Irish', *Studies*, lv (1966), p. 51.
11   DD vol. 29, 11 April 1929, col. 297 [dangerous to the spirit of nationalism].
12   *Report of the Board of Education, Journal of the General Synod* (1923), p. 213, quoted in Valerie Jones, 'The Attitudes of the Church of Ireland Board of Education to Textbooks in National Schools, 1922–67', *Irish Educational Studies* 11 (Spring, 1992), p. 74.
13   Valerie Jones, 'The Attitudes of the Church of Ireland Board of Education to Textbooks in National Schools, 1922–67', *Irish Educational Studies* 11 (Spring, 1992), p. 73.
14   Michael Tierney, DD vol. 23, 1 June 1928, col. 2515.
15   Valerie Jones, 'The Attitudes of the Church of Ireland Board of Education to Textbooks in National Schools, 1922–67', *Irish Educational Studies* 11 (Spring, 1992), p. 75.
16   *The Leader*, Nov. 1939. Quoted in Bernard Shane, *The Emergency: Neutral Ireland 1939–45* (Dublin, 1987), p. 107.
17   INTO, *A Plan for Education* (Dublin, 1947), p. 118.

18 Irish Labour Party, *Challenge and Change in Education* (Dublin, 1963), p. 33.
19 Minutes of meeting between Eamon de Valera and private secretary, 3 July 1945 (N.A., D/T, Publications in Irish: An Gúm, S 9538).
20 INTO, *Official Programme of Annual Congress* (1955), p. 26.
21 *Report of the Department of Education, 1960–61*, p. 12.
22 *Report of the Department of Education, 1924–26*, p. 93.
23 J.M. O'Sullivan, DD vol. 19, 11 May 1927, col. 2200.
24 *Report of the Department of Education, 1927–28*, p. 49. The phrase used was 'dá chonstaic is mó'.
25 Ibid., p. 50 [high academic qualifications].
26 Radio broadcast, 17 March 1943, in Maurice Moynihan (ed.), *Speeches and Statements by Eamon de Valera* (Dublin, 1980), p. 468; Dublin, 7 Feb. 1949 in ibid., p. 524.
27 Letter from Comhdháil to Department of Education dated 9 Feb. 1954 (N.A., D/T, Irish Language: Development in the Schools, S 7801b) [the great lack of texts in Irish].
28 Letter from Sáirséal agus Dill to Frank Aiken, n.d. (N.A., D/T, Irish Language: Development in the Schools, S 7801b) [something positive].
29 Briefing from Sáirséal agus Dill of 14 June 1954 explaining situation (N.A., D/T, Irish Language: Development in the Schools, S 7801c).
30 *Report of the Council of Education: Curriculum of Secondary Schools* (Dublin, 1962), p. 310.
31 Ibid.
32 Irish Labour Party, *Challenge and Change in Education*, p. 33.
33 *Irish Schools Weekly*, 22 Sept. 1928.
34 *An Coimisiún um Athbheochan na Gaeilge: An Tuarascáil Dheiridh* (Dublin, n.d. [1964]), p. 251.
35 N.A., D/Fin., Scheme for production of works of general literature in Irish: form of type to be used in printing, S 018/0018/30.
36 James Fitzgerald-Kenny, DD vol. 29, 8 May 1929.
37 N.A., D/Fin., Scheme for production of works of general literature in Irish: form of type to be used in printing, S 018/0018/30.
38 Letter from D/Education to D/Finance, 31 Jan. 1931 (N.A., D/Fin., Scheme for production of works of general literature in Irish, S 018/0018/30).
39 Letter from D/Education to D/Finance, 19 May 1930 (N.A., D/Fin., Secondary School Irish Texts Scheme: Typing in Gaelic Characters of Fr. Dineen's Virgil, *Aeneid I*, S18/20/30).
40 D/Finance, Circular 15/31, 18 April 1932 (N.A., D/Fin., Scheme for production of works of general literature in Irish: form of type to be used in printing, S 018/0018/30).
41 Letter from Irish Publishers' Association to D/Education, 29 April 1953 (N.A., D/T, Publications in Irish: An Gúm, S 9538).
42 *An Páipéar Bán um Athbheochan na Gaeilge: Tuarascáil don Tréimhse Dár Chríoch 31 Márta 1968* (Dublin, 1969), p. 22.
43 Dr Johanna Pollak, 'On Teaching Irish', 26 May 1943 (N.A., D/T, Irish Language: Development in Schools, S 7801).
44 INTO, *Inquiry into Use of Irish as a Medium of Instruction* (Dublin, 1942), pp. 63–4.
45 Department of Education, *Litriú Simplithe Caighdeánach Gaeilge a Thabhairt isteach i Scola Náisiúnta*, circular 8/48 [the use of old and unusual forms of spelling is an obstacle in the development of Irish].

46 Ibid.
47 Ibid., [standard spelling].
48 Department of Education, 'Irish Spelling', circular 14/50.
49 Letter from Comhdháil to D/Education 25 June 1953 (N.A., D/T, Publications in Irish: An Gúm, S 9538) [what is correct and incorrect].
50 *Gramadach na Gaeilge agus Litriú na Gaeilge* (Dublin, 1958), p. viii.
51 INTO, *Inquiry into Use of Irish as a Medium of Instruction*, p. 63.
52 *Irish Schools Weekly*, 18 July 1936.
53 Ibid.
54 Frank MacDermott (Fine Gael /Independent), DD vol. 65, 17 Feb. 1937, col. 428.
55 N.A., D/T, Publications in Irish: An Gúm, S 9538.
56 Memo dated 3 Oct. 1945 (N.A., D/T, Publications in Irish: An Gúm, S 9538).
57 Letter from D/Education to D/Finance, 13 Jan. 1937 (N.A., D/Fin., An Gael Óg, S 018/0002/37).
58 Memo, 24 July 1936 (N.A., D/Fin., An Gael Óg, S 018/0002/37).
59 Letter from D/Education to D/Finance, 17 Jan. 1937 (N.A., D/Fin., An Gael Óg, S 018/0002/37).
60 A newspaper, described as 'the first Irish newspaper for children' (*Irish Schools Weekly*, 24 Feb. 1923), with a similar title was launched on St Patrick's Day, 1923, but subsequently appears to have folded.
61 INTO, *A Plan for Education*, p. 112.
62 *Irish Independent*, 16 Dec. 1936.
63 For a survey of work in Irish see David Greene, 'Fifty Years of Writing in Irish', *Studies*, lv (1966), pp. 51–9; Proinsias MacCana, *Literature in Irish* (Dublin, 1980); Breandán Ó Doibhlin, 'Irish Literature in the Contemporary Situation', *Léachtaí Cholm Chille*, 1970; Aodh de Blacam, *Gaelic Literature Surveyed* (Dublin, 1929, 1973); and J.E. Caerwyn Williams and Máirín Ní Mhuiríosa, *Traidisiún Liteartha na nGael* (Dublin, 2nd edn, 1985).
64 *Sunday Independent*, 17 June 1990.
65 *Irish Independent*, 16 Dec.1936.
66 *Irish Independent*, 28 Dec. 1936.
67 Letter from S.C. Ó Faoilleacháin to D/Finance dated 20 Jan. 1937 (N.A., D/T, Publications in Irish: An Gúm, S 9538).
68 Francis MacManus, 'The Literature of the Period', in Francis McManus (ed.), *The Years of the Great Test, 1926–39* (Dublin, 1967).
69 Julia Carlson (ed.), 'Introduction' in *Banned in Ireland: Censorship and the Irish Writer* (London, 1990), p. 1. See also Donal Ó Drisceoil, *Censorship in Ireland: 1939–1945* (Cork, 1996).
70 Letter dated 4 Oct. 1951 (N.A., D/T, Publications Irish: An Gúm, S 9538).
71 *Irish Times*, 6 Sept. 1952.
72 N.A., R/Gael., Bord na Leabhar Gaeilge: Fiosrúcháin, C 1/8/1 [for books published as school text books].
73 Ibid. [and that it was necessary to make them available as part of the new Irish literature].
74 For short biographies of these writers see Ciarán Ó Cúlacháin, *Tobar na Gaeilge: Litríocht agus Teanga* (Dublin, 1980), ch. 8 and Donncha Ó Riain, *Stair na Gaeilge: Litríocht agus Teanga* (Dublin, 1996), chs 12 and 13.
75 N.A., D/T, Publications in Irish: An Gúm, S 4538.
76 DD vol. 44, 26 Oct. 1932, col. 382–3.

77 Letter from D/Education to D/Finance, 17 Feb. 1931 (N.A., D/Fin., Publication of books in Irish: production of short stories suitable for children, S 18/4/31).

78 *Comisiún um Athbheochan na Gaeilge: Summary in English of Final Report*, p. 85.

79 N.A., R/Gael., An Ghaeilge; nuachtáin agus irisláir; deontais, clodóireacht Gaeilge, C 1/7.

80 INTO, *Inquiry into Use of Irish as a Medium of Instruction*, p. 63.

81 *Report of the Department of Education, 1960–61*, p. 12.

Notes on Chapter Five

1 *Report of the Council of Education* (Dublin, 1955), p. 168.

2 N.A., D/Fin., Financial provision be made in the breac-Gaeltacht to pay old people to teach Irish to their grandchildren, S 18/6/31.

3 N.A., D/T, Staid na Gaeilge: Scéim Scoileanna Oíche, S 11282. See also Tomás Ó Deirg, DD vol. 87, 1 June 1942, col. 653–4 and INTO, *A Plan for Education* (Dublin, 1947), p. 121 [they would hardly have sufficient Irish to speak it fluently … all sorts of entertainment].

4 Statement by Eamon de Valera on the Civil Service and the Irish revival, April 1940 (N.A., D/T, Advancement of Irish: Appeal by Taoiseach to Civil Servants, S 11700) [to give the general public direction in terms of the work regarding Irish].

5 *Comisiún um Athbheochan na Gaeilge: Summary in English of Final Report* (Dublin, 1963), p. 18.

6 DD vol. 34, 21 May 1930, col. 2195–6.

7 *Commission of Inquiry into the Civil Service: Memoranda of Evidence, 1932–35* (Dublin, n.d.[1935]), p. 6.

8 Ibid.

9 *Commission of Inquiry into the Civil Service, 1932–35: Interim and Final Report* (Dublin, n.d. [1935]), p. 170.

10 *Commission of Inquiry into the Civil Service: Memoranda of Evidence, 1932–35*, p. 6.

11 *Irish Schools Weekly*, 19 Nov. 1927.

12 Quoted in Leon Ó Broin, *No Man's Man* (Dublin, 1982), p. 128.

13 Letter from D/Finance to D/Taoiseach, 4 Aug. 1933 (N.A., D/T, Irish: Facilities for Study—Special Leave for Civil Servants, S 6671 A).

14 *Commission of Inquiry into the Civil Service, 1932–35: Interim and Final Report*, p. 104.

15 *Comisiún um Athbheochan na Gaeilge: Summary in English of Final Report*, p. 23.

16 Statement in April 1940 on Civil Service and the Irish revival (N.A., D/T, Advancement of Irish: Appeal by Taoiseach to Civil Servants, S 11700).

17 DD vol. 76, 23 May 1939, quoted in Donal O'Sullivan, *The Irish Free State and its Senate* (London, 1940).

18 Donal O'Sullivan, *The Irish Free State and its Senate*, p. 19.

19 DD vol. 168, 4 June 1958, col. 1240.

20 DD vol. 182, 25 May 1960, col. 193–4.

21 Liam McNiffe, A *History of the Garda Síochána* (Dublin, 1997), pp. 44, 55.

22 Ibid., p. 126.

23 Ibid., p. 131.

24 Ibid., p. 128.

25 J.J. Lee, *Ireland 1912–1995: Politics and Society* (Cambridge, 1989), p. 135.

26 *Comisiún um Athbheochan na Gaeilge: Summary in English of Final Report*, p. 22.

27 *Report of Public Services Organisation Review Group, 1966–69* (Dublin, 1969), p. 91.
28 Ibid.
29 *Commission of Inquiry into the Civil Service, 1932–35: Interim and Final Report*, p. 104.
30 Department of the Public Service, Circular concerning Irish requirements in the Civil Service, 9/74.
31 Department of the Public Service, Circular concerning Irish requirements in the Civil Service, 43/75.
32 Further relevant circulars are Department of the Public Service, Circular concerning proficiency in Irish for promotion purposes: Civil Service Commission tests, 17/81 and Department of Finance, Circular concerning credit for proficiency in both Irish and English in confined promotion competitions, 30/90.
33 Basil Chubb, *The Government and Politics of Ireland* (England, 1986), p. 12.
34 See Adrian M. Kelly, 'The Gaelic League and the introduction of compulsory Irish into the Free State Education System', *Oideas*, vol. 41 (Winter 1993), pp. 46–57.
35 As quoted in Leon Ó Broin, *No Man's Man*, p. 127.
36 Ibid., pp. 127–8.
37 DD vol. 94, 13 June 1944, col. 277–8.
38 E. Brian Titley, *Church, State and the Control of Schooling in Ireland, 1900–1944* (Belfast, 1983), p. 135.
39 Irish was used in the following columns in DD vol. 21: 17, 19–20, 70, 158, 169, 170, 178, 179, 210, 281, 282, 365, 452, 583, 728, 857–9, 935, 1023, 1053–4, 1056, 1057, 1268, 1280, 1360, 1368, 1436, 1538–40, 1542, 1558–60, 1591, 1722, 1725, 1842, 1869, 1870, 1871, 1875 and 1936–40.
40 E.g. DD vol. 21, 19 Oct. 1927, col. 169–70.
41 DD vol. 21, 2 Nov. 1927, col. 585.
42 E.g. DD vol. 44, 26 Oct. 1932, col. 382–3.
43 Maurice Moynihan (ed.), *Speeches and Statements by Eamon de Valera 1917–1973* (Dublin and New York, 1980), p. 190.
44 Ibid., pp. 372–3.
45 Ibid., p. 230.
46 Ibid., p. 342.
47 Donal O'Sullivan, *The Irish Free State and its Senate*, p. 572.
48 Richard Anthony, DD vol. 44, 2 Nov. 1932, col. 799.
49 DD vol. 61, 24 March 1936, col. 111.
50 DD vol. 182, 24 May 1960, col. 12.
51 Noel Browne, *Against the Tide* (Dublin, 1986), pp. 119–20.
52 Ronan Fanning, *Independent Ireland* (Dublin, 1983), p. 148.
53 *Fianna Fáil: An Chéad Tréimhse* (Dublin, 1960), p. 85. [From the outset Fianna Fáil recognised the importance of Irish in the life of the nation. The cry 'Ireland free; Ireland Irish speaking' was not without meaning.]
54 Speech by Seán Lemass at a meeting of election workers at Fianna Fáil headquarters, 20 Sept. 1961 (N.A., D/T, Irish language policy, 6689 D/61).
55 *Irish Times*, 14 Sept. 1961.
56 *Leinster Express*, 16 Sept. 1961.
57 Speech by Seán Lemass at a meeting of election workers at Fianna Fáil headquarters, 20 Sept. 1961 (N.A., D/T, Irish language policy, 6689 D/61).
58 See for example, *Irish Times*, 14 Sept. 1961; *Galway Observer*, 16 Sept. 1961; *Longford Leader*, 16 Sept. 1961.
59 Department of the Public Service, Circular concerning Irish requirements in the

Civil Service, 9/74.

60   *Irish Times*, 4 April 1977.

61   See Mary E. Daly, 'Literacy and Language Change in the Late Nineteenth
     Century and Early Twentieth Century' in Mary E. Daly and David Dickson (eds),
     *The Origins of Popular Literacy in Ireland: Language Change and Educational Development,
     1700–1920* (Dublin, 1990), p. 165.

62   *Comisiún na Gaeltachta* (Dublin, 1926), pp. 6–7.

63   Problem with £2 grant in Athboy (N.A, R/Gael., Grants of £2 by D/Education
     to parents of Irish-speaking children at Athboy settlement, F 7/4/36).

64   Copy in N.A., D/T, University Courses in Irish: Scholarships and Prizes, S14109.

65   Nóta—An Fhíor-Ghaeltacht (N.A., D/T, University Courses in Irish: Scholar-
     ships and Prizes, S 14109). [Currently, the entirely Irish speaking areas comprise:
     (1) Corca Dhuibhne to the west and north west of Dingle; (2) the Aran Islands
     and Connemara from the outskirts of Galway City to Caiseal; (3) the centre west
     of Donegal and some areas on a line from Ard na Rátha to Cealla Beaga.]

66   *Comisiún na Gaeltachta*, p. 10.

67   Ibid., pp. 15–16.

68   Ibid., pp. 16–17.

69   Ibid., p. 25.

70   DD vol. 23, 31 May 1928, col. 2477. [The area which includes Clanna Caoilte
     and An Sciobairín is Irish speaking, and there are at least twelve schools there
     which are not bilingual while Irish is taught badly as a subject in half of them.
     Irish is being destroyed in such schools.]

71   *Comisiún na Gaeltachta*, p. 58.

72   Ibid.

73   *Report of the Department of Education, 1930–31*, p. 24. This was later quoted in Shán
     Ó Cuív, *The Problem of Irish in the Schools* (Dublin, 1936), p. 14.

74   *Statement of Government Policy on Recommendations of the Commission* (Dublin, n.d.), p. 9.

75   Department of Education, *Rules and Regulations* (Dublin, 1932), p. 15.

76   Letter from Sean MacEntee, Minister for Finance, to Eamon de Valera, Aug.
     1935 (N.A., D/T, Galway: Development as an Irish-Speaking Centre, S 9303).

77   N.A., D/T, Galway: Development as an Irish-Speaking Centre, S 9303.

78   *Irish Press*, 27 May 1936 [as Irish as this town].

79   *Report of the Council of Education: Curriculum of the Primary School* (Dublin, 1955), p. 156.

80   John MacNamara, *Bilingualism and Primary Education* (Britain, 1966), p. 318.

81   *Irish Times*, 15 Sept. 1938. [The people living in Irish speaking areas did not show
     much interest in those offering them advice; they knew they had to make a living
     irrespective of Irish. They could speak Irish, but the majority of people with the
     best jobs in the country could not … those in power thought a little was good
     enough for the Irish speaking areas.]

82   Tomás Ó Deirg, DD vol. 51, 21 Mar. 1934, col. 1347–8.

83   Coiste Eadar Roinne, minutes of meeting 12 Feb. 1952 (N.A., R/Gaeltacht,
     Deontas £5, C 2/6).

84   *Report of the Department of Education, 1934–35*, p. 24. [According to reports the
     position of Irish in the totally Irish speaking areas and the areas in which Irish is
     spoken by many people has improved over the past year, and the £2 grant is
     helping a lot in terms of the language. It is said that those on the edges of Irish
     speaking areas are trying to stop the use of English so they can claim the grant.]

85   See for example *Irish Schools Weekly*, 21 March 1936.

86   Letter dated 5 Nollaig 1957 (N.A., D/T, Advancement of Irish: State Support,

S 11193) [in the very heart of the English speaking areas].

87   An Deontas £5: Treoracha do Chigirí, June 1957 (N.A., R/Gael., An Deontas £5: Modha Oibre, R 5).

88   Tomás Ó Deirg, DD vol. 101, 22 May 1946, col. 553.

89   *Comisiún na Gaeltachta*, p. 56.

90   Summary of committee's observations on the Comhdháil memorandum, 23 Nov. 1953 (N.A., D/T, Development of the Irish Language: Use of Radio and Television, A 13756).

91   Comhdháil Náisiúnta na Gaeilge: memorandum for the Taoiseach regarding a Board for the Gaeltacht (N.A., R/Gael, Aireacht na Gaeltachta—bunú, A 22).

92   Ruairí Mac Aoidh, SD, vol. 45, 2 Nov. 1955, col. 459 [the expansion and preservation of Irish speaking areas … an independent board].

93   Notes on motion put down in Seanad Éireann regarding establishment of a board to preserve and develop the fíor-Ghaeltacht, Oct. 1955 (N.A., R/Gael., Aireacht na Gaeltachta—bunú, A 22).

94   SD, vol. 45, 2 Nov. 1955, col. 488. [Clearly, a ministry would have strength and advantages. The minister would have a definite job to do and would have the ear of the other ministers who would listen to him.]

95   Ministers and Secretaries (Amendment) Act, 1956.

96   *Derry Journal*, 17 Aug. 1956.

97   *Pictorial*, 20 Oct. 1956.

98   *Connacht Sentinel*, 28 Feb. 1956. See also *The Kerryman*, 28 April 1956, and *Pictorial*, 18 Feb. 1956.

99   *Connacht Sentinel*, 28 Feb. 1956.

100   *Pictorial*, 18 Feb. 1956.

101   DD vol. 192, 15 Nov. 1961, col. 157.

102   *Report of the Public Services Organisation Review Group, 1966–69*, pp. 313–4.

103   *Páipéar Bán um Athbheochan na Gaeilge*, p. 170.

104   *Comisiún na Gaeltachta*, p. 58.

105   See Brian Ó Cuív, 'Irish Language and Literature, 1691–1845', in T.W. Moody and W.E. Vaughan (eds), *A New History of Ireland*, vol. iv (Oxford, 1986), pp. 376–7.

106   John Edwards, 'Irish Revival: Success or Failure', unpublished paper delivered to the international conference on language revival in honour of the centenary of modern Hebrew, Jerusalem, Oct. 1990, p. 2. See also D.H. Akenson, *The Irish Education Experiment: The National Education System in the Nineteenth Century* (London and Toronto, 1970), p. 380.

107   *An Claidheamh Soluis*, 30 June 1900 and 25 Aug. 1900.

108   Lecture given by Micheál Ó Síothcháin to the Society of Colm Cille, Maynooth, in Peader MacLoingsigh (ed.), *A Call to Ireland* (Ireland, 1911, 1944), p. 14.

109   M.P. O'Hickey, *Language and Nationality* (Waterford, 1918), pp. 4, 5.

110   *Irish Schools Weekly*, 22 Jan. 1927.

111   Ibid.

112   *Irish Catholic Directory*, 21 Dec. 1932, p. 571.

113   Maurice Moynihan, *Speeches and Statements*, p. 342.

114   N.A., D/T, Staid na Gaeilge: Scéim Scoileanna Oíche, S 11282. [Even outside the context of learning Irish, the scheme is closely tied in with the work of the church, namely, the effort to keep young people in the countryside and to provide them with pastimes with which the church would agree.]

115   *Comisiún um Athbheochan na Gaeilge: Summary in English of Final Report*, p. 94.

116   Maurice Moynihan, *Speeches and Statements*, p. 606. [Clerics from every church are

supportive of Irish—bishops, priests and ministers. The majority of teachers, brothers and nuns are on side.]

117 *Acta et decreta concilii plenarii episoparum Hiberniae quod habitum est apud Maynutiam die 2 Augusti et diebus sequentibus usque Ad Diem 15 Augusti 1927* (Dublin, 1929), p. 109.

118 N.A., D/T, An Baile is Gealaí in Éirinn: Request for Patronage of President', S 17198/61. For a short history of Glór na nGael see Pádraig Ó Fiannachta, 'Stair Ghlór na nGael', *An Sagart*, 3, xxx (1987), 19–28.

119 Gearóid Ó Tuathaigh, 'The State and the Language since 1922', *Irish Times*, 4 April 1977.

120 Patrick Coogan (Ind.), DD vol. 94, 13 June 1944, col. 354.

121 Department of Education, Circular re showing of health films in national schools, 8/49.

122 Department of Education, Circular re Gael-Linn: An Scannán *Saoirse?*, 14/62.

123 *Radio Éireann: Report on Broadcasting, 1937*, p. 1.

124 Quoted in David O'Donoghue, *Hitler's Irish Voices: The Story of German Radio's Wartime Irish Service* (Belfast, 1998), p. 46.

125 Conradh na Gaeilge, *An Gaedheal agus an Radio* (Dublin, 1936). [A pamphlet giving information to Irish people on the use that can be made of the radio and what is necessary in that regard.]

126 *Radio Éireann Report*, 1939, p. 11.

127 Report in *Irish Independent*, 15 Oct. 1951.

128 Report on the use of Irish in Radio Éireann, June 1953 (N.A., D/T, Development of the Irish Language: Use of Radio and Television, A 13756).

129 Meeting between Comhdháil Náisiúnta na Gaeilge and the Taoiseach, 1 Aug. 1952 (N.A., D/T, Irish Language: Development in the Schools, S 7801).

130 INTO, *Official Programme of Annual Congress* (1957), resolution 38 [that will light in their hearts a love for Irish].

131 *Comisiún um Athbheochan na Gaeilge; Summary in English of Final Report*, p. 87.

132 Risteárd Ó Glaisne, *Radio na Gaeltachta* (Galway, 1982), p. 3.

133 N.A., D/T, Staid na Gaeidhilge: Moltaí P.A. Uí Síothcháin, S 11321.

134 *Comisiún um Athbheochan na Gaeilge: Summary in English of Final Report*, p. 87.

135 *An Páipéar Bán um Athbheochan na Gaeilge*, p. 28.

136 Gearóid Ó Tuathaigh, 'The State and the Language since 1922', *Irish Times*, 4 April 1977.

137 Letter from Connradh na Gaeilge to Private Secretary of the Taoiseach, 23 Feb. 1961 (N.A., D/T, Advancement of Irish: Proposals of Coiste Gnótha Connradh na Gaeilge, S 11197, D/61) [an additional subject on the school programme, something that caused people to fail in exams, or that helped them get minor State jobs].

Notes on Conclusion

1 J.J. Lee speaks of the language recovering some of its 'dignity' through the work of the Gaelic League (*Ireland 1912–1984: Politics and Society* (Cambridge, 1990), p. 673).

2 DD vol. 83, 27 May 1941, col. 1023.

3 See for example John Costello, DD vol. 66, 1 April 1937, col. 195; J.M. O'Sullivan, DD vol. 90, 12 May 1943, col. 104; James Dillon, DD vol. 90, 12 May 1943, col. 122.

162   *Compulsory Irish: Language and Education in Ireland, 1870s–1970s*

4   DD vol. 159, 18 July 1956, col. 1279.
5   DD vol. 168, 3 June 1958, col. 1080–1.
6   *Comisiún na Gaeltachta* (Dublin, 1926), p. 12.
7   N.A., D/T, Irish Language: Development in the Schools, S 7801. See ch. 1.
8   Dr Johanna Pollak, 'On Teaching Irish', 26 May 1943 (N.A., D/T, Irish Language: Development in Schools, S 7801).
9   *Irish Independent*, 25 Aug. 1954 [examination].
10 See J.J. Byrne, DD vol. 29, 17 April 1929, col. 405.
11 INTO, *Report of Committee of Inquiry into Use of Irish as a Teaching Medium to Children whose Home Language is English* (1942), p. 24.
12 Letter in *Irish Times*, 6 Sept. 1944.
13 Richard Anthony (Labour Party), DD vol. 35, 31 May 1930, col. 2190.
14 DD vol. 83, 27 May 1941, col. 1022.
15 *Report of the Department of Education, 1930–31*, p. 24.
16 John MacNamara, *Bilingualism and Primary Education* (Britain, 1966), p. 318. See ch. 5.
17 *Report of the Department of Education, 1933–4*, p. 21 [a time of experimentation for teachers].
18 'Comisiún i dtaobh na Gaedhilge san stát sheirbhís i dtaobh scéime ar mhaithe leis an nGaedhilg ar fuaid na tuaithe', c.1939 (N.A., D/T, Staid na Gaeilge: Scéim Scoileanna Oíche, S 11282). See also Tomás Ó Deirg, DD vol. 87, 1 June 1942, col. 653–4 and INTO, *A Plan for Education* (Dublin, 1947), p. 121.
19 'Comisiún i dtaobh na Gaedhilge san Stát Sheirbhís i dtaobh scéime ar mhaithe leis an nGaedhilg ar fuaid na tuaithe', c.1939 (N.A., D/T, Staid na Gaeilge: Scéim Scoileanna Oíche, S 11282). [Some people aged eighteen years or over would be entering who would hardly have enough Irish to speak it as it would be four or more years since they had left school. Even those who had just left primary school would hardly have enough Irish to speak it fluently.]
20 Ibid.
21 DD vol. 110, 4 May 1948, col. 1103.
22 *Report of the Council of Education: Curriculum of the Secondary School* (Dublin, 1962), p. 118.
23 Fine Gael, *Policy for a Just Society: 3. Education* (Dublin, 1966), p. 63.
24 J.J. Lee, *Ireland, 1912–1985: Politics and Society*, p. 134.
25 This was pointed out by Dr Johanna Pollak in her report submitted to the Department of the Taoiseach in May 1943 (N.A., D/T, Irish Language: Development in the Schools, S 7801).
26 See Ronan Fanning, *Independent Ireland* (Dublin, 1983), p. 82.
27 *Irish Schools Weekly*, 6 April 1929. See also Thomas Mullen (Fianna Fáil), DD vol. 29, 17 April 1929, col. 410 and DD vol. 87, 1 June 1942, col. 693.
28 DD vol. 29, 17 April 1929, col. 404.
29 Shán Ó Cuív, *The Problem of Irish in the Schools* (Dublin, 1936), p. 11.
30 *Report of the Department of Education, 1934–35*, p. 24 [in most schools rather than being spoken by young people outside of school].
31 DD vol. 80, 9 June 1940, col. 1579–80. [What is the key that will open that lock?]
32 DD vol. 86, 20 May 1942, col. 2446 [the entire nation … still viewing Irish as though it was nothing more than an ordinary academic subject].
33 *Irish Schools Weekly*, 22 Jan. 1949.
34 *Comisiún um Athbheochan na Gaeilge: Summary in English of Final Report* (Dublin, 1963), p. 58.

35 *Report of the Council of Education: Curriculum of the Secondary School*, p. 128.
36 *Comisiún um Athbheochan na Gaeilge: Summary in English of Final Report*, p. 16.
37 John Edwards, 'Irish Revival: Success or Failure?' A paper to the international conference on language revival in honour of the centenary of modern Hebrew, Jerusalem, 15–18 Oct. 1990 (Typescript).
38 *An Páipéar Bán um Athbheochan na Gaeilge: Progress Report for the Period Ended 31 March 1968* (Dublin, 1968), pp. 38–42.
39 *Irish Times*, 22 Sept. 1966.

Appendix I

Irish National Teachers Organization
Inquiry into the use of Irish as a Teaching Medium
ORDERED BY CONGRESS, 1936.

QUESTIONNAIRE

INTRODUCTORY

The Killarney Congress directed the C.E.C. to have an inquiry made into the use of Irish as a teaching medium, and to issue a detailed report of their investigation.

In order to obtain evidence which will enable them to arrive at well considered conclusions, they have directed that the following Questionnaire be issued, and **that all members who have at any time made use of Irish as a teaching medium** should be invited to assist the Executive by answering the queries set out thereon.

It should be particularly noted:

1. That only those teachers who themselves have taught through Irish should answer the Questionnaire.
2. That teachers should answer the queries in the particular section in which they have had experience.
3. That all replies should be given as a result of personal **experience**, irrespective of one's **opinions** or of the experience or opinions of others.
4. That this Questionnaire will be regarded as a **strictly confidential** document. The facts and opinions set down will be used to enable the Committee to come to general decisions, but the contents will not be disclosed to any person or body outside the Executive.

Your assistance in this matter will be appreciated.

Replies to the Questionnaire **should be sent to Head Office** not later than November 1st, 1936.

By order of the C.E.C.

T.J. O'CONNELL,

General Secretary.

Head Office:
9 GARDINER PLACE, DUBLIN,
Sept. 7th, 1936.

**N.B. – The information set out in this Form will be regarded as
strictly confidential.**

SECTION I.

(*a*) THE TEACHER

Name of Teacher .... Position in School ....

If trained .... No. of years' service .... Present Rating ....

Qualifications in Irish .... Native Speaker? ....

(*b*) THE SCHOOL

Name of School .... Roll No. .... County ....

Average attendance (year ending 30/6/36) .... No. of Teachers in the School ...

Is school district officially scheduled as **Fior Gaeltacht**, Gaeltacht, Breac Gaeltacht
or Galltacht?

....

SECTION II. – Infants.

*(To be answered only by Teachers who have taught Infant Standards.
Reasons for answers should be given where possible.)*

1. Number of pupils enrolled in Infants ....

2. Specify whether Junior, Senior, or both inclusive ....

3. How long have you taught the "all Irish" programme to Infants? ....

4. Do all the pupils derive benefit from Instruction through the medium of Irish
   equal to what they would receive through the medium of English?

   ....

   If not, state the Percentage who:

   (*a*) derive equal benefit ....

   (*b*) derive a good measure of benefit ....

   (*c*) derive very little benefit ....

6. Does the child get a sound grasp of numerical values and processes when taught
   entirely through Irish?

   ....

   ....

   ....

7. Does the child acquire adequate powers of expression in regard to his everyday experiences when taught solely through the medium of Irish?

....

....

....

....

....

8. Is there any connection between the medium of instruction (Irish or English) and the extent of the strain on the pupils?

....

....

....

....

....

9. Apart from the question of the revival of Irish, do you consider it better from the point of view of the mental and physical development of the child that he should be taught entirely through Irish or that Irish and English should be used?

....

....

....

....

....

10. From the point of view of the language revival alone, do you consider it better that the use of Irish as a medium of instruction should be continued throughout the entire school day? (Give reasons and suggestions, if any)

....

....

....

....

....

SECTION III. – Standards, I, II, and III.

(To be answered only by Teachers who have taught these Standards.
Reasons for answers should be given where possible.)

Give hereunder your experience in teaching **Arithmetic** through Irish:

TABLE I.

Standard	(a) Number of years you have taught Arithmetic through Irish	(b) Pupils' previous experience in this subject through Irish	(c) Was instruction in (a) Bilingual or solely through Irish?
I.	....	....	....
	....	....	....
II.	....	....	....
	....	....	....
III.	....	....	....

11. Do all the pupils derive benefit from instruction through Irish equal to that which they would receive through English? ....

    If not, state the Percentage who:

    (a) derive equal benefit ....

    (b) derive a good measure of benefit ....

    (c) derive very little benefit ....

12. In teaching Arithmetic through the medium of Irish, what has been your experience *re*:
    (a) Ready reproduction of tables? ....

    ....

    ....

    (b) Pupils' grasp of numerical processes? ....

    ....

    ....

    (c) Solution to problems? ....

    ....

    ....

13. To what extent does teaching Arithmetic through Irish in these standards contribute to fluency in the language?

....

....

....

14. Apart from the question of the revival of Irish, do you consider that the mental and physical development of the child is adequately catered for when Arithmetic is taught entirely through Irish?

....

....

SECTION IV. – Standards IV to VII.

(To be answered only by Teachers who have taught these standards.
Reasons for answers should be given where possible.)

Give hereunder your experience in teaching the following subjects through the medium of Irish:

TABLE II

Subject	A. Standard to which Teacher has taught this subject through Irish	B. Number of years Teacher has taught this subject to standard in A through Irish	C. Standards (if any) in which this subject had been taught to same pupils through Irish (other than that in A.)	D. Was instruction in A Bilingual or solely through Irish?
Arithmetic	....	....	....	....
Algebra	....	....	....	....
Geometry	....	....	....	....
History	....	....	....	....
Geography	....	....	....	....
Needlework	....	....	....	....
Singing	....	....	....	....

15. Do all the pupils derive benefit from instruction through Irish equal to that which they would receive through English?

....

If not, state:

TABLE III

Subject	(a) Percentage who derive equal benefit	(b) Percentage who derive a good measure of benefit	(c) Percentage who derive very little benefit	(d) Can content of present programme be effectively covered through Irish?
Arithmetic	....	....	....	....
Algebra	....	....	....	....
Geometry	....	....	....	....
History	....	....	....	....
Geography	....	....	....	....
Needlework	....	....	....	....
Singing	....	....	....	....

16. Apart from the question of the revival of Irish, and regarding only the mental and physical development of the child, what subjects may, **with advantage**, be taught through the medium of Irish?

....

....

17. State which of the subjects in Table III above, when taught through Irish, contribute to fluency on the part of the pupils, and name them in order of preference

....

....

18. Is the teaching of Arithmetic through the medium of Irish in the junior standards a necessary preliminary to its effective teaching through Irish in the Senior standards, and, if so, to what extent?

....

....

SECTION V. – Religious Programme.

19. Do you give religious instruction through the medium of Irish? ....

20. If so, state in which of the following is instruction given
    (*a*) Prayers; (*b*) Catechism; (*c*) Explanation of Catechism and Christian Doctrine; (*d*) Church History; (*e*) Bible History, etc.

    ....

    ....

    ....

21. Do you fulfil the requirements of your Diocesan programme by teaching in Irish alone?

    ....

22. Are you obliged by Diocesan regulation to teach through Irish in whole or in part, or is it a matter of individual choice?

    ....

    ....

SECTION VI. – General.

23. Is it, in your opinion, possible to revive Irish unless subjects are taught through that medium?

    ....

    ....

    ....

    ....

24. Have you – as a result of official suggestion and contrary to your own judgment – taught subjects through the medium of Irish when the necessary conditions were not present – namely, teacher qualified and pupils competent to benefit by the instruction?

    ....

    ....

    ....

    ....

25. Have any of your pupils who have been taught subjects solely through the medium of Irish competed at public examinations?

....

....

....

Did those pupils answer their examination papers through the medium of Irish?

....

....

....

26. What is your opinion regarding the suitability of the Text Books used in Irish?

....

....

....

27. Are the same Text Books in Irish suitable to Galltacht and Gaeltacht?

....

....

....

28. What is your opinion regarding the suitability of Text Books, in Irish, on the other subjects?

....

....

....

SECTION VII. – Observations.

Members are invited to give their observations regarding any aspect of this question not dealt with in the Questionnaire, and which, in their opinion, will help the Executive in coming to a proper conclusion.

Bibliography

Primary Sources

National Archives, Dublin
Department of Education files
Department of Finance files
Roinn na Gaeltachta/Department of the Gaeltacht files
Department of Taoiseach files

Department of Education and Science, Dublin
Library Archives

Works of Reference
Browne, Vincent *The Magill Book of Irish Politics* (Dublin, 1981).
Edwards, John *The Irish Language: An Annotated Bibliography of Sociolinguistic Publications, 1772–1982* (New York, 1983).
Flynn, William J. *The Oireachtas Companion and Saorstát Guide for 1930* (Dublin, 1930).
Flynn, William J. *Irish Parliamentary Handbook 1939* (Dublin, 1939).
Flynn, William J. *Irish Parliamentary Handbook 1945* (Dublin, 1945).
Hickey, D.J. and Doherty, J.E. *A Dictionary of Irish History 1800–1980* (Dublin, 1989).

Official Government Publications
An Páipéar Bán um Athbheochan na Gaeilge: Progress Report for the Period ended 31 March 1966 (Dublin, 1966).
An Páipéar Bán um Athbheochan na Gaeilge: Progress Report for the Period ended 31 March 1968 (Dublin, 1968).
Athbheochan na Gaeilge: Arna Leagan ag an Rialtas faoi Bhráid Gach Tí den Oireachtas, Eanair 1965 (Dublin 1965).
Comisiún na Gaeltachta (Dublin, 1926).
Comisiún um Athbheochan na Gaeilge: Summary in English of Final Report (Dublin, 1963).

Commission of Inquiry into the Civil Service, 1932–35: Interim and Final Report (Dublin, n.d. [1935]).

Commission of Inquiry into the Civil Service: Memoranda of Evidence, 1932–35 (Dublin, n.d. [1935]).

Dáil Éireann, Díospóireachtaí Pairliminte, 1922–1970.

Department of Education, *Notes for Teachers: Irish* (Dublin, 1933).

Department of Education, *Programme for Students in Training, 1924–25.*

Department of Education, *Regulations Regarding Curricula, Certificates, Examinations and Scholarships, with Programme for the Year 1927–8.*

Department of Education, *Regulations Regarding Curricula, etc. 1929–30– 1931–32.*

Department of Education, *Reports of the Department of Education, 1922–1975.*

Department of Education, *Revised Programme of Primary Instruction* (Dublin, 1934).

Department of Education, *Rules and Regulations for National Schools under the Department of Education* (various years).

Department of Education, *Secondary Schools Programme* (various years).

Department of Education, *Secondary School Rules, 1926–27–1974–75.*

Intermediate Education Commissioners, *Rules and Programme, 1924–25* (Dublin, 1925).

Investment in Education: Report of Survey Team Appointed by the Minister for Education in October 1962 (Dublin, 1965).

National Programme Conference, *Report of the First National Programme Conference of Primary Instruction* (Dublin, 1922).

National Programme Conference, *Report of the Second National Programme Conference* (Dublin, 1926).

Public Statutes of the Oireachtas.

Report of Public Services Organisation Review Group, 1966–1969 (Dublin, 1969).

Report of the Council of Education as Presented to the Minister for Education (Dublin, 1955).

Report of the Council of Education as Presented to the Minister for Education: The Curriculum of the Secondary School (Dublin, 1962).

Saorstát Éireann Official Handbook (Dublin, 1932).

Seanad Éireann, Díospóireachtaí 1922–1970.

Statement of Government Policy on Recommendations of the Commission (on the Gaeltacht) (Dublin, n.d.).

Other Printed Primary Sources

Acta et decreta concilii plenarii episcoparum Hiberniae quod habitum est apud Maynutiam Die 2 Augusti et Diebus sequentibus usque Ad Diem 15 Augusti 1927.

Coll, Thomas 'Are We Reviving Irish', *The Bell*, xvii (1951), no. 1, 52–5.

Comhairle na Gaeilge, *Irish in Education* (Dublin, 1974).

Conradh na Gaeilge/Gaelic League pamphlets:

An Gaedheal agus an Radio (Dublin, 1936).

Bilingual Instruction in National Schools (1901).

Butler, Mary *Irishwomen and the Home Language* (Dublin, 1901).

Forde, Patrick *The Irish Language Movement: Its Philosophy* (1901).

Hyde, Douglas *A University Scandal* (Dublin, 1901).

Martyn, Edward *Ireland's Battle for Her Language* (Dublin, 1901).

O'Hickey, M.P. *Irish in the Schools* (Dublin,1901).

Parliament and the Teaching of Irish (Dublin,1901).

Revd. Dr Walsh, *Bilingual Education* (Dublin, 1901).

The Case for Irish (Dublin, n.d.)

The Case of Bilingualism (Dublin, 1901).

The Future of Irish in the National Schools (Dublin, 1901).

The Irish Language and Irish Intermediate Education (Dublin, 1901).

Corcoran, Timothy 'The New Secondary Programmes in Ireland', *Studies*, 11 (1922).

Corcoran, Timothy 'The Irish Language in the Schools', *Studies*, 14 (1925).

Fine Gael, *Policy for a Just Society: 3. Education* (Dublin, 1966).

Hyland, Áine and Milne, Kenneth *Irish Educational Documents*, vol. II (Naas, 1992).

INTO, *Report of Committee of Inquiry into Use of Irish as a Teaching Medium to Children whose Home Language is English* (1942).

INTO, *A Plan for Education* (Dublin, 1947).

INTO, *Official Programme of INTO Annual Congress* (various years).

Irish Labour Party, *Labour's Policy on Education* (Dublin, 1925).

Irish Labour Party, *Challenge and Change in Education* (Dublin, 1963).

Mac Loinsigh, Peadar (ed.), *A Call to Ireland* (Ireland, 1911, 1944).

Moynihan, Maurice (ed.), *Speeches and Statements by Eamon de Valera, 1917–73* (Dublin, 1980).

National University of Ireland, *The National University Handbook, 1908–1932* (Dublin, 1932).

National University of Ireland, *The National University of Ireland, 1932–39* (Dublin, 1939).

Ó Cuív, Shán *The Problem of Irish in the Schools* (Dublin, 1936).

Ó Faoláin, Seán 'The Death of Nationalism', *The Bell*, 2, xvii (1951), 44–52.

Ó Droighneáin, Muiris *Taighde i gcomhair Stair Litridheachta na Nua-Ghaedhilge* (Dublin, 1936).

O'Growney, Eugene *Simple Lessons in Irish*, vols i, ii, iii, iv (Dublin, 1918).

O'Hickey, M.P. *Language and Nationality* (Waterford, 1918).

Pearse, P.H. *The Murder Machine and Other Stories* (Dublin, 1976).

Programme of Religious Instruction in the Catholic Colleges and Secondary Schools for 1928–9 (Dublin, 1928).

RTÉ, *Annual Reports* (various years).

RTÉ, *Education Broadcasting for Children and Young People* (1972).

St Patrick's College, Maynooth, *Kalandarium* (various years).

Trinity College, Dublin, *Calendars*.

University College, Cork, *Calendars*.

University College, Dublin, *Calendars*.

Secondary Sources

General Survey Texts

Browne, Terence *Ireland: A Social and Cultural History, 1922–1985* (London, 2nd ed., 1985).

Daly, Mary E. *Social and Economic History of Ireland since 1800* (Dublin, 1981).

Fanning, Ronan *Independent Ireland* (Dublin, 1983).

Foster, R.F. *Modern Ireland* (Great Britain, 1988).

Hoppen, K.T. *Ireland since 1800: Conflict and Conformity* (Britain, 1989).

Lee, J.J. (ed.), *Ireland 1945–70* (New York, 1980).

Lee, J.J. *Ireland 1912–1985* (Cambridge, 1990).

Lyons, F.S.L. *Ireland since the Famine* (London, 1979).

Murphy, J.A. *Ireland in the Twentieth Century* (Dublin, 1975).

Books and Articles

Adams, G.B. 'The 1851 Language Census in the North of Ireland', *Ulster Folklife*, 20 (1974).

Adams, Michael *Censorship: The Irish Experience* (Dublin, 1968).

Akenson, D.H. *The Irish Education Experiment: The National Education System in the Nineteenth Century* (London, 1970).

Akenson, D.H. *A Mirror to Kathleen's Face: Education in Independent Ireland, 1922–1960* (Canada and London, 1975).

Andrews, L.S. *The Decline of Irish as a School Subject in the Republic of Ireland* (Armagh, 1978).

Breatnach, R.A. 'The End of a Tradition: A Survey of Gaelic Literature', *Studia Hibernica*, 1 (1961).

Breatnach, R.A. 'Irish Revival Reconsidered', *Studies*, liii (1964), 18–30.

Brennan, Martin 'The Restoration of Irish', *Studies*, liii (1964), 263–77.

Browne, Noel *Against the Tide* (Dublin, 1986).

Chubb, Basil *The Government of Ireland* (England, 1986).

Comerford, R.V. 'Nation, Nationalism and the Irish Language' in Thomas Hachey and Lawrence McCaffrey (eds), *Perspectives on Irish Nationalism* (Lexington, 1989).

Coolahan, John *Irish Education: Its History and Structure* (Dublin, 1981).

Corcoran, Timothy *State Policy in Irish Education, 1536–1816* (Dublin, 1916).

Corish, Patrick J. *Maynooth College, 1795–1995* (Maynooth, 1995).

Corkery, Daniel *The Fortunes of the Irish Language* (Cork, 1956).

Daly, Mary 'The Development of the National School System, 1831–40' in Art Cosgrave and Donal McCartney (eds), *Studies in Irish History* (Dublin, 1979).

Daly, Mary *The Buffer State: The Historical Roots of the Department of the Environment* (Dublin, 1997).

Daly, Mary and Dickson, David (eds), *The Origins of Popular Literacy in Ireland: Language Change and Educational Developments, 1700–1920* (Dublin, 1990).

de Bhaldraithe, Tomás *Nuascéalaíocht* (Dublin, 1952).

de Blacam, Aodh *Gaelic Literature Surveyed* (Dublin, 1929, 1973).

de Fréine, Seán *The Great Silence* (Dublin, 1978).

Dooney, Sean *The Irish Civil Service* (Dublin, 1976).

Fanning, Ronan *The Irish Department of Finance, 1922–58* (Dublin, 1976).

Farrell, Brian *Seán Lemass* (Dublin, 1983).

Fianna Fáil, *Fianna Fáil: An Chéad Tréimhse* (Dublin, 1960).

Gleeson, D.A. and O'Neill, Joseph 'Father Corcoran, S.J.', *Studies* 32 (1943), 153–62.

Gorham, Maurice *Forty Years of Irish Broadcasting* (Dublin, 1967).

Hartnett, Micheal 'No Longer the Language of Officialdom', *Irish Times*, 20 April 1970.

Hartnett, Micheal *Collected Poems* (Dublin, 1984).

Hindley, Reg *The Death of the Irish Language* (New York, 1990).

Hoctor, D. *The Department's Story: A History of the Department of Agriculture* (Dublin, 1971).

INTO, *80 Years of Progress* (Dublin, 1948).

Jones, Valerie 'The Attitudes of the Church of Ireland Board of Education to Textbooks in National Schools, 1922–67', *Irish Educational Studies*, 11 (Spring, 1992).

Kelly, Adrian 'The Gaelic League and the Introduction of Compulsory Irish into the Free State Education System', *Oideas*, vol. 41 (Winter, 1993).

Kelly, Adrian 'Women in Twentieth-Century Ireland: Activism and Change' in Ilka Kangas (ed.), *The Situation of Elderly Women: Rour Lifestories of Grandmothers on the Fringes of the European Union* (Finland, 1997).

MacArdle, Dorothy *The Irish Republic* (Dublin, 4th edn, 1951).

MacCana, Prionnsias *Literature in Irish* (Dublin, 1980).

MacDonagh, Oliver *States of Mind: A Study of Anglo-Irish Conflict, 1780–1980* (London, 1983).

MacManus, Francis (ed.), *The Years of the Great Test, 1926–39* (Dublin, 1967).

MacNamara, John 'The Commission on Irish: Psychological Aspects', *Studies*, liii (1964).

MacNamara, John *Bilingualism and Primary Education* (Britain, 1966).

Manning, Maurice *Irish Political Parties* (Dublin, 1972).

McDowell, R.B. and Webb, D.A. *Trinity College Dublin, 1592–1952* (London and New York, 1982).

McRedmond, Louis (ed.) *Written on the Wind: Personal Memories of Irish Radio, 1926–76* (Dublin, 1976).

Mescal, John *Religion in the Irish System of Education* (Dublin, 1957).

Murphy, Ignatius 'Primary Education' in P.J. Corish (ed.), *A History of Irish Catholicism*, vol. V (Dublin, 1971).

Murray, C.H. *The Irish Civil Service Observed* (Dublin, 1990).

Ní Mhuiríosa, Máirín and Caerwyn Williams, J.E. *Traidisiún Liteartha na nGael* (Dublin, 2nd edn., 1985).

Ó Broin, León *No Man's Man* (Dublin, 1982).

Ó Buachalla, Séamus *Education Policy in Twentieth Century Ireland* (Dublin, 1988).

O'Callaghan, Margaret 'Language, Nationality and Cultural Identity in the Irish Free State, 1922–7: the *Irish Statesman* and the *Catholic Bulletin* Reappraised', *IHS*, 24 (1984–5).

Ó Céileachair, Séamas *Nuafhilí* (Dublin, 1956).

Ó Cobhthaigh, Diarmid *Irishmen of Today: Douglas Hyde* (Dublin, 1917).

Ó Coindealbháin, Seán 'Schools and Schooling in Cork City, 1700–1831', *Journal of the Cork Historical and Archaeological Society*, 48 (1943).

O'Connell, T.J. *A History of the INTO: 100 years of Progress* (Dublin, 1968).

O'Connor, Sean *A Troubled Sky: Reflections on the Irish Educational Scene, 1957–1968* (Dublin, 1986).

Ó Cróinín, Breandán 'An Ghaeilge sa Chóras Bunoideachais in dTús an Chéid Seo', *Oideas* (Fomhar, 1988).

Ó Cuív, Brian 'Irish Language and Literature, 1691–1845' in T.W. Moody and W.E. Vaughan (eds), *N.H.I.*, vol. iv (Oxford, 1986).

Ó Culacháin, Ciarán *Tobar na Gaeilge: Litríocht agus Teanga* (Dublin, 1980).

Ó Danachair, Caoimhín 'The Irish Language in County Clare in the Nineteenth Century', *North Munster Antiquarian Journal*, xiii (1970).

O'Doherty, E.F. 'Bilingual School Policy', *Studies*, 47 (1958).

O'Doherty, E.F. 'Bilingualism: Educational Aspects', *Advancement of Science*, 56 (1958).

Ó Doibhlin, Breandán 'Irish Literature in the Contemporary Situation', *Leachtaí Cholm Chille* (1970).

O'Donoghue, David *Hitler's Irish Voices: The Story of German Radio's Wartime Irish Service* (Belfast, 1998).

O'Donoghue, T.A. 'The Dáil Commission on Secondary Education, 1921–22', *Oideas* (Samhradh, 1989).

Ó Drisceoil, Donal *Censorship in Ireland: 1939–1945* (Cork, 1996).

Ó Fiaich, Tomás 'Cumann na Sagart', *An Sagart*, vol. 1 (1958), no. i.

Ó Fiaich, Tomás *Má Nuad* (Má Nuad, 1972).

Ó Fiannachta, Pádraig 'Stair Ghlór na nGael', *An Sagart*, vol. 30 (1987), no. iii.

Ó Gadhra, Nollaig *An Gaeltacht Oifigiúil agus 1992* (Dublin, 1989).

Ó Glaisne, Risteárd *Radio na Gaeltachta* (Gaillimh, 1982).

Ó hÉilí, Séamus 'The Preparatory Training Colleges', *Oideas* (Samhradh, 1984).

Ó hEithir, Breandán 'Where Do We Go from Here?', *Irish Times*, 22 April 1977.

Ó Loinsigh, Pádraig 'The Irish Language in the Nineteenth Century', *Oideas* (Earrach, 1975).

Ó Muimhneacháin, Aindrias *Dóchas agus Duaineis* (Dublin, 1974).

Ó Murchú, Máirtín *The Irish Language* (Dublin,1985).

Ó Riain, Donncha *Stair na Gaeilge: Litríocht agus Teanga* (Dublin, 1996)

Ó Ruairc, Maológ 'The Decline of the Irish Language: A Possible Explanation', *Leachtaí Cholm Chille* (1972).

Ó Súilleabháin, Donnchadh *An Piarsach agus Conradh na Gaeilge* (Dublin, 1981).

Ó Súilleabháin, Donncha *Cath an Gaeilge sa Chóras Oideachais, 1893–1911* (Dublin, 1987).

Ó Súilleabháin, S.V. 'Secondary Education' in P.J. Corish (ed.), *A History of Irish Catholicism*, vol. V (Dublin, 1971).

O'Sullivan, Donal *The Irish Free State and its Senate* (London, 1940).

Ó Tuama, Seán *Nuabhéarsaíocht* (Dublin, 1950).

Ó Tuathaigh, Gearóid 'Language, Literature and Culture in Ireland since the War' in J.J. Lee (ed.), *Ireland 1945–70* (New York, 1980).

Ó Tuathaigh, Gearóid 'Maigh Nuad agus Stair na Gaeilge' in Etáin Ó Síocháin (eag.), *Maigh Nuad: Saothrú na Gaeilge* (Maigh Nuad, 1995).

Ó Tuathaigh, Gearóid 'The State and the Language', *Irish Times*, 4 April 1977.

Ó Tuathaigh, Gearóid and Lee, J.J. (eds) *The Age of de Valera* (Dublin, 1982).

Paulin, Tom *A New Look at the Language Question* (Derry, 1983).

Peillon, Michel *Contemporary Irish Society: An Introduction* (Dublin, 1982).

Rockett, Kevin, Luke, Gibbons and Hill, John *Cinema and Ireland* (London, 1988).

Shane, Bernard *The Emergency: Neutral Ireland 1939–45* (Dublin, 1987).

Sheehan, John 'Education and Society in Ireland, 1945–70' in J.J. Lee (ed.), *Ireland 1945–70* (New York, 1980).

Titley, E. Brian *Church, State and the Control of Schooling in Ireland, 1900–1944* (Belfast, 1983).

Tobin, Fergal *The Best of Decades: Ireland in the 1960s* (Dublin, 1984).

University College Dublin, *UCD: the Past, the Present, the Plans* (UCD, 1976).

Wall, Patrick J. 'The Bishops and Education', *Oideas* (Earrach, 1982).

Walsh, R.B. 'The Death of the Irish Language' in Liam de Paor (ed.), *Milestones in Irish History* (Dublin, 1991).

White, Jack *Minority Report: The Protestant Community in the Irish Republic* (Dublin, 1975).

Whyte, J.H. *Church and State in Modern Ireland, 1923–1979* (Dublin, 1980).

Williams, J.E. and Ní Mhuiríosa, Máirín *Traidisiún Liteartha na nGael* (Dundalk, 1985).

Williams, T.D. 'Conclusion' in Francis MacManus (ed.), *The Years of the Great Test* (Dublin, 1967).

Wilson Foster, John 'Yeats and the Folklore of the Irish Revival', *Éire—Ireland*, 2, xvii (1982).

Theses and Unpublished Works

Edwards, John 'Irish Revival: Success or Failure?': A Paper to the International Conference on Language Revival in Honour of the Centenary of Modern Hebrew, Jerusalem, October 1990, (typescript).

McNamara, John 'The Use of Irish in Teaching Children from English-Speaking Homes: A Survey of Irish National Schools' (Ph.D. thesis, Uni. of Edinburgh, 1963).

Ó Riagáin, Pádraig 'The Irish Language' (typescript).

Ó Síoradáin, Micheál 'Cigire ag Féachaint Siar', 1986 (typescript, Library, Department of Education and Science).

Index